"Tony Merida is an outstanding expositor and a superb teacher of preaching. The unique blend of both gifts shines brightly throughout this superb work. I cannot commend it highly enough. I will use it again and again personally as well as in my own teaching on the high calling of proclaiming the unsearchable riches of Christ."

—**Daniel L. Akin,** president,
Southeastern Baptist Theological Seminary

"The New Testament is clear: the entire Bible is about Jesus. But I am often asked by fellow pastors, 'How can I preach Jesus week after week from all the Scriptures?' That's why I love Tony Merida's book. He teaches us how to be Christ-centered preachers who preach Christ-centered sermons."

—**Jonathan Akin,** senior pastor, Fairview Church

"Tony Merida is an extraordinary church planter, preacher, and professor. In this excellent book, *The Christ-Centered Expositor: A Field Guide for Word-Driven Disciple Makers,* he provides the single best introductory volume on faithful, Christ-centered preaching. Highly recommended."

—**Bruce Ashford,** provost and dean of faculty and professor of
theology and culture, Southeastern Baptist Theological Seminary

"During my doctoral studies in expositional Christ-centered preaching, I literally read dozens of books on the subject from scholars and practitioners, past and present. Tony Merida's *Faithful Preaching* was hands-down my favorite. And now this expanded and revised version is even better! *The Christ-Centered Expositor* is a must-read for every preacher."

—**Matt Carter,** pastor of preaching and vision,
The Austin Stone Community Church

"As a pastor, I am always on the lookout for books on preaching, especially when they come from men whose preaching is effective and whose lives are the real deal. And so I was very pleased to see *The Christ-Centered Expositor* by Tony Merida, who meets both of these criteria. Pastor, I highly recommend this book. It will serve your preaching, your soul, and most importantly, your church."

—**C. J. Mahaney,** senior pastor,
Sovereign Grace Church of Louisville

"Tony Merida has a reputation across the country for the weightiness of his ministry and the power of his proclamation. This book will show you why the reputation is deserved and will help you build a ministry rooted in the person and work of Jesus."

—**Russell Moore**, president, Ethics & Religious Liberty Commission
of the Southern Baptist Convention

"The glory of God is the goal of preaching, and Tony Merida has sounded a call for a new generation of preachers to be faithful to the purpose God has entrusted to them. This revision of *Faithful Preaching* provides a fresh and needed exhortation for preachers and teachers young and old alike to proclaim the Bible with conviction, courage, and compassion in the church and to the nations. I highly recommend it."

—**David Platt**, president, International Mission Board
of the Southern Baptist Convention

Numerous scholars, pastors and preachers have helped us think through exposition. And a host of others have helped us think through Christ-centered hermeneutics and homiletics. But few have helped us think through how they all play together in the same symphony of faithful preaching. And none have done it like Tony Merida does in *The Christ-Centered Expositor*. This brother captivatingly helps us see that exposing the text means exposing Christ. Just like biblical exposition isn't a sermon form but a preaching process, so Christ-centered preaching isn't a homiletical genre but a divine mandate. If you're going to preach, then preach Christ. If you're going to preach Christ well, then read Merida.

—**Jim Shaddix**, W. A. Criswell chair of expository preaching,
Southeastern Baptist Theological Seminary

"This is wonderful. You could put this book in someone's hands, and they could go seamlessly from text to sermon. The process is very clean. As well, Tony Merida does a wonderful job of framing expository preaching both biblically and historically. I'm very grateful for his passion and scholarship; it bleeds all over this book!"

—**Steven Smith,** vice president for student services and professor of
communication, Southwestern Baptist Theological Seminary

"Merida, with the heart of a pastor and the skill of a teacher, proves a great guide for preachers, both aspiring and seasoned. Here is a book that is succinct, pastoral, informative, and challenging."

—**Steve Timmis,** executive director, Acts 29 Network

"Tony Merida's content in this book is the primary resource I use in training pastors and church planters how to preach. Tony's balance between piety and preaching makes it an ideal text for those who aspire to preach or for those looking to refresh themselves on the core components of gospel-centered expository preaching. I reread it at least once every two years."

—**Harvey Turner,** lead pastor of preaching and vision, Living Stones
Church, and regional director, Acts 29 West Network

The
Christ-
Centered
Expositor

TONY MERIDA

The
Christ-Centered
Expositor

A Field Guide for
Word-Driven
Disciple Makers

ACADEMIC
NASHVILLE, TENNESSEE

To Imago Dei Church,
my brothers and sisters
whom I love and serve,
my joy and crown.
Stand firm in the Lord, beloved.

CONTENTS

Foreword by Bryan Chapell   xi
Acknowledgments   xv
Preface   xvii

Chapter 1   The Making of an Effective Expositor   1

PART 1: THE EXPOSITOR'S HEART

Chapter 2   Watch Your Life and Doctrine   25
Chapter 3   Love the Christ-Centered Scriptures   41
Chapter 4   Proclaim Christ from the Scriptures   59
Chapter 5   Rely on the Spirit's Power   81
Chapter 6   Cultivate a Vibrant Prayer Life   97
Chapter 7   Preach and Teach for God's Glory   115

PART 2: THE EXPOSITOR'S MESSAGE

Chapter 8   Step 1: Study the Text   133
Chapter 9   Step 2: Unify the Redemptive Theme   151
Chapter 10   Step 3: Construct an Outline   163
Chapter 11   Step 4: Develop the Functional Elements   175
Chapter 12   Step 5: Add an Introduction and a Conclusion   199
Chapter 13   Deliver the Word   211
Chapter 14   Contextualize the Message   227

Conclusion   243

APPENDIXES

A Historical Sketch of Preaching   245
Advice on Doing Exposition in Non-Pulpit Contexts   261
Sermon Outline Sheet   269
Sermon Evaluation Form   271

Selected Bibliography   275
Name Index   287
Subject Index   289
Scripture Index   293

FOREWORD

WHY SHOULD A PREACHER'S exposition of Scripture be "Christ-centered," as Pastor Tony Merida advocates in this wonderful text?

In part, the answer must be that Jesus teaches us to expound Scripture with his ministry in constant view. The Gospel of Luke tells us that after Jesus rose from the dead and was walking with his disciples on the road to Emmaus, he explained the Bible this way: "And beginning with Moses and all the Prophets, he interpreted to them in all the Scriptures the things concerning himself" (Luke 24:27 ESV).

Does this mean that Jesus used some magical formula or secret decoder ring to show how every verse in the Bible makes some mention of him? Sometimes we hear well-meaning people try to explain the Bible this way.

Such interpreters may tell us things like the wood of Noah's ark symbolizes the wood of the cross. Or they may stretch a bit further and suggest that the wood of the ark was made of "gopher" wood, and that is supposed to remind us of the resurrection—since gophers live in the ground and Jesus came up out of the ground.

Hopefully we recognize that such fanciful explanations are more about what is in the imagination of the interpreter than what is actually being communicated in the pages of Scripture. Such imaginative explanations could make the Bible mean anything we want it to mean (e.g., the wood could also symbolize the wood of the manger, or the wood Jesus used for his carpentry, or the wood of the boat from which he stilled the storm).

Jesus was not playing such imagination games when he told his disciples that all the Scriptures revealed him. He was teaching that he was the fulfillment of all the promises the Scriptures had made and the full revelation of the grace that God had been beaconing throughout the biblical record.

Prior to Jesus, the Scriptures had been progressively and consistently revealing the nature of the grace of God that would culminate in Jesus. Throughout the Bible, God had provided for people who could not provide for themselves (food for the hungry, strength for the weak, rest for the weary, forgiveness for the flawed, faithfulness to the unfaithful, freedom for slaves, sacrifices for the sinful, etc.). By all of these means, God's people were learning about the character and care of God that would be fully revealed in Christ. He is the culmination of the grace God's Word had been unfolding since the dawn of humanity.

When Jesus said that all the Scriptures spoke of him, he was not requiring us to make him magically appear in every Old Testament mud puddle or camel track by some acrobatic leap of verbal or symbolic gymnastics. Not every verse in the Bible mentions Jesus, but every passage does reveal aspects of God's character and care that relate to his saving work. Thus, for us to try to interpret a passage of Scripture and *only* speak of the commands that we should do or the doctrines that we should know actually misses the gospel truth Jesus said the passage contains.

Finding that gospel truth is not only required so that we will get the right and full meaning of the text. Consider what happens if *all* we do is teach a passage's moral instructions or doctrinal information. If that is all we do, then we are saying this passage is *only* about increasing the quality of our human performance or competence. The message basically gets entirely focused on broken humans doing better—straightening up and flying right.

There are only two possibly human responses to messages that entirely focus on us doing better. One possible response is *pride*. Like the rich young ruler of Mark 10, we could conclude, "I have done all that God requires." The problem with this conclusion is that our best works are like "filthy rags" to God (Isa 64:6) and, according to Jesus, when we have done all that we should do, we are still "unworthy" servants (Luke 17:10).

The other possible human response to a message that focuses entirely on increasing human performance or competence is *despair*. When we actually face the holiness that God requires in the context of our own human brokenness, we will inevitably despair that heaven will ever receive or bless us (Isa 6:5).

The Bible, of course, is not moving us toward pride or despair but toward faith in a Savior who makes gracious provision beyond the limits of our performance or competence. When we really understand how holy are God's requirements, then we are forced to seek help beyond our own resources to satisfy God and have a loving relationship with him. That's what the apostle Paul taught when he said that the law (the holy requirements of God) were a "schoolmaster" or "guardian" to lead us to Christ (Gal 3:24).

Paul would never want us to believe that the moral and doctrinal standards of Scripture don't apply to our lives, but neither would he want anyone to teach that our path to God is made by the perfections of our obedience. Jesus makes our path to God. When we put our faith in him, he provides the holiness that God requires.

Christ's perfect life and sacrificial death were provided for us so that we would have his righteousness in our place (2 Cor 5:21). Love for him and dependence on the enabling power of his Spirit are required for us to have the proper motivation and enablement to serve him—not only at the moment of our justification but for every step of our sanctification.

So, when we are interpreting a text from the Old or New Testament, we need to do more than show the duty others should do or the doctrine they should know. We also need to explain how the Scriptures are pointing us to dependence on our Lord for the grace that makes us his own and enables us to do as he requires.

We must take care to remember that apart from Christ we can do nothing (John 15:5). Such biblical mindfulness will encourage us to excavate the aspects of grace glistening throughout Scriptures that point us to the character and care of our Savior. Such Christ-centered exposition will lead God's people to heart responses of devotion and praise—not to gain God's affection but to return love to him who has been so gracious to us.

Bryan Chapell
Senior pastor, Grace Presbyterian Church; president emeritus, Covenant
Theological Seminary; distinguished professor of preaching, Knox Theological
Seminary and Gordon-Conwell Theological Seminary

ACKNOWLEDGMENTS

THIS WORK IS THE fruit of many colaborers in the gospel. I am indebted to Dr. Jim Shaddix, my mentor and friend, who emphasized the difference between "good stuff" and "God stuff" in preaching. His faithful exposition, classroom instruction, and prayerful support continue to shape me. He not only taught me about the sufficiency of Scripture but also illustrated it by his life and ministry.

I must also say thank you to other professors and pastoral models: to Dr. Charlie Ray, thank you for teaching me the value and use of the original languages; to Dr. Stan Norman, thank you for teaching me the importance of theology; to Dr. John Piper, thank you for inspiring and instructing me through your writings and ministry; to Dr. Bryan Chapell, thank you for your emphasis on Christ-centered expository preaching; to Dr. Timothy Keller, thank you for helping me think about preaching Christ to the unbeliever and the believer in the modern world.

To Andrew Arthur, John Blackmon, Stephen McDonald, and Seth Brown, thank you for your friendship and helping with parts of this book.

To Dr. Daniel Akin, thank you for the opportunity to teach at Southeastern Baptist Theological Seminary and for giving me a godly example of leadership and exposition.

To the elders at Imago Dei Church, thank you for your friendship and for your labor in the local church; it is my highest joy in ministry to serve alongside each of you.

To my bride, Kimberly, where would I be without you? You are my dear companion in life and ministry. My love and admiration for you grow by the day. Thank you for your faithfulness and grace. You are an amazing wife and mother.

To my children, James, Joshua, Angela, Jana, and Victoria, I pray that you will grow up to love the Scriptures and will make disciples among all nations. I love being your dad.

Most of all, I must thank my Lord and Savior Jesus Christ. Thank you for the cross and the empty tomb. Apart from you, I have no hope and nothing to preach. I pray that you will receive this little book as an offering of my worship to you, my King.

PREFACE

THE BELIEVER'S TASK OF making disciples among all nations involves *teaching* (Matt 28:18–20). If you take our Lord's commission seriously, then this book is for you. If you have (or aspire to have) an official teaching position in the church, then this book is especially for you.

There is more to the church than teaching, but the church's ministry is built on the understanding and application of Scripture. We know we should pray, but where do we learn to pray? The Bible. We know we should sing, take communion, care for one another, give generously, evangelize the world, care for orphans, and do a host of other things as a church, but where do we learn these things? The Bible. Husbands are to love their wives, but from where should we derive our view of marriage and family? The Bible. A healthy church is filled with healthy teaching.

In Acts 2, Peter stands up on the day of Pentecost and answers the question of a perplexed crowd, "What does this mean?" (Acts 2:12 ESV). He tells the crowd that Pentecost means that prophecy has been fulfilled (2:16; Joel 2:28–32); that the last Days have dawned (Acts 2:17); that all believers are "prophets" (2:17); and that Jesus has ascended to the throne (2:22–36). There is much to learn from Peter's sermon, but his point about all believers being "prophets" is quite important for supporting the view that while God appoints some men to the office of a pastor, *every believer* is called to teach in some capacity.

In the book of Numbers, Moses was exhausted from leadership, and so elders were appointed, filled with the Spirit, and they prophesied. When some were disturbed by this, and complained to Moses, then Moses said, "If only all the LORD's people were prophets and the LORD would place His Spirit on them!" (Num 11:29). What Moses longed for and Joel prophesied about, Peter says has arrived with the pouring out of the Spirit.

Of course, Peter is not saying that every believer has the "gift of prophecy" (1 Cor 12:10), but he does mean that every believer shares (in a general sense) the privilege and responsibility of Old Testament prophets. What did this involve? Prophets were able *to know God intimately* and were commissioned *to speak God's Word faithfully.* We too can know God truly and fully through Jesus Christ. And we can grow in this knowledge through the revealed Word of God. And we are commissioned to speak God's Word faithfully—both to believers and unbelievers.

The book of Acts recounts the story of the Word of God increasing and multiplying across geographical and cultural barriers by the power of the Holy Spirit (2:42; 6:7; 11:24; 12:24; 13:49; 16:5; 19:20; 28:30–31). Luke says that God's people taught others about Jesus, who is the hero of the Bible, in all sorts of contexts: "And every day, in the temple, and from house to house, they did not cease teaching and preaching Jesus as the Christ" (Acts 5:42 ESV). In many cases, it was the "nonprofessional" Christians proclaiming the Word. For instance, in Acts 8:4, Luke writes, "Now those who were scattered [the nonapostles] went about preaching the Word" (ESV).

While it is most certainly true that God has gifted some in the church with a unique ability to teach and preach (Rom 12:7; Eph 4:11; 1 Tim 3:1–7; Titus 1:5–9; Heb 13:7; 1 Pet 4:10–11), all believers share this responsibility in different ways. To the Colossian believers, Paul says, "Let the word of Christ dwell in you richly, *teaching and admonishing one another* in all wisdom" (Col 3:16a ESV, my emphasis). He told the Romans, "[Y]ou yourselves are full of goodness, filled with all knowledge and *able to instruct one another*" (Rom 15:14b ESV, my emphasis). Peter urged believers to be ready to teach unbelievers saying, "But in your hearts honor Christ the Lord as holy, always being prepared to make a defense to anyone who asks you for a reason for the hope that is in you" (1 Pet 3:15 ESV; see Col 4:5).

All this means that every believer must read, ponder, and love the Scriptures and be skillful at teaching and applying the message to others. If you are a disciple of Christ, then you should listen to sermons not merely as a "receiver" but as a "reproducer." Listen to learn and apply the text to yourself first, but also listen to teach others (such as your friends, neighbors, small group, or family members). When you study the Bible, do not merely study for information's sake, but study to know God personally and deeply, and study that you may instruct others.

Some believers will have a unique role in the church that involves the weekly labor of sermon preparation and delivery, and of course, they must take their task with the utmost seriousness (Acts 20:17–35; Heb 13:7, 17; Jas 3:1). We will give an account for how we have taught God's Word. We should tremble at this task.

So, here goes. Even though I have a bias toward those who are in the pulpit weekly, I hope to address both the heart and the message of all Word-driven disciple makers. If you are familiar with the original version of this book, entitled *Faithful Preaching*, you will find the same basic theology and methodology. Hopefully this new version is organized better; the newer sections make things clearer, and various concepts are emphasized more appropriately.

My prayer is that we all teach the Word of Christ more faithfully and effectively, and that we will treasure the Christ of the Word more deeply.

1

The Making of an Effective Expositor

Until I come, devote yourself to the public reading of Scripture, to exhortation, to teaching . . . Practice these things, immerse yourself in them, so that all may see your progress.
— *1 Timothy 4:13, 15 (ESV)*

Part of me wishes to avoid proving the sordid truth: That preaching today is ordinarily poor. But I have come to recognize that many, many individuals have never been under a steady diet of competent preaching.[1]
— *T. David Gordon*

My bible exposition students enter the room on the first day of the semester with a host of questions. Some of them aspire to the office of pastor, while others want to make disciples among unreached people groups, and still others are unsure how the Lord will use them to minister the Word. But they all come with questions. I assume because you are reading this book, you have an

---
[1] T. David Gordon, *Why Johnny Can't Preach* (Phillipsburg, NJ: P&R, 2009), 17.

inquiring mind too. Let us begin with some basic questions and foundations for proclaiming the Word.

WHAT MAKES A GREAT PREACHER/TEACHER?

"If I take this class, will it make me a great preacher?" On the first day of class, I tell students upfront that I cannot manufacture expositors. I wish I could. Why do I say this? For this reason: much of great preaching and teaching rests on the individual's personal life and with the sovereign Spirit of God. One has to take personal responsibility for spiritual and theological depth, and for personal and ministry growth, and one must acknowledge that God sovereignly works in people's lives by his own pleasure and for his own glory.

To highlight this reality, allow me to offer nine ingredients that contribute to the making of a great expositor. Examine your own heart as you read through this list.

1: Love for the Word of Christ and the Christ of the Word. Good preaching and teaching are an overflow of love for the Savior. It is actually possible to preach a Christ-centered message without having a Christ-centered heart. Guard against this. Good preaching and teaching come through a person who treasures the Christ of the Word. Let the Word drive you to the pulpit; do not let the pulpit (only) drive you to the Word.[2] Avoid studying only to preach sermons. Beware of becoming "The Sermonator," mechanically churning out sermons weekly but failing to meet with the risen Christ personally. Be renewed in the gospel personally. Sit under your own preaching. Let the Word pass through you before it passes from you.

After giving a few answers to the question "Where and how did you learn to preach?," preaching giant John Piper said, "I don't think there is much you can do to become a preacher except know your Bible and be unbelievably excited about what's there. And love people a lot."[3] Heed this counsel. Be personally enamored by the Savior, and then out of love for the bride, lead them down the aisle to the Groom.

---

[2] Tim Keller, *Preaching* (New York: Viking, 2015), 205.

[3] "Where and How Did You Learn to Preach?," Desiring God Ministries, accessed February 5, 2015, http://www.desiringgod.org/interviews/where-and-how-did-you-learn-to-preach.

2: Love People. Those who feed the flock must love the flock. Preparing messages is often lonely, and it is always tiring. Remember why you do it! Jesus loves his church, and we are called to love who Jesus loves. Avoid being a machine gun behind the podium, just firing content at people. Preach from a heart of love. The goal is not only to get through a message but also to get through to the hearts of people. Make sure when you are speaking to unbelievers that you do so with the compassion of the Father, who invites both hedonistic prodigals and moralistic Pharisees to enjoy his transforming grace. Do not replace truthfulness with "tolerance" but speak the truth in love. Bryan Chapell said that as an early preacher he wrote at the top of his notes "Love the people" as a reminder of this important point.[4]

3: Gifts. I cannot hand out teaching gifts to people. To quote the instructor from the movie *Chariots of Fire,* "I can't put in what God has left out!" God in his sovereign grace has equipped people with unique gifts for building up the body. Teaching may or may not be your primary gift. That is OK. We need all types of people to serve the body faithfully. Rest in the grace of God. Use the gifts and abilities that he has given you.

4: Experience. With the exception of giving students a few reps in sermon delivery class, I cannot give anyone experience. To grow as an expositor, you need to find ways to preach and teach a lot. Your early sermons may be like your first days riding a bike. You and the bike will get scratched up a bit, but keep riding. Most do not start out as proficient riders. And even the best preachers have improved from their early days. Take every opportunity you have to teach the Bible to people. Churches are not the only places where you can expound the Bible. Visit prisons, nursing homes, or shelters. Take a young person out for lunch weekly and teach him the Bible. It will bless him, and it will improve your skills.

5: A Mentor. I try to mentor nine or ten guys in our pastoral training program. I was blessed to have an incredible mentor in Jim Shaddix. If you do not have such a mentor, then be not dismayed. You can benefit from three types of mentors: life-on-life mentors, a mentor from a distance, and a deceased mentor. If you do not have a life-on-life mentor yet, start with the other two. Watch someone from a distance closely via technology. Not only can you watch

---

[4] "Why Expository Preaching?," The Gospel Coalition, accessed February 5, 2015, http://resources.thegospelcoalition.org/library/why-expository-preaching.

sermons online, but you may also communicate to them directly through various devices. (I have a faculty colleague who video chats with his mentor monthly.) By a "deceased mentor" I mean someone like Spurgeon, Luther, Calvin, Knox, or someone who faithfully taught God's Word and walked with Jesus. Read and study about them. Ideally, the perfect combination is all three. The Lord may allow you to have multiple mentors (of all types), and if so, thank him for such a privilege.

6: Models. Related to the previous point, when it comes to preaching and teaching, you can learn a lot by watching how someone goes about his craft. A mentor may or may not be a great model for exposition. You will do well to have many skilled models of exposition in your life. Danny Akin's words are correct: "Great preachers listen to great preachers."[5] You should not copy another's style (unless you want to look silly), but it is wise to watch and learn from faithful examples.

Here are a few of my models. D. A. Carson is my favorite Christ-centered expositor. I love to watch him dissect a particular text in context then fan out and show how it fits within the redemptive storyline of the Bible.[6] Akin does a tremendous job outlining passages in a book of the Bible. Alistair Begg, Mark Dever, Dick Lucas, Jim Shaddix, and Sinclair Ferguson have been wonderful models for weekly pastoral preaching. Tim Keller has impacted me more than anyone in the past five years. His ability to speak the gospel to the unbelieving skeptic, while doing substantive biblical preaching, is remarkable.

7: Holiness and Prayer. You must have a *lifestyle* that reflects a love for Scripture. People need to see the pastor/teacher exemplifying his teaching. You must accept responsibility for pursuing God and exemplifying Christ. You cannot separate your life and your ministry; the two are tied together. Lack of character will make you both *unfaithful* and *ineffective*. Involved in this pursuit is the need to cultivate a vibrant prayer life. Faithful preachers are faithful prayers. They commune with God regularly. I will say more about these things in chapters 2 and 6.

---

[5] Quoted in a PhD seminar at Southeastern Baptist Theological Seminary (SEBTS) that we co-teach.

[6] For example, watch this sermon on "The Temptation of Joseph," preached from Genesis 39 at Champion Forest Baptist Church on April 28, 2013; accessed February 5, 2015, https://www.youtube.com/watch?v=oS0iVA5UtN4.

8: Instruction. Here is where I try to be of most help to aspiring preachers in class (and with this book). You need to learn things such as how to exegete a passage of Scripture, how to incorporate biblical theology into expository preaching, how to apply the text in a gospel-centered manner instead of a moralistic manner, how to preach Christ from the Old Testament, how to prepare a sermon manuscript, and how to excel in other hermeneutical and homiletical skills. This book will provide some homiletical instruction that will hopefully be helpful to your Word-driven ministry. But this is an introductory book, so I encourage you to read other works, such as Bryan Chapell's *Christ-Centered Preaching,* John Stott's *Between Two Worlds,* and others referenced in the following chapters.

9: The Sovereign Spirit of God. Much in the preaching and teaching event is "mysterious." I cannot explain all the spiritual dynamics involved in delivering the Word. God has blessed all sorts of Word-driven disciple makers through the years for his own reasons, by his own power. The wind blows where he wants it to blow. God does miraculous things with weak vessels who may or may not be polished in the pulpit. Praise his holy name.

WHAT DOES THE BIBLE SAY ABOUT PREACHING AND TEACHING?

Before discussing biblical preachers, it is important to note that God himself was the "first preacher." Dever writes, "From the first page of the Bible, words are enormously important to the God who made the universe."[7] Throughout the pages of the Bible, we see that one feature that sets God apart from idols is the fact that *God speaks* (Ps 115:4–5).

As we read on, we see how God used people to speak his Word in order to reveal his truth and give life. When Jesus (the Word made flesh) began his earthly ministry, he did so by preaching (Matt 4:12–17). In the pages of the New Testament, we read of how God built his church by his Word (e.g., Acts 2:14–47). Declaring the Word is tied to the very nature and purpose of our great Creator and Redeemer.

Preachers in the biblical period were characterized by two primary factors: *calling* and *content.* Regarding *calling,* God set apart prophets, apostles, and preachers for the particular task of declaring

---

[7] Mark Dever and Greg Gilbert, *Preach* (Nashville: B&H, 2012), 13.

his Word publicly. On the other hand, God did not send false prophets who failed to proclaim the Word of God. In Jeremiah 23, God rebuked the false prophets, saying, "I did not send these prophets, yet they ran with a message. I did not speak to them, yet they prophesied" (v. 21). Surely this is one of the reasons why the special callings of the true prophets are included in the Old Testament. God's calling was important. It showed the people the difference between the two kinds of prophets. False prophets did not receive the vision of an Isaiah or experience the calling of a young Jeremiah or Samuel. Similarly, Paul often described his apostolic calling in order to set himself apart from the false apostles of the day (Gal 1:6–17). Old Testament scholar C. Hassell Bullock commented, "We cannot ignore the basic fact that the prophets found their legitimacy and valid credentials first of all in Yahweh's call."[8]

In addition, the *content* of the prophets set them apart from false prophets. God told Moses to proclaim the law of God (Exod 20:22). As the prophet Samuel grew, "the Lord was with him and let none of his words fall to the ground" (1 Sam 3:19 ESV). Ezra stood up and read "the book of the law" after God's people gathered together after exile (Neh 8:1). The Holy One commissioned Isaiah for the purpose of proclaiming his message to hard-hearted people (Isa 6:9–13). God put his words in Jeremiah's mouth for the purpose of proclamation (Jer 1:7–9). God told Ezekiel to say, "Thus says the Lord God" (Ezek 2:4 ESV). True prophets preached God's Word alone, and their message proved true in time (Deut 18:21–22).[9]

Similarly, true preachers in the New Testament continued the pattern of the Old Testament prophets by proclaiming divine truth, as commanded by the Lord. God appointed John the Baptist to prepare the way of the Lord by "preaching in the wilderness" (Matt 3:1); and as mentioned, Jesus began his earthly ministry by preaching and continued to preach and teach until his death—then after his resurrection as well (e.g., Luke 4:14–22, 43–44; 24:25–49)! In

---

[8] C. H. Bullock, *An Introduction to the Old Testament Prophetic Books*, updated (Chicago: Moody, 2007), 20.

[9] Of course, prophets are different from current preachers in the sense that they made future predictions. Nevertheless, they were preachers. Bullock said, "Although it can accurately be said that the prophets were basically preachers—that is, they spoke to their own times and situations, interpreting current events of history in light of God's will for Israel—the predictive element was a distinctive part of their message." Ibid., 16.

Acts, the apostle Peter preached "the first Christian sermon" by expounding and applying the Old Testament (and one-fourth of the book of Acts is sermonic material!). Paul preached his first recorded sermon by expounding on the Old Testament story (Acts 13:17–41). He spent many days teaching the Word in places like Corinth and Ephesus. He exhorted Timothy to devote himself "to the public reading of Scripture, to exhortation, to teaching" (1 Tim 4:13 ESV). Paul sent Titus to Crete and commissioned him to "teach what accords with sound doctrine" (Titus 2:1 ESV). Peter stated that those who are gifted to speak should declare "the oracles of God" (1 Pet 4:11). And the book of Hebrews is essentially a sermon, which the author calls "a word of exhortation" written for a group of believers (Heb 13:22 ESV).

The metaphors for God's messengers in the New Testament illustrate the preacher's responsibility to the Word. God calls the messenger a "sower" (*ho speiroun*) who sows the seed of the Word; a "steward" (*oikonomos*) who is entrusted with the mysteries of God; a "herald" (*keryx*) who proclaims the news of God; an "ambassador" (*presbus*) who represents God; a "shepherd" (*poimen*) who feeds and protects the flock of God; and a "workman" (*ergateus*) who rightly divides the truth of God. Concerning these images, John Stott stated, "It is impressive that in all these New Testament metaphors the preacher is a servant under someone else's authority, and the communicator of someone else's word."[10] Do not forsake your responsibility. Keep sowing, stewarding, heralding, representing, feeding, and rightly dividing God's Word.

Alistair Begg described the role of the preacher in a vivid way. The church where he attended as a boy had the type of sanctuary that required the pastor to ascend several steps before reaching a cone-shaped pulpit, located high above the people. Prior to his ascension, about three minutes prior to commencement, the parish official (beadle) went up first, carrying a large Bible. The beadle opened the Bible to the text for the day and then descended. The pastor then walked up into the pulpit. After this, the beadle ascended a final time to shut the door. This process illustrated something quite important: apart from the Scriptures, the preacher basically had nothing to say. However, if the preacher had Scriptures

---

[10] John Stott, *Between Two Worlds* (Grand Rapids: Eerdmans, 1982), 137. See Matt 13:1–23; 1 Cor 4:1; 2 Cor 5:20; 2 Tim 2:15; 4:2; 1 Pet 5:2.

before him, then he should not come down until he preached the text! And the people sitting below should submit to the authority of the text.[11]

The fact that true preaching involves the giving of a particular message makes sense when you realize that the gospel is *news*. What do you do with news? You speak it! The frequently quoted remark allegedly uttered by Francis of Assisi, "Preach the gospel at all times and if necessary, use words," sounds good, but it is nonsense. No television news anchor will say, "Tonight, I'm going to give you the news, and if necessary, I'll use words."[12] The gospel is news, and it therefore requires the act of speaking. It is better to say, "Preach the gospel at all times, and if necessary, use a microphone!" The New Testament is filled with references about the importance of *announcing* the good news (see Mark 1:37–38; 3:14; Luke 4:18–19; Rom 1:15; 10:14; 1 Cor 1:18–2:5; 9:16; 15:1–8).

Preaching has fallen on hard times because of the antiauthoritarian mood of our day. When preachers appear on television shows or movies, they are rarely portrayed in a respectful way. Some churches do not even like to use the word *preach*. Many claim, "Preaching doesn't work." But none of these realities should keep us from embracing the centrality of heralding the Word.

The fact is every generation bristles at the idea of submission to God's Word. Yet God's plan has not changed, and neither should ours. The number of biblical examples that illustrate the importance of the preached Word is stunning. After commenting on the book of Deuteronomy, which is essentially a book of Moses's sermons, Christopher Ash says, "True prophets were preachers of the written covenant. God did not just give them a book. He gave them preachers of the book so that face-to-face they could be taught, challenged, rebuked and exhorted to repentance and faith."[13] Similarly, after describing the God-breathed Scriptures in 2 Timothy 3:14–17, Paul tells Timothy to "preach the word" (4:2 ESV).

So preach *the Bible*. When God's Word is truly proclaimed, the voice of God is truly heard. Believe this, and go deliver it to your generation.

---

[11] Alistair Begg, *Preaching for God's Glory* (Wheaton, IL: Crossway, 1999), 9.

[12] I heard D. A. Carson use this illustration at a chapel service at Southeastern Baptist Theological Seminary.

[13] Christopher Ash, *The Priority of Preaching*, repr. (London: Proclamation Trust Media, 2010), .

DEFINITIONS AND DISTINCTIONS

Preaching, then, is about making God's Word known publicly to a particular audience. More specifically, faithful preaching involves *explaining what God has said in his Word, declaring what God has done in his Son, and applying this message to the hearts of people.* The best approach for accomplishing this agenda is expository preaching.

Ranting is not preaching; ranting is dangerous. Today we have "new school" ranting. "Old school" ranting involved a preacher lifting a verse from a passage and building a sermon around this verse or phrase. It was/is often filled with decent theology and delivered artistically, but these sermons tend to ignore the context of the passage and be presented to congregations with an anti-intellectual spirit.

A "new school" ranting sermon looks like this: Deal with a passage about John the Baptist for a bit and then do a thirty-minute rant on biblical manhood, regardless of the fact that the text is not about biblical manhood. New school ranters often say things that are helpful, and even Bible-based, but ranting is not exposition. Expository proclamation requires you to keep your focus on the text. It means rooting your application in the text. Say what God has said, and declare what God has done.

Ranting is dangerous for many reasons. In fact it is the same method prosperity preachers use. They lift a verse or idea out of a text without considering the context then go on about a self-serving agenda. Avoid this method. When you rant, you can easily depart from the meaning of a text. You also lose authority, feed carnality, perpetuate celebrity culture, and confuse people about what God did and did not say. Preach the Word, not your opinions and hobbyhorses, so that people put their faith in Christ, not in man's wisdom.

What Is the Difference Between Preaching and Teaching?

We should recognize that there are many similarities between *teaching* and *preaching.* Scholar Sidney Greidanus notes, "The New Testament uses as many as thirty-three different verbs to describe what we usually cover with the single word *preaching.*"[14] In one sense, preaching is telling the good news—which all believers should do (Acts 8:4). But

---

[14] Sidney Greidanus, *The Modern Preacher and the Ancient Text*, repr. (Grand Rapids: Eerdmans, 2000), 6.

there seems to be something unique about preaching God's Word publicly in a worship assembly (1 Tim 4:13; 2 Tim 4:1–4).[15]

Some think that one has gone from teaching to preaching when the speaker starts yelling! But I think the difference has more to do with *content* than with *volume*. The act of preaching involves three characteristics that are *not* always present in the act of teaching: exhortation, evangelism, and exultation.

Preaching involves *exhortation* because it calls people to respond or to act. Teaching does not always do this. Teachers may simply transfer information. Preachers urge hearers to repent and obey.

Preaching involves *evangelism* because it is tied up with the heralding of the gospel. If you do a word study for "preaching," you will find that the gospel usually accompanies it. One may teach for two hours about how archaeologists found a particular Psalm scroll in a Qumran cave, but they would not be preaching because educating is not evangelizing. It would not be "*declaring* what God has done through his Son."

Preaching involves *exultation* because it is an act of worship. The preacher should "exult" over the Word.[16] One may teach for information, but preaching aims at adoration. True preaching is an act of worship on the part of the preacher and the receiver (e.g., Neh 8:1–8). My goal every week is not merely to transfer information but to lead people to see the glory of Christ and be changed.

When people ask me if "I'm more of a teacher or a preacher," I say, "I'm a teaching preacher and a preaching teacher." I cannot preach well without careful teaching. But I do not want to merely teach people stuff; I want to preach the gospel, exult in Christ, and exhort people to respond. Interestingly, Paul incorporates the charge to "teach" in the same charge to "preach the Word" (2 Tim 4:1–4). We may herald the facts of the gospel (preaching), but we have to come behind that announcement and explain it (teaching). We proclaim that the tomb is empty and the throne is occupied, so repent and believe in the King (preaching); but we have to then explain who Jesus was, why people should believe in the

---

[15] John Piper states that in 2 Timothy 4 Paul has a worship assembly in mind. See "The Essential and Prominent Place of Preaching in Worship," sermon online, preached at SEBTS. Accessed February 5, 2015, https://www.youtube.com/watch?v=P8CMrjT62Vo. In 1 Timothy 4, Paul seems to also have a corporate gathering in view.

[16] John Piper emphasizes "exultation" in various places, such as in *The Supremacy of God in Preaching*, rev. ed. (Grand Rapids: Baker, 2004).

resurrection, and what repentance and faith mean (teaching). Not all teaching involves preaching, but all good preaching contains careful teaching.

What Are Some Classical Definitions of Preaching?

In the world of *homiletics*, "the science and art of preaching," many teachers provide more descriptive definitions, calling our attention to certain nuances. Though some debate what Phillips Brooks meant, this definition is regularly given to define preaching: "Preaching is the bringing of truth through personality."[17] We certainly cannot divorce the *personality* of the preacher from the preaching event, which is why we should not try to copy others' preaching style. We should proclaim the Word authentically. Of course, some parts of our personalities need purification by the Holy Spirit. We should not assume that "being ourselves" means that we have complete liberty to preach in any manner apart from moral boundaries. However, God has made us with unique traits and graced us with unique skills and mannerisms; therefore, we should not see preaching as conforming to one particular style.

Other teachers focus more on *content* in their definition of homiletics. V. L. Stanfield said, "Preaching is giving the Bible a voice."[18] Karl Barth stated, "Preaching must be the exposition of Holy Scripture. I have not to talk about Scripture but from it. I have not to say something, but merely repeat something."[19] Stanfield and Barth remind us that preaching is different from giving a "sermon," a "talk," or a "speech." In fact, a person can deliver a sermon or talk about anything. What makes preaching unique is its divine content.

Passion has also been emphasized through the years. Extraordinary expositor D. Martyn Lloyd-Jones asserted, "Preaching is theology coming through a man who is on fire."[20] Contemporary preacher John Piper called true preaching "expository exultation."[21] Both of these pastor-theologians remind us of the need for theological depth and fervency in the pulpit. While passion is expressed

---

[17] Phillips Brooks, *Lectures on Preaching* (New York: E. P. Dalton; repr., Grand Rapids: Baker, 1969), 5.

[18] John A. Broadus, *On the Preparation and Delivery of Sermons*, 4th ed., rev. Vernon L. Stanfield (San Francisco: Harper and Row, 1979), 19.

[19] Karl Barth, *Homiletics*, trans. Geoffrey W. Bromiley and Donald E. Daniels (Louisville: WJK, 1991), 49.

[20] D. Martyn Lloyd-Jones, *Preaching and Preachers* (Grand Rapids: Zondervan, 1971), 97.

[21] Piper, *The Supremacy of God in Preaching*, 11.

in different ways by preachers—such as volume, gestures, tears, sincerity, or pace—it is an important element in the preaching event for conveying a sense of gravity and gladness in worship. Genuine passion is also contagious and convincing. You will look hard to find any preaching in the Bible that does not contain expressions of passion.

Jerry Vines and Jim Shaddix define preaching as "the oral communication of a biblical truth by the Holy Spirit through a human personality to a given audience with the intent of enabling a positive response."[22] Vines and Shaddix add to the personality characteristic, *the Spirit's ministry* and a *positive response*. Certainly, we must emphasize the work of the Spirit in Christian preaching. And it is only by the Spirit that positive responses can occur. Preachers should expect God to work when his Word is accurately proclaimed.

I might add to this brief survey that true preaching is *trinitarian*. We must aim to *responsibly, passionately, and authentically declare the Christ-exalting Scriptures, by the power of the Holy Spirit, for the glory of God*. In my opinion, the approach that best fulfills this quest is *expository preaching*. John Stott went so far as to say that "all true Christian preaching is expository preaching."[23]

What Is Expository Preaching?

Many definitions of expository preaching/teaching exist. The general understanding is that the text of Scripture drives expository preaching. The Bible is at center stage. The confusion exists in answering the following particular questions about expository preaching:

1. Does expository preaching have to do with the *form* of the sermon?
2. Does expository preaching have to do with the *process* of preparing the sermon?
3. Does expository preaching have to do with the *content* of the sermon?
4. Does expository preaching have to do with the *style* of the sermon?
5. Does expository preaching include a *combination* of some of these elements?

---

[22] Jerry Vines and Jim Shaddix, *Power in the Pulpit* (Chicago: Moody, 1999), 27.
[23] Stott, *Between Two Worlds*, 125.

Expository preaching as a sermon *form* means to preach "verse *by* verse" instead of preaching "verse *with* verse." By this classification, only sermons that move through a particular passage are considered expository. Verse-with-verse preaching is known as "topical preaching," where the preacher selects a number of verses in order to support his idea.

Expository preaching as a sermon *process* means that exposition deals with the in-depth study of the text for the purpose of communicating the message the original author intended. The process (as we will discuss later in part 2) includes looking at certain features in the text such as authorship, date, context, words, and sentence structure. The expositor is then trying to uncover the meaning of a passage, which has been covered up by time, culture, language, and our presuppositions.

Expository preaching, when understood as the *content* of the message, means the essence of the sermon is biblical—regardless of the form or style of the message. With this idea, expository preaching is simply Word-centered preaching. One may choose various texts in a sermon, but the texts that are used are to be understood in their proper context. The verses must be treated in a way that does not offend the author whom God chose to write the texts.

Expository preaching as a sermon *style* means that there is a certain way to deliver an expository sermon. Usually one has a particular preacher in mind when defining exposition in this way. Unfortunately, those who react negatively to exposition often react to poor styles of delivery by particular preachers. These critics often claim that expository preachers only give the hearers boring background information sprinkled with Greek grammar and other irrelevant excerpts from commentaries.

The clearest option to reject is exposition as a *style*. We have many contemporary examples of preachers who are being faithful to the text while maintaining their own personality. No one likes boring exposition that includes no application for real life, and no one likes cloned exposition—trying to imitate a certain preacher.

Most proponents of exposition emphasize the need for the preacher to explain and apply a particular text or texts by understanding it in context. They emphasize the need for exegetical study and biblical content. Consider the following examples:

- John Broadus: "An expository discourse may be defined as one which is occupied mainly with, or at any rate very largely, with the exposition of Scripture."[24]
- John Stott: "It [exposition] refers to the content of the sermon (biblical truth) rather than the style (a running commentary). To expound Scripture is to bring out of the text what is there and expose it to view."[25]
- Haddon Robinson: "Expository preaching is the communication of a biblical concept, derived from and transmitted through the historical, grammatical, and literary study of a passage in its context, which the Holy Spirit first applies to the personality and experience of the preacher, then through the preacher, applies to the listeners."[26]
- Sidney Greidanus: "Expository preaching is 'Bible-centered preaching.' That is, it is handling the text in such a way that its real and essential meaning as it existed in the mind of the particular writer and as it exists in the light of the over-all context of Scripture is made plain and applied to the present-day needs of the hearers."[27]
- John MacArthur: "Expository preaching involves presenting a passage entirely and exactly as God intended."[28]
- Bryan Chapell: "[Expository preaching] attempts to present and apply the truths of a specific biblical passage."[29]
- Mark Dever and Greg Gilbert: "Expositional preaching is preaching in which the main point of the biblical text being considered becomes the main point of the sermon being preached."[30]
- Vines and Shaddix: "[An expository sermon is] a discourse that expounds a passage of Scripture, organizes it around a central theme and main divisions which issue forth the given text, and then decisively applies its message to the listeners."[31]

---

[24] John Broadus, *On the Preparation and Delivery of Sermons*, new and rev. ed. Jesse Witherspoon (New York: Harper and Row, 1944), 144.

[25] Stott, *Between Two Worlds*, 125–26.

[26] Haddon Robinson, *Biblical Preaching*, 2nd ed. (Grand Rapids: Baker, 2001), 21.

[27] Greidanus, *The Modern Preacher and the Ancient Text*, 11.

[28] John MacArthur Jr. and The Master's Seminary Faculty, *Rediscovering Expository Preaching* (Dallas: Word, 1982), 23–24.

[29] Bryan Chapell, *Christ-Centered Preaching*, 2nd ed. (Grand Rapids: Baker, 2005), 30.

[30] Mark Dever and Greg Gilbert, *Preach* (Nashville: B&H, 2012), 36.

[31] Vines and Shaddix, *Power in the Pulpit*, 29.

- D. A. Carson: "At its best, expository preaching is preaching which however dependent it may be for its content, upon text(s) at hand, draws attention to inner-canonical connections (connections within Scripture) that inexorably moves to Jesus Christ."[32]

The *form* of the sermon is the most often disputed part of expository preaching. Are only sermons that move verse by verse through passages to be considered expository? Are only sermons that move through entire books to be considered expository? Can you preach expository sermons by preaching on more than one text so long as those texts are not stripped from their original context? Some have even argued that a sermon is only expository when it is a sermon based on a particular passage longer than a few verses. Consider the following definitions:

- F. B. Meyer: "We are able to define expository preaching as the consecutive treatment of some book or extended portion of Scripture."[33]
- Andrew Blackwood: "Expository preaching means that the light for any sermon comes mainly from a Bible passage longer than two or three consecutive verses."[34]
- Harold Bryson: "[Expository preaching] involves the art of preaching a series of sermons either consecutively or selectively from a Bible book."[35]

I personally hold that the form of the message is secondary to the *process* of study and *content* of the sermon. Exposition, or Word-centered preaching, may be achieved in various ways. A person may preach a "topositional" sermon, which means the sermon addresses a particular doctrine that requires a verse-with-verse approach. This approach still holds the expositional commitment of seeking the intent of those various authors. I also believe that the preacher may select various themes through a book, such as the "I Am" statements in John. Another way of doing exposition is to overview a book, attempting to cover the major themes of a Bible book in a single

[32] D. A. Carson, "The Primacy of Expository Preaching," Bethlehem Conference for Pastors, 1995, cassette.
[33] F. B. Meyer, *Expository Preaching* (London: Hodder & Stoughton, 1910; repr., Eugene: Wipf and Stock, 2001), 25.
[34] Andrew Blackwood, *Expository Preaching Today* (Grand Rapids: Baker, 1975), 13.
[35] Harold Bryson, *Expository Preaching* (Nashville: B&H, 1995), 39.

sermon. A preacher may also do a series of sermons on a particular theme, where the series is made up of individual texts that relate to that theme, so long as these texts are treated faithfully.

In short, expository preaching is *Word-centered*, *Word-driven*, or *Word-saturated* preaching. It involves explaining what God has said in his Word, declaring what God has done in his Son, and applying this message to the hearts of people. Word-driven expositors are committed to the careful explanation and application of the biblical text.

Even though there is some liberty in the form of the sermon, I believe the best way to grow healthy disciples is by moving verse by verse through books of the Bible—simply allowing the main point of selected passages to drive the main point of your weekly sermon. While there may be times in which a pastor thinks another approach would be helpful for his people, I believe these occasions should not be the norm. Over time I believe the pastor will see the wonderful benefits of systematic exposition. I like to say that moving systematically through books is the diet of our congregation, but occasionally we go out to eat (preaching a *topositional* sermon or a thematic series).

One may also preach expositionally through books of the Bible in other contexts, such as Bible studies, Sunday school, or over coffee with two or three people. When the *Christ-Centered Exposition* commentary series was released, it was encouraging to hear about all the "non-preachers" using it. Moms, dads, small group leaders, youth ministers, military chaplains, and more have reported using these books as they seek to expound God's Word to a given audience. Let me encourage you to be an expositional student.

My mentor, Jim Shaddix, often used an analogy of a swimming pool to explain the Word-saturated nature of exposition. He said that preachers and teachers generally use the Bible in one of three ways. One approach is that they use the Word as a *diving board*. In this method, the preacher reads the text but never returns to it. Another approach is for the preacher to use the Word as *patio furniture*, occasionally returning to the text. Expository preachers, however, use the Word as the *pool*. They take the listeners for a swim in the biblical text.[36] At its most basic level, expository preaching is

---

[36] Jim Shaddix is my mentor, friend, and former pastor and professor. I highly recommend his two books, which support much of this book: *The Passion-Driven Sermon* (Nashville: B&H, 2003) and Vines and Shaddix, *Power in the Pulpit*.

preaching in such a way that the listeners get wet with God's Word after the sermon. Their Bibles remain open as the preacher continues to explain and apply the meaning of a particular text or texts. Of course, some sermons are not even in the vicinity of the pool! They have no text, and at this point, the hearers should go elsewhere to look for water.

More Questions About Expository Preaching

Frequently, three particular questions are raised when I discuss exposition in general and expository preaching in particular. The benefits of exposition, the dangers of exposition, and the alternatives to exposition are always questions of concern and discussion. Both the champions and critics of this approach to preaching should take these questions seriously.

What Are the Benefits of Expository Preaching?

Expository preaching is an approach that is founded on certain theological beliefs, such as the role of the preacher according to Scripture, the nature of the Scriptures, and the work of the Spirit. Therefore, many of the benefits of doing exposition are difficult to measure. However, nine practical and theological benefits are worth noting.

First, exposition calls for attention to biblical doctrine. One has to preach on every doctrinal issue if he preaches the whole counsel of God. This keeps the preacher from only dealing with his favorite subjects, and it will give the hearers theological stability.

Second, exposition, done well, is good for both audiences: believers and unbelievers. If one preaches the Scriptures in view of their redemptive history that culminates in Jesus, then the gospel will be integrated naturally into every sermon. The unbeliever will be confronted with his need for repentance and his need for hope in Christ. On the other hand, exposition will edify the believers in the church and remind them that they do not work for grace but from grace and by grace. So I am a huge fan, and hopefully a practitioner, of gospel-filled exposition. When you preach Christ-centered sermons, you are able to "evangelize as you edify and edify as you evangelize."[37]

---

[37] Tim Keller, *Center Church* (Grand Rapids: Zondervan, 2012), 79.

Third, exposition gives authority to the message. Preachers who try to be cutting-edge or fill their sermons with endless stories lose authority. The authority of the sermon is not in the preacher's suggestions, stories, or observations. Authority comes from God's Word.

Fourth, exposition magnifies Scripture. Preachers may claim to believe in the sufficiency of God's Word, but if they do not take people for a swim in the text, they betray their beliefs. You will show your people what you believe about the Bible by how you use it. This is how you magnify the nature of Scripture with something more than repeated clichés.

Fifth, exposition is God centered, not man centered. By starting with God's Word instead of a popular idea or a perceived need, the preacher will expose the nature and truth of the triune God to people—which is their greatest need.

Sixth, exposition provides a wealth of material for preaching. By moving through the Scriptures, you will avoid reductionism; that is, picking only the topics that seem important (money, sex, and power). The Bible will provide you with more subjects to preach on than you ever dreamed. A holistic approach will produce holistic Christians.

Seventh, exposition edifies the person delivering the Word. This is the most enjoyable part of committing to exposition. By studying the text each week, you will be developed as a disciple, and you will continue to fill your soul with spiritual nourishment.

Eighth, exposition ensures the highest level of biblical knowledge for the congregation. By regularly expounding the Word of God, you will train a group of people to know the Scriptures. Further, you will not only remind them of who they are in Christ and how to glorify God, but you will also train them to think biblically. Other types of preaching may put a bandage on people's felt needs, but such will not transform their worldview unless they understand the mind of the Holy Spirit in the Word. Exposition is a primary means of transforming people by the renewal of their minds (Rom 12:2).

Finally, exposition teaches people how to study the Bible on their own. The old saying is true, "Give a man a fish and you will feed him for a day; teach him how to fish and you will feed him for a lifetime." By moving systematically through passages and books, you will teach the people how to engage the text. They will understand the importance of context, words, and biblical genres.

After doing exposition in various places, I have discovered that the people are able to predict my next point, and see how I got it. Expository preaching will produce expository preachers and expository students.

Therefore, the benefits of exposition are numerous. No other approach to preaching seems to provide such advantages. Why would we want to do anything else?

What Are the Dangers of Exposition?

In championing expository preaching, I must point out that there are several dangers to avoid. One problem is *dullness.* The Word needs to pass through us before it passes from us. If we are dull, then it probably means that we have not let the Word do its work in our own hearts first. Another danger related to this one is *irrelevancy.* The goal of exposition is not information but personal transformation. The preacher must show how the text has implications for the hearers' lives.

Expositors should also watch out for *monotony.* The preacher should work hard at presenting the Word in fresh ways. Starting the sermon off the same way or using the same types of illustrations becomes predictable and frustrating to the hearer. Creativity and freshness are not bad, especially when they are part of the preacher's personality.

In addition, preachers should watch out for *detail overload.* Sometimes the hardest part of preparing expository sermons is deciding what to leave out. Good expository preaching has one dominant theme. The preacher takes this theme and supports it in order to drill this truth into the minds of the hearers. Simplicity and clarity are especially important to remember if you begin doing exposition in a church that has never heard it before.

Intellectual pride is a deadly shark to avoid as well. It comes in two ways. One way is when the preacher tries to impress the audience with his knowledge of biblical backgrounds and biblical languages. Our role is not to impress people but to present the Word plainly and clearly to them. Pride also creeps in when a preacher dogmatically preaches a difficult text, insisting that his interpretation is the only correct view. My philosophy is to present all of the views on such texts and then state my own view, giving reasons to support it. Balancing authority with humility is often difficult for preachers who cannot distinguish between first-, second-, and third-tier doctrines. By giving options, you will help people develop a Christian mind and learn to study on their own. You will also build credibility with your hearers as you practice humble exegesis.

The final shark is quite deadly. We must avoid *Christ-less* sermons. Often expositors miss the forest of the Bible (God's redemption in Jesus) for the trees (a particular passage). According to some hermeneutical plans, one could preach through the book of Nehemiah verse by verse yet never mention Jesus—and the sermon would be classified as expository! What is wrong with this method? It has missed the greater context of the whole Bible. Every expositor should try to identify where the selected passage is located in redemptive history. Is it before the cross or after it? I am not proposing that we try to "find Jesus under every rock," but I do want to contend that despite some discontinuity, the Bible is one Christian book. I am not advocating "extra-Jesus" but faithful exegesis and theological application, which consider both the details of a text and the broad contours of Scripture. D. A. Carson says, "The entire Bible pivots on one weekend in Jerusalem about two thousand years ago."[38] We must remember this as we dive into any passage. In fact, Jesus told the disciples that the Old Testament pointed to himself (Luke 24:25–27, 44–47). No Jewish rabbi should be able to sit comfortably under our preaching from the Old Testament. Expositors should work hard at finding the redemptive connections within the text and make a grace-filled application of it.

What Are Some Alternative Approaches to Expository Preaching?

Preachers today have many alternatives to exposition. *Narrative preaching* is often the method of choice. Certainly, narrative preaching can be done expositionally; that is, preaching through narrative texts without imposing an unnecessary rhetorical outline. Preachers may do exposition of narrative texts by simply following the natural parts of the story (i.e., character, plot, conflict, resolution).

Sometimes, however, those who call for narrative preaching do not mean preaching from narrative texts in a story-based way alone. They encourage preachers to tell interesting stories and give moral examples for people to follow. The problem with this type of narrative preaching is that it sometimes does more to fascinate than to change. Keeping people's attention does not mean that anyone

---

[38] D. A. Carson, *Scandalous* (Wheaton, IL: Crossway, 2010), 11.

will be changed necessarily. It also is less likely to incite a hunger for God's Word because the sermon is primarily a story.

Many pastors have also embraced the *topical-felt-need* approach in recent years. Pastors using this method often start by doing surveys in order to find out the needs of people then preach messages that deal with these issues. These sermons are extremely practical. The points of the sermon, however, seem like suggestions. Sometimes I wonder if a Mormon, a pop psychologist, or any other moral person would have a difficult time with some of these sermons. Practical tips for daily living may not be explicitly Christian. It is not what people are getting that concerns me but, rather, what they are *not* getting: namely, the gospel and God's revelation.

Recently, the *dialogical* approach to preaching has become popular among the emergent church leaders. That does not mean they have people talk back to them during the sermon. Rather, these advocates believe that we should let everyone participate in the sermon by giving everyone a chance to stand up and speak—with virtually no boundaries. Usually, this approach comes from a rejection of truth and authority.

While dialogue is needed in some contexts (such as small groups), it fails to be true preaching. Further, it invites misguided people into the discussion. What do you do when someone stands up and reads *The Watchtower*? Practically, this method cannot accommodate for large growth either. How do you have a dialogue with two thousand people in attendance? Theologically, there also seems to be a failure to understand how the body of Christ works. The ones who have the gift of teaching and preaching should be doing it. The dialogue idea seems to suggest that church is exclusively for Sundays. People with some spiritual gifts find their context of service elsewhere, like in orphanages, the mission field, and administration.

SUMMATION

Faithful preaching involves saying what God has said in his Word, declaring what God has done in his Son, and applying this message to the hearts of people. Christ-centered exposition is the best approach for accomplishing this goal. This Word-driven ministry offers wonderful spiritual benefits to both the expositor and to the congregation. To be faithful expositors today, we must avoid the common problems such as boredom, pride, detail overload, irrelevancy, and Christ-less messages. Effective expositors usher the people through the text passionately and authentically, pointing them to the Savior.

QUESTIONS

1. In the opening section, "What Makes a Great Preacher/Teacher?" which ingredient struck you the most and why?
2. Regarding this statement, "Preaching has fallen on hard times because of the antiauthoritarian mood of our day," how have you seen negativity about preaching expressed?
3. What is preaching? What are some key aspects of effective preaching? How is preaching different from teaching?
4. What are some of the benefits of expository preaching?
5. What are some of the dangers of expository preaching?

PART I

THE EXPOSITOR'S HEART

2

Watch Your Life
and Doctrine

Keep a close watch on yourself and on the teaching. Persist in this,
for by so doing you will save both yourself and your hearers.
                                            —1 Timothy 4:16 (ESV)

My people's greatest need is my personal holiness.[1]
                                            —Robert Murray M'Cheyne

I HAVE A WOODEN CHARLES Spurgeon head on my bookshelf. I
know it sounds idolatrous, but I do not bow down to him! I do,
however, wish he would preach to me sometimes. If Spurgeon
could still speak to ministry leaders and aspiring ministers, I think
he might choose to speak on 1 Timothy 4:16. In Spurgeon's classic book *Lectures to My Students*, the opening chapter is entitled
"The Minister's Self-Watch." Using Paul's words in 1 Timothy 4:16,
Spurgeon launched into an appeal for personal godliness/holi-
ness among ministers. Spurgeon said, "We have all heard the story
of the man who preached so well and lived so badly, that when
he was in the pulpit everybody said he ought never to come out

---

[1] Robert Murray M'Cheyne, quoted in J. I. Packer, *Rediscovering Holiness* (Ann Arbor:
Servant Publications, 1999), 33.

again, and when he was out of it they all declared he never ought
to enter it again . . . Our characters must be more persuasive than
our speech."[2]

It is essential that we understand the importance of our character in a book about speaking the Word. Apart from personal holiness, we do not have an expositional ministry. We do not need for
Spurgeon to come back to life and preach this message to us. We
have something better: the Scriptures. Let us consider the concept
of holiness in general, and then the importance of it in the lives of
ministers of the Word in particular, using the words of both Peter
and Paul as a primary biblical foundation.

UNDERSTANDING PERSONAL HOLINESS

God calls all believers to personal godliness. Peter opens his first
epistle with the glorious good news of the gospel and then transitions to call Christians to "be holy" as the God who called them is
holy (1 Pet 1:15–16). He urges these born again, blood bought,
recipients of divine mercy to live in the hope and power of their
new identity (1:13); to make war on sin (1:13–14; 2:11); to set their
hope on the grace that is in Jesus (1:13); to live before the all-see-
ing eye of God (1:17); to revel in the gospel regularly (1:18–21);
to feast on the living and abiding Word of God (1:22–25; 2:2); to
put away relational sins that harm the body of Christ (2:1); and to
always remember that Jesus is better than sin (1:13–2:3).

In this section, Peter shatters modern concepts of sin. Many
want to rename sin, redefine sin, minimize sin, manage sin, or
blame others for their sin. But Peter reminds us about the gravity of God's holiness, the vile nature of sin, and the need to fight
sin by the Spirit's power. Puritan John Owen said there are only
two options: "Be killing sin, or it will be killing you."[3] This message
of battling for personal godliness is absent today—both inside and
outside the church. The consequences of this reality are devastat-
ing. When one minimizes the holiness of God, he minimizes the
sinfulness of sin, and this leads to them being unmoved by the

---

[2] Charles Spurgeon, *Lectures to My Students*, repr. (Grand Rapids: Zondervan, 1954), 17.
[3] John Owen, quoted by Kelly Kapic, *Overcoming Sin and Temptation* (Wheaton, IL:
Crossway, 2006), 30.

glorious gospel of grace and the kindness of God that leads sinners to repentance.

To expose the need for holiness, we need to clarify several misconceptions. First, we must distinguish between *positional* holiness and *personal* holiness (or practical holiness). Positional holiness means that we are made perfectly righteous through faith in Christ. We stand accepted, loved, and totally justified before God. Personal holiness means that we are now becoming in practice what God has already declared us to be in position. We must not confuse the order. Because we are positionally holy, we can pursue a life of personal holiness. We are not trying to be holy in order to be made righteous. All who have repented of sin and placed faith in Christ for salvation now work *from* righteousness, not *for* righteousness.

On a street level, we also have to clarify some popular ideas. Personal holiness does not mean isolationism. The holiest person to ever live was Jesus (1 Pet 2:22), but Jesus was around sinners so much that he was labeled as a friend of sinners. Personal holiness means that we are separated from sin but not isolated from people. (I will talk more about engaging culture without falling into the sins of the culture in chap. 14).

Further, personal holiness is not primarily about outward appearances either. Your heart matters more than how you dress. Both businessmen and hipsters can commit adultery. Jesus rebuked religious people for displaying outer appearances of righteousness while being full of hypocrisy and lawlessness (see Matt 23:27–28).

Another misconception is that holiness is boring. We must remind others (and ourselves) that Jesus taught, "Blessed are the pure in heart, for they shall see God" (Matt 5:8 ESV). Jesus essentially says, "Happy are the holy." The reason there is so little happiness in the world is there is so little holiness in the world. We do not find boredom when we pursue holiness; we find excitement, joy, wonder, beauty, and freedom.

Finally, many assume other things are more important than personal holiness. But remember what Paul says before going on to talk about sexual purity: "For *this is God's will*, your sanctification" (1 Thess 4:3, my emphasis). What is more important than God's will? How many Christians want to "find God's will for their life" but do not take personal holiness seriously? Many have their priorities upside down. God cares more about who you are than whether you live in Detroit or Dayton. God's will is for you to be more like Christ in every way (Rom 8:29). We are called to pervasive holiness. God calls us to be holy in "all our conduct" (1 Pet 1:15), which includes not only our relationship to God but also holiness in all other relationships: within the church (2:1; 4:8–12), with unbelievers (2:9–12; 3:13–17; 4:12–19), with the government (2:13–17), within marriage (3:1–7), and between elders and the church (5:1–5). Let us give the utmost attention to this highest of callings.

PURSUING HOLINESS AS MINISTERS OF THE WORD

After telling Christians how to pursue holiness in an unholy, hostile world, Peter directs his attention to the pastors/elders (1 Pet 5:1–5). He urges his fellow pastors to pursue ministerial integrity: "Shepherd God's flock among you, not overseeing out of compulsion but freely, according to God's will; not for the money but eagerly; not lording it over those entrusted to you, but being examples to the flock. And when the chief Shepherd appears, you will receive the unfading crown of glory" (vv. 2–4).

In this appeal, Peter addresses the hearts of ministers. He challenges them to examine their motives and methods. He calls ministers to shepherd the flock because it is God's will, not because they feel compelled to do so. He says they should be eager to fulfill their holy responsibility and should not serve for financial gain. And he urges them to live as examples for the church instead of using their position to domineer the church. The ultimate motivation for such a ministry is that Jesus is the Chief Shepherd, and he will reward faithful service. Therefore, setting a godly example for the flock is essential for ministers if they desire to live faithfully before God and if they desire to bless the people of God.

In 1 Timothy, Paul urges Timothy to live as an example to the flock. In 1 Timothy 3:1–7, he lists the qualifications of overseers, which include godly character qualities and the ability to teach (see Titus 1:7–9). In 1 Timothy 4:16, Paul summarizes this list saying, "Pay close attention to your life and your teaching" (see Acts 20:28). This shows that the list of pastoral qualifications should always be in front of the minster.

Other than having the ability to teach, everything in the list applies to Christians in general. To be a faithful pastor, then, you must first be a faithful Christian. This appeal to godliness echoes powerfully in the following chapter of the epistle:

> If you point these things out to the brothers, you will be a good servant of Christ Jesus, nourished by the words of the faith and the good teaching that you have followed. But have nothing to do with irreverent and silly myths. Rather, train yourself in godliness, for the training of the body has a limited benefit, but godliness is beneficial in every way, since it holds promise for the present life and also for the life to come.
>
> This saying is trustworthy and deserves full acceptance. In fact, we labor and strive for this, because we have put our hope in the living God, who is the Savior of everyone, especially of those who believe.
>
> Command and teach these things. Let no one despise your youth; instead, you should be an example to the believers in speech, in conduct, in love, in faith, in purity. Until I come, give your attention to public reading, exhortation, and teaching. Do not neglect the gift that is in you; it was given to you through prophecy, with the laying on of hands by the council of elders. Practice these things; be committed to them, so that your progress may be evident to all. Pay close attention to your life and your teaching; persevere in these things, for by doing this you will save both yourself and your hearers. (1 Tim 4:6–16)

Paul addresses the private life and the public ministry of Timothy here. He calls Timothy (and us) to do the following: exercise for godliness passionately (4:6–10), exemplify your teaching personally (4:12), expound the Scriptures publicly (4:11, 13), exercise your gift practically (4:14–15), and examine your life and doctrine persistently (4:16). Let us give some time and attention to applying this first point to our lives.

Training for Godliness

Paul begins by saying that Timothy is to put "these things" before brothers, in order to "be a good servant of Christ Jesus" (1 Tim 4:6a). "These things" refers to the general summary of Paul's instructions to Timothy. Before putting these things before others, though, Paul tells Timothy that he must be "trained in the words of faith" and "good doctrine" (4:6b ESV).

The word for "trained" is better translated as "nourished." Timothy's spiritual diet was to consist of high quantities of good teaching. In addition, he was to avoid spiritual junk food. Paul says, "Have nothing to do with irreverent and silly myths" (4:7). The Greco-Roman world was full of folk religions of gods and goddesses. Myths and tales were everywhere. As in our day of the Internet, many lies, half truths, and irrelevant ideas were available for one to feed on. We too must reject bad teaching and feast on good teaching.

So behind the public ministry of the Word is the private study of the Word. We must digest it ourselves first. This word for "nourish" is also a present participle, which indicates continual nourishment. John Stott challenges busy pastors to use their time wisely for personal study: "But the minimum [time for study] would amount to this: every day at least one hour; every week one morning, afternoon or evening; every month a full day; every year a week. Set out like this, it sounds very little. Indeed it is too little. Yet everybody who tries it is surprised to discover how much reading can be done within such a disciplined framework. It tots up to nearly 600 hours in the course of a year."[4]

Our ministries will suffer if we do not consume sound doctrine. In his last letter, the apostle Paul asked Timothy to bring his "books" and "above all the parchments" (2 Tim 4:13 ESV). If anyone could go without books, it was Paul, right? He experienced things we will never experience, yet he still wanted his books! As someone quipped, "If you need shoes, buy books!" The call to exposition is a call to study.

I did not like to read before I became a Christian. I actually had a reading problem as a kid and was put into special reading classes. I even had a personal reading tutor in college. I could not remember anything that I read. But when God saved me from a life of sin as a sophomore in college, I developed a deep hunger for God's Word (and my personal study habits changed!). A love for reading books developed. When I eventually started my first semester of seminary, I could not believe the number of books required for a class. Three to five books for each of my five classes—with no

---

[4] John Stott, *Between Two Worlds* (Grand Rapids: Eerdmans, 1982), 204.

pictures! But I praise God for these requirements and for wonderful authors/teachers. Remember, leaders are readers. Nourish
your soul. Godliness begins with a healthy diet. Stay away from
junk food.

A Healthy Diet

The meat of our nourishment comes from the *memorization* and
meditation of Scripture. This will always be the protein. We cannot
develop strong spiritual muscles apart from large portions of this
meat.

Psalm 119 is a remarkable chapter about the value of Scripture,
written by a young man who desired purity and truth (vv. 9, 99–
100). Virtually every verse has something to say about the Word.
But it is not the book, for the book's sake, that the psalmist is after.
He is after the Giver of the Word: God himself. Virtually every verse
of this psalm also refers to the Author of Scripture. The Scriptures
get us to God. That is why the words of Scripture are more precious
than silver and more valuable than gold.

Because of the incomparable value of Scripture, we must "treasure it in our heart" (119:11). Of course, simply memorizing something does not necessarily change someone. Many prodigals can
quote verses such as "Every seed-bearing plant God made is good,"
and "Judge not, lest you be judged!" The difference is that we treasure the Word "in our heart." The heart, in the Old Testament, is
a place of both thinking and feeling. Treasure God's Word in the
heart, where we can think about its truths and taste its delights.

Paul tells the Colossians, "Let the word of Christ dwell in you
richly" (3:16 ESV). This is what is needed. Whatever you need to do
for the Word to dwell in you richly, do it. I call this "meditation."
Not in the sense that you are "emptying your mind" but that you
are filling your mind (and heart) with the glories of the gospel in
the Bible. You may do this by listening to sermons on your morning commute, by memorizing large portions of Scripture, by praying through the Psalms and Proverbs, by meeting regularly with
a Christian brother to discuss your Bible reading plan, by writing
songs based on the Scriptures, or many other ways. Just make sure
the Word is dwelling in you!

Meditation on Scripture is necessary for many reasons. God
intends to sanctify us primarily by the Word and Spirit. Jesus
prayed, "Sanctify them by the truth; Your word is truth" (John

17:17). By seeing Christ in his Word, we are conformed to his likeness (2 Cor 3:18).

Additionally, you should memorize the Scriptures for the purpose of counseling others. The author of Proverbs says, "A word spoken at the right time is like golden apples on a silver tray" (25:11). Through the Scriptures we also overcome spiritual attacks (Eph 6:17a). We better not go into battle without a sword! I love the words of Luther: "And though this world, with devils filled, should threaten to undo us, we will not fear, for God hath willed his truth to triumph through us. The Prince of Darkness grim, we tremble not for him; his rage we can endure, for lo, his doom is sure; one little word shall fell him."[5]

These and other benefits demand that the minister of the gospel treasure God's Word. Scripture memorization is one of the disciplines that has impacted me greatly. I agree with Chuck Swindoll:

> I know of no other single practice in the Christian life more rewarding, practically speaking, than memorizing Scripture. . . . No other single exercise pays greater spiritual dividends! Your prayer life will be strengthened. Your witnessing will be sharper and much more effective. Your attitudes and outlook will begin to change. Your mind will become alert and observant. Your confidence and assurance will be enhanced. Your faith will be solidified.[6]

When it comes to memorizing large portions of Scripture, several excuses typically surface. The first is usually "I don't have time." But the fact is that we make time for things that are important to us. It reminds me of the cartoon in which the doctor looks at the out-of-shape patient and says, "What fits your busy schedule better, exercising one hour per day or being dead twenty-four hours per day?" Think about the busy saints in our history who memorized Scripture. Henry Martin, pioneer missionary to India, memorized Psalm 119 in the midst of great stresses and workload while translating the Bible into an Indian dialect.[7] Before dying of exhaustion in 1812, he said that it was the Scriptures that sustained him.

---

[5] Martin Luther, "A Mighty Fortress Is Our God," trans. Frederick H. Hedge in *The Baptist Hymnal* (Nashville: Convention Press, 1991), 8.

[6] Chuck Swindoll, *Growing Strong in the Seasons of Life* (Grand Rapids: Zondervan, 1994), 61.

[7] Quoted in J. M. Boice, *Psalms*, vol. 3 (Grand Rapids: Baker, 1998), 973.

William Wilberforce, the British statesman who was largely responsible for the abolition of slave trade throughout the empire, wrote in his diary in 1819, "Walked from Hyde Park Corner, repeating the Psalm 119 in great comfort."[8] The busy Wilberforce fed himself on Psalm 119. The sad reality is that lack of time is a cover-up for "I am too lazy."

What would happen if you suddenly had no access to the Bible? If you got kidnapped on a mission trip and imprisoned for more than twenty years, would you know enough of the Bible by heart to copy it down and teach it to others? Could you teach Ephesians, word for word, by heart?

At the end of the day, the greatest problem with the practice of memorizing and meditating on Scripture is one of unbelief. Do you really believe that God will change you through the Spirit as you meditate on his Word? Do you value the spiritual profit of marinating on Scripture more than money? Test yourself. If I offered you a hundred bucks for every book you memorized in the next year, would you memorize only a verse or two? Remember, the Scriptures are "better to me than thousands of gold and silver pieces" (119:72 ESV).

It is a sad day when children are memorizing the Koran in Madrassas at age five, and many Christian ministers have not memorized their own book, with the help of the Holy Spirit. Where are the David Livingstones, who memorized Psalm 119 at age nine? There is no reason that you and I cannot memorize the book of Romans.[9] It simply requires that you train for godliness.

So in addition to good theology books and other helpful Christian literature, feast upon the riches of God's Word. Get alone with your Bible and your books, and come out of the study ready to overflow. As Stott says, plan some shorter and longer retreats to give special time and attention to allowing the Word to affect your soul—daily, weekly, monthly, and yearly.

Spiritual Exercise

The words for godliness (*eusebeia*) and godly (*eusebeus*) in 1 Timothy 4:6 occur fifteen times in the New Testament. Thirteen of these occurrences are in the Pastoral Epistles. Nine of the thirteen

---

[8] Ibid.
[9] For free help on Scripture memory, see Pastor Andrew Davis's "An Approach to Extended Memorization of Scripture," http://www.fbcdurham.org/pages.php?page_id=5.

occurrences are in 1 Timothy. This word basically means "reverent" or "respect" or "awe." A godly person is in awe of God. This was a matter of first importance to the apostle, who at the end of his life had seen many wander from the faith. The other important word in verse 7 is "train." This word *gumnazou* is the word from which we get our word *gymnasium* or *gymnastics*. It implies sweat and effort. In ancient Greek games, the participants removed clothing to avoid hindrances. By New Testament times the word meant to train in general. In other words, it means to take exercise passionately. Today we might say, "Put your game face on." This is serious business.

We will not grow in godliness if we do not exercise spiritually every day. Spiritual fitness, like physical fitness, takes time and attention. Of course, this spiritual discipline is not about legalism, that is, making a list and trying to keep it in order to gain merit with God. We are talking about grace enabled, Spirit-empowered discipline that flows from a heart that loves God and is satisfied in Christ above all things. The difference between legalism and spiritual discipline is one of *motive*. We practice the disciplines because we love the One who first loved us. These disciplines are the means of grace by which we know our Savior better. Spiritual discipline, then, is motivated by delight, not duty.

Paul also shows us the difference in spiritual discipline and legalism in that spiritual discipline has a different power source. He says in 1 Timothy 4:10, "For to this end we toil and strive, because we have our hope set on the living God, who is the Savior of all people, especially of those who believe" (ESV). Here Paul puts human responsibility and God's sovereign power together, as he does in other places when describing the process of godliness (e.g., Phil 2:12–13). He tells Timothy to "labor" but then says that his hope is in the "living God." The living God empowers our growth in godliness. And it is Jesus, the Savior, who is our Mediator and Helper in the process (1 Tim 2:5). Jesus stands with us, and the Spirit fills us as we train for godliness.

Paul did not specify which exercises Timothy should practice, but I suggest a few important disciplines to implement.

Reading Scripture. Maintain a plan for dwelling in the Scriptures personally. There are many ways to do this. I like James Stalker's advice: "Have a large, varied, and original communion with God."[10]

----

[10]James Stalker, quoted by Joel Beeke, "The Utter Necessity of a Godly Life," in *Reforming Pastoral Ministry*, ed. John H. Armstrong (Wheaton, IL: Crossway, 2001), 61.

Make time for it; mix up your pattern if necessary; and find something that impacts you specifically (do not just copy someone else).

Praying and Repenting. Prayer is a wonderful gift to the Christian. For the pastor, prayer is a large part of our calling (see Acts 6:4). We should meet with God throughout the day to *intercede* for others, realizing that it is a privilege to call upon the Father on behalf of others (more on this in chap. 6). But we also need to pray in order to care for our own soul. For example, here is Tim Keller's practice of prayer and repentance:

> Besides morning prayer (M'Cheyne, Psalms, meditation, and petition) and evening prayer (Psalms and repentance) I try as often as possible to take five minutes in the middle of the day to take a spiritual inventory, either by remembering the more spiritually radioactive ideas from my morning devotion, or by a quick look at my most besetting sins and idols. I do that to see whether so far that day I've given in to bad attitudes such as pride, coldness and hardness of heart, anxiety, and unkindness. If I see myself going wrong, the mid-day prayer can catch it. The problem with mid-day prayer is finding a time for it, since every day is different. All I need is to get alone for a few minutes, but that is often impossible, or more often than not I just forget. However, I carry a little guide to mid-day prayer in my wallet which I can take out and use.
>
> The last form of prayer that I do daily is prayer with my wife, Kathy. About nine years ago Kathy and I were contemplating the fact that we had largely failed to pray together over the years. Then Kathy exhorted me like this. "What if our doctor told us that we had a serious heart condition that in the past was always fatal. However, now there was a pill which, if we took it every night, would keep us alive for years and years. But you could never miss a single night, or you would die. If our doctor told us this and we believed it, we would never miss. We would never say, 'oh I didn't get to it.' We would do it. Right? Well, if we don't pray together every night, we are going to spiritually die." I realized she was right. And for some reason, the penny dropped for us both, and we can't remember missing a night since. Even if we are far away from each other, there's

always the phone. We pray very, very simply—just a couple of minutes. We pray for whatever we are most worried about as a couple, anyone or anything on our hearts that day. And we pray through the needs of our family. That's it. Simple, but so, so good.[11]

I am not necessarily recommending that you take Keller's approach, but I find it illustrative of the need for personal prayer in the life of a minister. He knows the importance of dealing with his own soul daily, through prayer and repentance. Indeed, our hearts are also prone to be cold, scared, ensnared, or proud. We must cultivate a life of gospel-oriented repentance and prayer to combat these problems.

Living in Community. If you are a pastor, do not neglect sharing life together with other believers. You do not need to live in isolation. Sanctification is a community project. Participate in the functions of your church, like a normal Christian. Not only should we be part of the weekly worship gathering, where the Word is read and expounded (1 Tim 4:13); we also need other brothers and sisters exhorting us in community (Heb 10:19–25).

Pursuing Christ-centered Humility. Humility must be the mark of shepherds who follow the way of the Great Shepherd. A note of humility is struck throughout the Pastoral Epistles. At the end of 2 Timothy, Paul says that many in culture are "lovers of self" (2 Tim 3:2).

Sadly, self-glory creeps into the hearts of ministers, as well. Paul Tripp states, "Perhaps there is no more powerful, seductive, and deceitful temptation in ministry than self-glory. Perhaps in ministry there is no more potent intoxicant than the praise of men, and there is no more dangerous form of drunkenness than to be drunk with your own glory. It has the power to reduce you to shocking self-righteousness and inapproachability."[12] He then lists ten problems associated with the absence of humility and the presence of self-glory:

1. Self-glory will cause you to parade in public what should be kept in private.
2. Self-glory will cause you to be way too self-referencing.

---

[11] Tim Keller, "Scraps of Thoughts on Daily Prayer," accessed February 11, 2015, http://www.thegospelcoalition.org/article/scraps-of-thoughts-on-daily-prayer.
[12] Paul Tripp, *Dangerous Calling* (Wheaton, IL: Crossway, 2012), 167.

3. Self-glory will cause you to talk when you should be quiet.
4. Self-glory will cause you to be quiet when you should speak.
5. Self-glory will cause you to care too much about what people think about you.
6. Self-glory will cause you to care too little about what people think about you.
7. Self-glory will cause you to resist facing and admitting your sins, weaknesses, and failures.
8. Self-glory will cause you to struggle with the blessings of others.
9. Self-glory will cause you to be more position oriented than submission oriented.
10. Self-glory will cause you to control ministry rather than delegate ministry.[13]

Sadly, I have fallen many times in these areas. But there is hope for all of us in Christ Jesus. By the Spirit's power, let us serve people. Let us fill our minds with the message of the gospel, in order to be free from an addiction to self (2 Cor 5:15). Let us prayerfully and intentionally kill self-glory and boast only in Christ's cross (Gal 6:14).

Setting an Example. In 1 Timothy 4:12, Paul told Timothy to put his teaching on display personally. Timothy was called to a position beyond his years. He was probably in his early thirties. It takes spiritual discipline to avoid the common ministerial pitfalls. Stott helps us relate to Timothy's temptations:

> Perhaps some were jealous of Timothy being promoted over their heads. Others may have looked down their noses at this pretentious youth, much like Goliath despised young David. Older people have always found it difficult to accept young people as responsible adults in their own right, let alone as leaders. And young people are understandably irritated when their elders keep reminding them of their immaturity and inexperience, and treat them with contempt.[14]

How should we respond when some look down upon our youth? Not in boastful, crass, or aggressive behavior. Paul tells Timothy to do the opposite of what his flesh may want to do. Notice the "but"

---

[13] Ibid., 167–80.
[14] Stott, *Guard the Truth*, 119.

(*alla*) in verse 12b. It is a word of sharp contrast: "But set the believers an example." Paul tells Timothy to follow after Christ, who is the embodiment of exemplary speech, conduct, love, faith, and purity. Many will forget about your age when they admire your example. Be above reproach in regard to your family life, your church life, and your social life. Love your wife. Love your people. Love your kids. Love your community. And may that love flow out of an honest heart that loves Christ above all things.

Growing in Ministry. In 1 Timothy 4:15, Paul says that Timothy should display "progress." A disciplined minister should grow in his ministry of proclamation. Use your gifts (1 Tim 4:14). Allow others to give you feedback. This evaluative process will sanctify you as a Christian and sharpen your skills as an expositor.

Practicing Self-Examination. In 1 Timothy 4:16, Paul emphasizes the need to watch our life and doctrine *persistently.* We cannot ever stop watching our life and our teaching because the call to godliness is too serious. Paul warns Timothy about a host of temptations that are particularly present in the lives of ministers, like greed (e.g., 1 Tim 6:3–11). We must beware of so many threats to our lives and ministries: pornography, love for power, love for controversy, anger, impatience, pride, despair, laziness, overwork, cowardice, hypocrisy, jealousy, anxiety, and so on. We must be on our guard constantly. Sin never sleeps. Satan hates what we are doing. So keep your guard up and keep a close watch on your life and teaching.

I have observed the ruin of numerous people in ministry over the past ten years. They have dropped out of ministry for a variety of reasons, some over more grievous sins than others. But in every case, these men stopped walking carefully. Each name that I could give you is the name of a guy who was not only in ministry but was incredibly gifted for ministry. But it does not matter how gifted you are; if you do not have godliness, you do not have a ministry. M'Cheyne stated, "It is not great talents that God so much blesses, as it is great likeness to Jesus."[15] You may not have "great talents," but you can pursue likeness to Jesus.

---

[15] Robert Murray M'Cheyne and Andrew A. Bonar, *Memoir and Remains of the Rev. Robert Murray M'Cheyne* (Edinburgh; London: Oliphant Anderson & Ferrier, 1894), 241.

Godliness Makes Up for Your Deficiencies

Before concluding, I must point out one additional reason to pursue personal holiness. Not only is godliness essential for faithfulness to God; it also makes up for our own deficiencies in ministry.[16] This is not the primary motive for pursuing holiness, but it is true. If you are not a great preacher, but you are godly, people will listen to you. They will find you interesting because you walk with God. You can probably list a handful of people who are not the most gifted behind the lectern but who are effective because they are godly. Similarly, you may not be the most gifted leader, but if you are godly, people will respect you and follow your leadership. You may not be the most gifted counselor, but if you are fighting sin and pursuing Christlikeness, people will trust you, pour out their heart to you, and you can walk with them, weep with them, and pray with them. You will not be good at all the prophet-priest-king ministries of the church, but if you keep the utter necessity of godliness as your first priority, then many of your holes will be filled up by holiness. Pursue godliness for the sake of God-glorifying faithfulness and for ministry effectiveness.

SUMMATION

Watching our life and our doctrine are two priorities for one disciplined soldier. Avoid the mistake of thinking that you *only* need doctrine or that you *only* need spiritual discipline. You need both a diet full of healthy doctrine and a discipline that leads to Christlikeness. B. B. Warfield gave an apt illustration to a group of ministry students: "A minister must be learned, on pain of being utterly incompetent for his work. But before and above being learned, a minister must be godly. Nothing could be more fatal, however, than to set these two things over against one another. Recruiting officers do not dispute whether it is better for soldiers to have a right leg or a left leg: soldiers should have both legs."[17]

What the church needs are two-legged soldiers more than anything. E. M. Bounds said, "The church is looking for better

---

[16] Tim Keller made this point in "Ministry and Character." Article online http://static1.squarespace.com/static/5315f2e5e4b04a00bc148f24/t/537a7280e4b0d4555968 6de9/1400533632260/Ministry+and+Character.pdf. Accessed Feb 14, 2015.

[17] B. B. Warfield, *The Religious Life of Theological Students*, repr. (Phillipsburg, NJ: P&R, 1992), 1–2.

methods, God is looking for better men."[18] May God make you a two-legged soldier for the glory of the Triune God!

QUESTIONS

1. What is the difference between *positional* holiness and *practical* holiness? How should we pursue practical holiness? Why is this pursuit so important?
2. What does John Stott say about the wise use of study time?
3. What are the benefits of the memorization of Scripture?
4. In the list of spiritual exercises/disciplines emphasized for ministers of the gospel, which one impacted you the most and why?
5. Explain B. B. Warfield's analogy of a two-legged soldier. Why is this concept so important for ministers of the Word?

---

[18] E. M. Bounds, *Power Through Prayer* (Uhrichsville, OH: Barbour, 1984), 8.

3

LOVE THE CHRIST-CENTERED SCRIPTURES

But as for you, continue in what you have learned and firmly believed, knowing from whom you learned it and how from childhood you have been acquainted with the sacred writings, which are able to make you wise for salvation through faith in Christ Jesus. All Scripture is breathed out by God and profitable for teaching, for reproof, for correction, and for training in righteousness, that the man of God may be competent, equipped for every good work.
—*2 Timothy 3:14–17 (ESV)*

For although the Spirit is primarily responsible for producing the Bible as the inspired Word of God, the Bible is not primarily about the Spirit but rather it is about the Son.[1]
—*Bruce Ware*

A HIGH VIEW OF SCRIPTURE should lead to a high view of biblical preaching and teaching. Paul's words about the divine nature of Scripture in 2 Timothy 3:14–17 are followed immediately by the charge to "preach the word" (4:1–2 ESV). An unfortunate chapter

---

[1] Bruce Ware, *Father, Son, and Holy Spirit* (Wheaton, IL: Crossway, 2005), 110.

division interrupts the link between these two sections, but the relationship is obvious. If God inspired the Scriptures, then why would we want to preach anything else?

Strangely, many claim to have a high view of biblical inspiration in theory but fail to demonstrate this belief in practice. They wave the Bible in the air as the "inspired, inerrant, and infallible Word of God" but never actually preach Word-driven sermons.

Many Christians also claim to believe in the inspiration of Scripture but spend little time actually reading it. Popular agnostic Bart Ehrman tells of an annual scene in one of his classes at the University of North Carolina, Chapel Hill. Ehrman asks the class, "How many of you believe that the Bible is the inspired Word of God?" He reports that quite a high percentage of the students raise their hands. He then asks, "How many of you have read [insert a popular author's latest book]?" Virtually everyone raises his hand. Then he asks, "How many of you have read the entire Bible?" Almost no one raises a hand. Ehrman points out the inconsistency of this practice, saying, "I understand why you would want to read this popular author, but *if you really believe God wrote a book, wouldn't you want to read it?*"[2]

Paul urges Timothy to keep "learning" and keep "believing" the God-breathed Scriptures. And if we really believe that the Bible is God's Word, that it leads us to Jesus, and that it equips us for every good work, then shouldn't we love it and read it and teach it? We should say with the psalmist,

- "Oh how I love your law! It is my meditation all the day" (Ps 119:97 ESV).
- "Your testimonies are my delight; they are my counselors" (Ps 119:24 ESV).
- "Your promise is well tried, and your servant loves it" (Ps 119:140 ESV).

We have a God who speaks. Do you understand how unique and amazing this is? Do you love the Christ-centered Scriptures?

This chapter will be divided into two sections: (1) "The Divine Nature of the Scriptures" and (2) "The Centrality of Christ in the

---

[2] I heard Ehrman use this illustration at a debate in New Orleans. Some of my students have been in his class at UNC and also told me about this experience. Questions are paraphrased.

Scriptures." In the first, I will emphasize four particular beliefs related to the nature of Scripture. In the second, I will emphasize the need to preach Christ as the Hero of Scripture.

THE DIVINE NATURE OF THE SCRIPTURES

What is the nature of Scripture? Religious pluralists believe the Bible is one good book among many other religious texts. Other skeptical theologians believe that only about 20 percent is historically accurate. Ehrman argues that we cannot "know" if the Bible is God's Word or not.[3] In every age, the nature of Scripture is questioned.

Biblical Inspiration

By the inspiration of Scripture, we mean that God is the source behind the Scriptures, and that he acted through the Holy Spirit, with the biblical writers, to pen his Word entirely and exactly as he intended. We do not mean that the Bible is *inspirational*. When someone on the street hears the word *inspiration*, one may think he means that the Bible is inspired, such as an artist or a playwright. But we actually mean that the Bible is *expired*. The word translated as "inspired" (*theopneustos*) means "breathed-out" by God (2 Tim 3:16). In other words, the Scriptures have their origin in God's revelation. Paul also affirmed the *total* inspiration of Scripture in 2 Timothy 3:16, saying that "all" Scripture is inspired.

Peter described how God revealed his Word to men, saying, "First of all, you should know this: no prophecy of Scripture comes from one's own interpretation, because no prophecy ever came by the will of man; instead, men spoke from God as they were moved by the Holy Spirit" (2 Pet 1:20–21). The Spirit carried Old Testament writers along like a sailboat in the wind to pen the words of God recorded in the Bible. Peter again affirmed this in the selection of Matthias: "Brothers, the Scripture had to be fulfilled that *the Holy Spirit through the mouth of David* spoke in advance about Judas" (Acts 1:16, my emphasis). According to Peter, David was the mouthpiece through whom the Lord spoke.

The witness of Old Testament writers and prophets validates this divine/human process. The phrase "Thus says the Lord" appears hundreds of times. Jeremiah states, "These are the words

---

[3] Bart Ehrman, *Misquoting Jesus* (San Francisco: HarperCollins), 2005.

the LORD spoke" (Jer 30:4). Isaiah says, "For this is what the LORD said to me with great power" (Isa 8:11). Amos declares, "This is the declaration of the Lord GOD" (Amos 8:11). David affirms, "The Spirit of the LORD spoke through me, His word was on my tongue" (2 Sam 23:2). These examples show how men were carried along by the Holy Spirit, and that they were aware of God's presence in the process of penning it.[4]

The casual reader cannot miss Jesus's emphasis on the divine nature of Scripture either. Jesus often debated with the Pharisees over the interpretation of Scripture, but he did not question the inspiration and authority of Scripture.[5] He quoted Scripture frequently in the Sermon on the Mount and in his temptation in the wilderness (Matt 4:1–11). He also affirmed many powerful truths about the nature of Scripture, such as, "Man must not live on bread alone but on every word that comes from the mouth of God" (v. 4), and "Heaven and earth will pass away, but My words will never pass away" (Matt 24:35). Jesus also affirmed the authority of the Old Testament by his use of it, and he taught that he was the fulfillment of it: "These are My words that I spoke to you while I was still with you—that everything written about Me in the Law of Moses, the Prophets, and the Psalms must be fulfilled" (Luke 24:44).

Regarding the inspiration of the New Testament, Peter added that Paul's words were to be taken as part of the Scriptures (2 Pet 3:16). This means that Peter and the early church considered Paul's words to be in the same category as the Old Testament writings.[6] Additionally, Paul stated, "For the Scripture says: 'Do not muzzle an ox while it is treading out the grain,' and, 'the worker is worthy of his wages.'" (1 Tim 5:18). His first quote comes from Deuteronomy 25:4, and the second quote is found in Luke 10:7. Paul called both these Old and New Testament references "Scripture." Paul's self-awareness of the inspiration process also led him to write, "What I write to you is the Lord's command" (1 Cor 14:37).

So why should we trust the Scriptures as reliable and inspired? For one, the Bible claims this for itself.[7] Jesus also affirmed the

---

[4] Millard Erickson, *Christian Theology*, 2nd ed. (Grand Rapids: Baker, 2000), 228.
[5] Ibid.
[6] Wayne Grudem, *Christian Beliefs*, ed. Elliot Grudem (Grand Rapids: Zondervan, 2005), 13.
[7] Critics argue that such reasoning is circular. The circular argument is: "We believe the Bible is God's Word because it claims that for itself; we believe the claims of the Bible because it is God's Word." Admittedly, this is a type of circular argument, but that does not invalidate

inspiration of Scripture by his statements and use of them. And every regenerated believer understands that there is a real mysterious, supernatural reason as well: God confirms that the Bible is his Word by the Spirit to our hearts. Peter says to born-again believers, "Like newborn infants, desire the pure spiritual milk, so that you may grow by it for your salvation" (1 Pet 2:2). In other words, the Spirit of God creates an appetite for the Word of God in the hearts of the people of God.

Other beliefs regarding the Bible flow out of inspiration, such as the belief in the *clarity of Scripture*, which means that any Christian can learn God's Word as he maintains a right relationship with God (Ps 19:7). Of course, sound interpretive principles should be applied in the reading of the Scripture, but those principles should merely assist the Christian in doing something that he is already able to do; namely, understand the Bible as a Spirit-filled follower of Jesus.[8]

Like Timothy, the faithful preacher should confidently proclaim and teach the inspired Word of God with complete patience. Spurgeon once quipped that the Bible is like a lion; we do not need to defend it as much as we need to turn it loose!

Biblical Authority

While teaching systematic theology to a group of high school students, I began my talk on authority by asking, "Does God have the right to tell you what to do?" Of course, they said yes (at least that is what they said in church). I then followed that question by asking, "How does God tell us what to do?" The clear answer was "the Bible."

When the Scriptures are interpreted rightly, the next step is obedience. According to Wayne Grudem, "The authority of Scripture means that all the words of Scripture are God's words in such a way as to disbelieve any word of Scripture is to disbelieve or disobey God."[9] Millard Erickson states, "By the authority of the Bible we

---

it. Wayne Grudem is correct in saying that "all arguments for an absolute authority must ultimately appeal to that authority for proof: otherwise the authority would not be an absolute or higher authority." See Wayne Grudem, *Systematic Theology* (Grand Rapids: Zondervan, 2000), 78. Additionally, if we cannot trust the Bible about its claims about its nature, then why should we trust it for doctrines such as salvation and the deity of Christ?

[8] My belief in the inerrancy of Scripture also comes from this high view of inspiration. For an excellent study on the reliability of the biblical text, see B. M. Metzger, *The Text of the New Testament: Its Transmission, Corruption, and Restoration*, 3rd ed. (New York: Oxford, 1992).

[9] Grudem, *Systematic Theology*, 73.

mean that the Bible, as the expression of God's will to us, possesses the right supremely to define what we are to believe and how we are to conduct ourselves."[10] Both theologians express the idea that God reserves the right to tell us how to live, and he has told us specifically in the Scriptures.

The implications for the authority of Scripture are numerous. First, we should develop our biblical doctrine from the Scriptures. A study of God must be rooted in God's revelation of himself. Second, we should evaluate our ministries by the Scriptures. The temptation to look for other means of evaluation often leads to unreal expectations and constant discouragement. Third, we should evaluate our lives based upon the Scriptures. Finally, we should preach from the Scriptures because God told us to do so, and we have nothing really to say apart from his Word!

The authority of Scripture is quite a practical doctrine for the church to think through as well. For example, older Christians should listen to the young preacher for one simple reason: he is the one with the Bible! Of course, many will look down upon your youth, but age is no excuse for tuning out God's Word. Remember, your authority does not come from your years of experience or your title. It comes from the Word. This is why expository preaching is so important. It best expresses a belief in the authority of Scripture. Piper is correct in saying, "Our authority as preachers sent by God rises and falls with our manifest allegiance to the text of Scripture."[11] Apart from the Scriptures we have no authority by which to preach. But with the Scriptures we have no reason for not proclaiming it boldly and faithfully.

Many faithful witnesses have passed on the precious doctrine of biblical authority and inspiration. For example, early leaders such as Clement of Rome, Polycarp, Justin Martyr, Irenaeus, Clement of Alexandria, and Origin each affirmed the inspiration of Scripture.[12] Later, the cry of the Reformers was *sola Scriptura* (Scripture alone). They believed that Scripture should be the final rule for faith and practice. The Reformers shared a desire to put the Bible in the language of the people in word and print. Brian Edwards, a biographer of English Reformer William Tyndale (1494–1536), stated,

---

[10] Erickson, *Christian Theology*, 267.
[11] John Piper, *The Supremacy of God in Preaching*, rev. ed. (Grand Rapids: Baker, 2004), 44.
[12] R. Saucy, *Scripture* (Nashville: Word, 2001), 190–96.

"Thus the two fundamental doctrines of men like Tyndale and Luther—the absolute authority of Scripture, and salvation by faith in the death of Christ alone, led to an inevitable conclusion: the Scriptures must be translated."[13] Tyndale was burned at the stake for such a pursuit. His final words were "Lord, open the King of England's eyes."[14] We must never forget how much these have suffered to pass on God's Word to our generation.

Biblical Revelation

Revelation is the act of God's self-disclosure and self-communication. As Christians, we believe that God is a talking God. Consequently, God is knowable. J. I. Packer stated, "God's friendship with men begins and grows through speech: His to us in revelation, and ours to Him in prayer and praise. Though I cannot see God, He and I can yet be personal friends, because in revelation He talks to me."[15] God has revealed himself generally in creation (Rom 1:19–20), specifically in Scripture (2 Pet 1:20–21), and most clearly and magnificently in the incarnation (John 1:14). Interestingly, Jesus, as God, was involved in all three aspects of revelation. He created the world (Col 1:16); he inspired, spoke, and fulfilled the Scriptures (Matt 5:17); and he was declared as Lord and God while on earth (John 20:28).

God's special revelation of himself in the written Word is especially relevant for a discussion on expository preaching and teaching. Unfortunately preachers often use the phrase "God revealed this to me." They then proceed to tell everyone what "the Lord has laid on their heart." Impressionable people often believe that everything said in the pulpit does indeed come from God. Such wolves often lead them astray. While God certainly speaks to our hearts through the Spirit, we should not think that these impressions ever contradict his written Word, nor should these impressions be perceived as having the same authority as the Scriptures.

Perhaps the reason that this issue is so misunderstood is because many assume preachers today are like preachers in the biblical period. Indeed, there is much to glean from biblical preachers, but there are also some big differences. While we do carry on

---

[13] Brian Edwards, *God's Outlaw*, 6th ed. (Darlington, England: Evangelical Press, 1988), 71.
[14] Ibid., 168.
[15] J. I. Packer, *God Has Spoken* (London: Hodder & Stoughton, 1965), 34.

the tradition of speaking for God, there is one major difference between preaching then and preaching today: biblical preachers often gave first-time revelation. Because God's revelation was given progressively, God revealed new things through them. In the case of the apostles, these men had the blessing of being physical eyewitnesses to Jesus. We do not share this privilege.

Therefore, it is important to remember that we do not give *new* revelation. We declare old revelation. In the words of D. A. Carson, we give "re-revelation"; that is, we "reannounce" the Word of God.[16] Contemporary preachers should never think that preaching today is to be *exactly* as it was in the biblical period. Sure, we have the same source of authority as the apostles and prophets, but it has come to us *fully* and *finally* in the written Word. Our present task is to take God's revelation deposited in the Bible and faithfully proclaim it to people. This is a liberating truth. The preacher today does not have to come up with "new stuff" every week. The old stuff is good and sufficient! Love it and give this old wine in some new wineskins.

The similarities, however, of preaching then and now certainly help us to understand the preaching event. First, the biblical preachers explained and applied God's revelation. In Nehemiah 8, Ezra read from the law, and it was explained and applied to the people (vv. 8–9). The Jewish synagogue also provided occasions for teaching, which became the pattern for the early church. Jesus also explained the Scriptures throughout his ministry. In the Sermon on the Mount, he began several sections saying, "You have heard it said" and then proceeded to offer a fuller understanding of the selected text and its implications. He also explained the Scriptures in the synagogue and on the Emmaus Road (Luke 4:16–21; 24:27, 32).

In addition, preaching in the biblical period was done publicly. Luke describes the pattern of the early church: "Every day in the temple complex, and in various homes, they continued teaching and proclaiming the good news that Jesus is the Messiah" (Acts 5:42). Paul urged Timothy and Titus to teach sound doctrine and expound the Scriptures publicly (1 Tim 4:13; 2 Tim 1:13–14; 2:2; Titus 2:1,15). Contemporary preachers follow this tradition of public exhortation, pointing people to Jesus.

---

[16] D. A. Carson, "Contemporary Challenges and Aims," in *Preach the Word*, ed. Leland Ryken and Todd A. Wilson (Wheaton, IL: Crossway, 2007), 176.

Next, the biblical preachers used rhetorical elements such as reasoning and persuasion in their preaching. In Acts 17:1–3, four words are used of Paul's preaching. Luke writes that he "*reasoned*. . . from the Scriptures, *explaining* and *showing* that the Messiah had to suffer and rise from the dead: 'This Jesus I am *proclaiming* to you is the Messiah'" (vv. 2–3). The word *reasoned* is used ten times in Acts (see Acts 17:17; 18:4; 19:8). It is the word from which we get the English word *dialogue*. The word *explain* literally means "opening." Like Jesus, Paul opened up the Scriptures and exalted the Messiah. The term for "showing" or "proving" means "to place beside" or "to set before." Paul provided reasonable arguments for the hearers to believe the message. Consequently, Luke adds that many were "persuaded" (18:4). This term is used at least seven times of Paul's preaching in Acts (cf., 13:43; 18:4; 19:8, 26; 26:28; 28:23–24). It means to act on the basis of what is recommended. Paul thus gives us an example of the use of rhetoric in preaching.[17]

Therefore, God's revelation deposited in the Bible provides the preacher with the necessary substance for faithful preaching. Contemporary preachers do not share the same experience of preachers in the biblical period in how God's revelation was received, but they do share many other features, such as explanation and application, public proclamation, and rhetorical persuasion. These elements should be used to proclaim God's revelation and story of redemption, which ultimately culminates in the person and work of Jesus.

Biblical Sufficiency

Another important doctrine that supports an expositional ministry is the sufficiency of Scripture. The sufficiency of Scripture means that God's Word contains everything we need for salvation, knowing God's will, being conformed into Christ's image, and trusting in God perfectly. In short, it is to believe that Scripture makes us "complete, equipped for every good work" (2 Tim 3:17). The sufficiency of Scripture does not mean, however, that we should not read other books at all. It does mean that God intends for his Word—coupled with the Spirit—to be the primary means for shaping people into the image of Christ.

---

[17] For more detail on Paul's rhetoric, see James Thompson, *Preaching like Paul* (Louisville: WJK, 2001).

The sufficiency of Scripture reminds us that the Bible is a spiritual book with a spiritual purpose of changing us from the inside out. We should rejoice in the fact that God's Word meets our deepest needs. We also should be committed to proclaiming it to people, who need God's Word more than man's observations and practical suggestions.

The benefits of Scripture are marvelous. In Psalm 19, Scripture claims to bring conversion, wisdom, joy, understanding, warning, and reward. In 119:9–11, Scripture is said to produce cleansing and protection from sin. Psalm 119:105 teaches that Scripture brings guidance. Jeremiah teaches us that God's Word brings joy and assurance (Jer 15:16). He adds that Scripture produces brokenness and humility (Jer 23:29). The Emmaus disciples discovered that the Scripture brought about a changed heart (Luke 24:32). Jesus prayed that the Father would sanctify his followers by the Scriptures (John 17:17). Paul affirmed that faith comes by hearing from the Word of God (Rom 10:17). Paul told Timothy that the Scriptures were sufficient enough to produce wisdom for salvation, content for instruction and reproof, and the necessary equipment for ministry (2 Tim 3:14–17). The author of Hebrews stated that Scripture searches the soul and examines the heart (Heb 4:12). Both James and Peter affirmed that salvation comes by way of the Word (Jas 1:21; 1 Pet 1:22–25). Peter added that Scripture produces spiritual growth (1 Pet 2:1–2).

These truths lead to one major question for preachers: If the claims of Scripture are true, then why would we want to give people anything other than God's revelation? Sure, there may be times to offer some practical suggestions and counsel or to read from a contemporary writer. However, we must distinguish between "good stuff" and "God's stuff."[18] Discerning expositors know the difference between helpful material and the life-changing gospel. They will also avoid "emotional sensationalism" and "pragmatic moralism."

Emotional sensationalism is the idea that a preacher does not need to study but instead should have a "word from the Lord" every week. Apparently, this "word" is supposed to come directly from God and may or may not be tied to the Bible. A belief in the sufficiency of Scripture, however, reminds the preacher that we always have "a word from the Lord." We have sixty-six books filled with God's Word! As I often tell high school students, "If you want to hear God speak, open the book. When you open the Word of God, you open

---

[18] Jim Shaddix, *The Passion-Driven Sermon* (Nashville: B&H, 2003), 65–66.

the mouth of God." Of course, there are times when God may lead us to particular passages from which to preach, but the idea that we should always have "the warm fuzzies" before we preach is unnecessary and dangerous. If you accurately expose the Scriptures, they are sufficient to perform God's redemptive work even on your worst day.

On the other extreme is *pragmatic moralism*. This view is expressed in the way many view the Bible as an answer book for all of mankind's questions and problems. To be sure, Scripture answers a lot of questions, but it does not answer *every* question people are asking. A pastor cannot possibly know every practical need of his people nor address them in every sermon. He can, however, meet the universal needs of everyone; namely, conforming people into the image of Christ (Rom 8:29). As God's Word is expounded week-by-week, spiritual growth takes place. Paul told the Galatians, "I am in the pains of childbirth for you until Christ is formed in you" (Gal 4:19). The expositor's role is to expound the Scriptures so that Christ may be formed in his people—not to try and address every perceived need of people. As transformation takes place, people's deepest needs are really met.

THE CENTRALITY OF CHRIST IN THE SCRIPTURES

Let us move from the nature of Scripture to the overall *message* of Scripture. What is the Bible about? Is there a unified message in Scripture? Is the same God revealed in both testaments? These are critical questions for those who wish to proclaim "the whole plan of God" (Acts 20:27). I believe that the redemptive purpose of Scripture (transforming people into Christ's image) is consistent with the redemptive message of Scripture. The Bible narrates the ongoing flow of redemptive history that moves ultimately to the person and work of Jesus.

Therefore exposition, at its best, will move inexorably to Jesus as the hero of Scripture. Certainly, evangelicals have emphasized the need to preach Christ historically. The sixteenth-century Puritan William Perkins summarized his theory of preaching, saying, "Preach one Christ, by Christ, to the praise of Christ. To God alone be the glory."[19] Likewise, John Broadus stated, "The subject

---

[19] William Perkins, *The Art of Prophesying*, rev. Sinclair Ferguson, first published in Latin, 1592, then in English, 1606 (repr., Carlisle, PA: Banner of Truth Trust, 1996), 79.

of preaching is divine truth, centrally the gospel as revealed and offered in Jesus Christ."[20] The problem, however, for the expositor, is that sometimes the selected text does not mention Jesus. How do you do justice to the selected text and still preach Christ where he does not seem to be present? The answer is found in seeing the Bible as a unified book. Every text stands somewhere in relation to Christ. Every text will point to Christ futuristically, refer to Christ explicitly, or look back to Christ implicitly.

Several writers in recent years have focused attention on Jesus as the hero of Scripture. For example, Arturo Azurdia argues that the Bible is "a record of the redemption of the people of God by His Son, Jesus Christ."[21] Norman Geisler states, "Christ is presented as the tie between the Testaments, the content of the whole canon, and the unifying theme within each book of the Bible."[22] Christopher J. H. Wright says, "The Old Testament tells the story which Jesus completes."[23] Similarly, Donald Juel posits, "The beginnings of Christian reflection can be traced to the interpretations of Israel's scriptures, and the major focus of that scriptural interpretation was Jesus, the crucified and risen Messiah."[24]

Integrating Biblical Theology

In order to effectively teach the details of a particular text, and give attention to the wider biblical narrative, we need to understand biblical theology. Biblical theology assumes that the many authors of the Bible are telling one overarching story, which culminates in Christ. You might liken this practice in Bible reading/teaching to the skill of a good point guard in basketball. Good point guards do not merely dribble the ball to the basket with their head down to the floor. Instead, they use full-court vision. They know where their teammates are (and where they are supposed to be), where defenders on the court are located, and what play should be called. Similarly, good Bible readers and teachers do not merely analyze the present passage (though they must); they also have enough "full-court

---

[20] John Broadus, *On the Preparation and Delivery of Sermons*, new and rev. ed. Jesse Witherspoon (New York: Harper and Brothers, 1944), 6.

[21] Arturo Azurdia, *Spirit-Empowered Preaching* (Ross-Shire, England: Christian Focus Publications, 1998), 52.

[22] Norman Geisler, *Christ: The Theme of the Bible* (Chicago: Moody, 1968), 7.

[23] Christopher J. H. Wright, *Knowing Jesus Through the Old Testament* (Downers Grove, IL: InterVarsity, 1995), 2.

[24] Donald Juel, *Messianic Exegesis* (Philadelphia: Fortress, 1988), 1.

vision" to know what is going on before and after the text, and how it all relates to overall progression of the biblical narrative.[25]

J. I. Packer defined biblical theology as "the umbrella-name for those disciplines that explore the unity of the Bible, delving into the contents of books, showing the links between them, and pointing up the ongoing flow of the revelatory and redemptive process that reached its climax in Jesus Christ."[26] Biblical theology deals with God's progressive revelation, whereas systematic theology deals more with topics that are supported by the Bible.

D. A. Carson also emphasizes how biblical theology focuses on the unity of the Bible and redemptive history, without sacrificing the individual documents and each historical context. He said, "On the one hand, biblical theology will try to preserve one glorious diversity of all the biblical documents; on the other, it will try to uncover all that holds them together, *sacrificing neither historical particularity nor the unifying sweep of redemptive history.*"[27] Therefore, when we expound a passage, we should also consider the wider biblical context, in order to make an appropriate Christological connection. Of course, what I am advocating is not a new idea. The *Baptist Faith and Message* in article 1, "The Scriptures," reads:

> The Holy Bible was written by men divinely inspired and is God's revelation of Himself to man. It is a perfect treasure of divine instruction. It has God for its author, salvation for its end, and truth, without any mixture of error, for its matter. Therefore, all Scripture is totally true and trustworthy. It reveals the principles by which God judges us, and therefore is, and will remain to the end of the world, the true center of Christian union, and the supreme standard by which all human conduct, creeds, and religious opinions should be tried. *All Scripture is a testimony to Christ, who is Himself the focus of divine revelation.*[28]

---

[25] Illustration adapted from an article by Jeramie Rinne, "Biblical Theology and Gospel Proclamation," accessed Feb 12, 2015, http://9marks.org/article/biblical-theology-and-gospel-proclamation/.

[26] J. I. Packer, "Foreword," in *The Unfolding Mystery* (Colorado Springs: Navpress, 1988), 7–8.

[27] D. A. Carson, "Systematic Theology and Biblical Theology," in *New Dictionary of Biblical Theology*, ed. T. Desmond Alexander, Brian S. Rosner, D. A. Carson, and Graeme Goldsworthy (Downers Grove, IL: InterVarsity, 2000), 100–101, my emphasis.

[28] Statement accessed February 13, 2015, http://www.sbc.net/bfm2000/bfm2000.asp, my emphasis.

Preaching Christ from All the Scriptures

A Christ-centered understanding of Scripture should lead us to a Christ-centered philosophy of expository preaching. So, what exactly does it mean to "preach Christ?" Sidney Greidanus defines *preaching Christ* "as preaching sermons which authentically integrate the message of the text with the climax of God's revelation in the *person, work,* and/or *teaching* of Jesus Christ as revealed in the New Testament."[29] To see Christ formed in our people, we should always emphasize, in our exposition, the unique person, work, and/or teaching of the Messiah. Graeme Goldsworthy expresses the heart of Christ-exalting exposition, saying, "It ought to be the aim of every pastor to bring all members of his or her congregation to maturity in Christ. But they cannot mature if they do not know the Christ in the Bible, the Christ to whom the whole Bible, Old and New Testaments, give a unified and inspired testimony."[30]

I want to underline four biblical reasons *why* we should read the Scriptures Christocentrically. First, Jesus clearly saw himself as the fulfillment of the Old Testament writings. Those who wish to challenge the unity of the Bible and its Christocentric emphasis must give an answer to several biblical texts that seem to demonstrate this idea. For example, one should consider the following texts:

- "You pore over the Scriptures because you think you have eternal life in them, yet they testify about Me" (John 5:39).
- "For if you believed Moses, you would believe Me, because he wrote about Me" (John 5:46).
- "He then rolled up the scroll, gave it back to the attendant, and sat down. And the eyes of everyone in the synagogue were fixed on Him. He began by saying to them, 'Today as you listen, this Scripture has been fulfilled'" (Luke 4:20–21).
- "Then beginning with Moses and all the Prophets, He interpreted for them the things concerning Himself in all the Scriptures" (Luke 24:27).
- "These are My words that I spoke to you while I was still with you—that everything written about Me in the Law of Moses, the Prophets, and the Psalms must be fulfilled" (Luke 24:44).

[29] Sidney Greidanus, *Preaching Christ from the Old Testament* (Grand Rapids: Eerdmans, 1999), 8.
[30] Graeme Goldsworthy, "Biblical Theology as the Heartbeat of Effective Ministry," in *Biblical Theology*, ed. Scott J. Hafemann (Downers Grove, IL: InterVarsity, 2002), 286.

A commitment to Christ-exalting exposition is consistent with the expositional principles of Jesus. Jesus said that the Scriptures were about him! Do not let enlightenment literary concepts or modern skepticism and relativism keep you from affirming this basic belief.

Second, the apostles knew that the Bible focused upon Jesus. Paul bookends his letter to the Romans with statements about the Old Testament and the Messiah (Rom 1:1b–3; 16:25–27). He tells the Corinthians that Christ died for our sins "according to the Scriptures," and that he was buried and raised on the third day "according to the Scriptures" (referring to the Old Testament Scriptures). He also told Timothy that the Old Testament is able to make a person "wise for salvation in Christ" (2 Tim 3:15).

The apostolic preaching in Acts also illustrates how the Old Testament was used as the means of preaching to unbelievers. Peter's first sermon consisted of an exposition of Joel and Psalm 16 and 110 (Acts 2:14–34). A few days later he preached about Jesus fulfilling God's promises and what the prophets foretold about the Messiah (3:18–25). In Acts 8, Philip explained to the Ethiopian eunuch that Isaiah 53 speaks of Jesus. Christ-exalting preaching from the Old Testament is powerfully demonstrated in Paul's first recorded sermon in Acts 13. Here, Paul preaches the death of Jesus and references several Old Testament texts (Ps 2:7; 16:10; Isa 49:6; 55:3; Hab 1:5). In Thessalonica, Paul does not hand out gospel tracts but, instead, reasons from the Scriptures in order to proclaim Christ (Acts 17:2–3). In Corinth, Paul is "occupied with the Word, testifying to the Jews that the Christ was Jesus" (Acts 18:5 ESV). When before Agrippa, Paul says, "I stand here testifying both to small and great, saying nothing but what the prophets and Moses said would come to pass: that the Christ must suffer and that, by being the first to rise from the dead, he would proclaim light both to our people and to the Gentiles" (Acts 26:22–23 ESV). At the end of Acts, Luke records, "From morning till evening he expounded to them, testifying to the kingdom of God and trying to convince them about Jesus both from the Law of Moses and from the Prophets" (28:23 ESV). This was how the apostles read the Bible, and how they preached it. Clearly they followed Jesus's words about the message of the Bible.

From Genesis to Revelation, the Bible is a Christian book. The whole Bible tells us the story of the Redeemer. It is more than an inspired book of moral virtues. It is a book about salvation. Sadly, many people know Bible stories but do not know the story of the Bible. While some Bible teachers are more "minimalists than maximalists" on the Christocentric emphasis scale, everyone should at least see that the whole Bible is Christian Scripture—and should seek to teach and apply Scripture in a redemptive manner.

In encouraging this type of reading, I am not advocating *allegory* or clever "Jesus-jukes" (also called *spiritualizing*). Some well-intended but misguided people, in their zeal to preach Christ, sometimes play fast and loose with the Bible, making cavalier and fanciful correspondences that are not in the text. Every time you read about *wood* in the Old Testament, it does not stand for the cross. Every time you see the color *red*, it does not signify blood. These are examples of silly, unfounded allegorical readings. What I am advocating is seeing the inner-biblical connections that lead us to Jesus—not allegory. The apostles saw them. Exegete responsibly and do good biblical theology. And if you do not think allegory is ridiculous, try to allegorize your wife's grocery list sometime! If you come home and say, "Well, you wrote down marshmallows, but I took that to mean toilet paper," she will not like your interpretative method! No, study the text in its historical context but then use your full-court vision to survey the entire biblical narrative, and lead people to the Redeemer with valid inner-biblical themes and connections. This leads to a third argument.

Third, we should see and expound Christ in all the Scriptures because of the thematic and climactic nature of Scripture. Some theologians propose one primary theme in Scripture over others, such as the kingdom of God, the presence of God, creation and new creation, or the offices of Jesus. I prefer to see these themes as many sides to the diamond of Scripture. Each displays a sense of glory and uniqueness to the beautiful unity of the Bible. These themes move climactically to the New Testament fulfillments. Again, Scripture is seen in a progressive nature, reaching its apex in Christ. So, I am not saying that every single verse in the Bible is directly speaking about Jesus. We should not go to Joshua 2:1 and say, "Oh, that's about Jesus," but what we should realize is that all the plot lines converge on Christ. All of the imbedded themes of salvation converge in him. Learn to look for these themes and see how these themes escalate until they reach their apex in the Messiah—and may you find your heart strangely "warmed" like those Emmaus disciples.

Finally, Christ-exalting exposition makes sense when you consider the primary purpose of the Spirit. Jesus said of the Spirit, "He will testify about Me" (John 15:26) and "He will glorify Me" (John 16:14). The primary role of the Spirit is to shine the spotlight upon the Son of God. The nature of the Bible illustrates his Christ-exalting work. Bruce Ware reminds us, "For although the Spirit is primarily responsible for producing the Bible as the inspired Word of God, the Bible is not primarily about the Spirit but rather it is about the Son."[31] On the day of Pentecost, the Spirit is poured out, Peter exalts Jesus from the Scripture (Acts 2:14–36), and people are converted. As the Scriptures are preached, the Spirit opens hearts of people to respond in repentance and faith to Jesus (Acts 16:14). The entire Godhead works in glad harmony in bringing people to faith in Christ (John 17:2–3).

SUMMATION

In this chapter, I have sought to identify four convictions about Scripture that drive preachers to an expositional ministry: inspiration, authority, revelation, and sufficiency. I have also noted the message of Scripture: God's work in redemptive history that culminates in Jesus. The implication of this understanding is that faithful expositors should proclaim the biblical text first in its original setting and then in view of its redemptive historical setting, exalting the person, work, and teaching of Jesus. Ultimately, the purpose of Christ-exalting exposition is to see Christ formed in his people for the glory of God.

QUESTIONS

1. How does our view of the Bible affect the way we handle the Bible in preaching and teaching?
2. How is preaching and teaching today both similar *and* different from preaching and teaching in *the biblical period?*

---

[31] Ware, *Father, Son, and Holy Spirit*, 110.

3. How can biblical theology help the expositor keep a Christ-centered focus in each message?
4. What is Sidney Greidanus's definition of preaching Christ?
5. What are four reasons why the preacher should desire to exalt Christ from the whole Bible?

4

PROCLAIM CHRIST FROM THE SCRIPTURES

Him we proclaim, warning everyone and teaching everyone with all wisdom, that we may present everyone mature in Christ. For this I toil, struggling with all his energy that he powerfully works within me.

—Colossians 1:28–29 (ESV)

If I have learned anything in 35 or 40 years of teaching, it is that students don't learn everything I teach them. What they learn is what I am excited about, the kinds of things I emphasize again and again and again and again. That had better be the gospel.[1]

—D. A. Carson

My GOAL IN THIS chapter is to challenge you with one main idea: *To passionately make the hero of the Bible (Jesus) the hero of every message you prepare.*[2]

---

[1] D. A. Carson online post, accessed February 15, 2015, http://www.thegospelcoalition .org/blogs/justintaylor/2010/11/19/carson-people-dont-learn-what-i-teach-them-they -learn-what-im-excited-about/.

[2] Much of this chapter first appeared in my e-book *Proclaiming Jesus* (Gospel-Centered Discipleship, 2012).

From where have you derived your view of teaching and preaching the Bible? You should think about this. If you are a pastor, think of how many times you will preach! Think of how many of your sermons people will hear (especially your wife!). If you are a regular teacher in the church at some level (small group, youth minister, college minister, etc.), then you should long to be effective, as well. Perhaps you are headed overseas to minister among an unreached people group. You have the holy and happy responsibility of declaring the Scriptures, and surely you want to do so faithfully. If you are a parent, then you have daily opportunities to teach your children God's Word, and surely you desire to do good biblical teaching.

I believe that the best book on preaching and teaching the Bible is *the Bible*. The Bible gives us the *convictions* we need for our task. Effective Christ-centered teachers and preachers are not those who have mastered certain techniques; they are those who *have been mastered by certain convictions.*[3]

In Colossians 1:24–29, we find some key convictions for the ministry of the Word. In verses 28 and 29, Paul says, "Him we proclaim, warning everyone and teaching everyone with all wisdom, that we may present everyone mature in Christ. For this I toil, struggling with all his energy that he powerfully works within me" (ESV).

Paul introduces us to the grand subject of Christian exposition saying, "Him we proclaim." One cannot miss this all-consuming passion of Paul and others in the New Testament. Luke records of the early church, "And every day, in the temple, and from house to house, they did not cease teaching and preaching that the Christ is Jesus" (Acts 5:42 ESV).

If Carson is correct—that people remember what we are most excited about—then everyone would have remembered that Paul preached Christ again and again. He was most excited about the Savior. To the Corinthians, Paul said the following:

> And I, when I came to you, brothers, did not come proclaiming to you the testimony of God with lofty speech or wisdom. For I decided to know nothing among you except Jesus Christ and him crucified. And I was with you in weakness and in fear and much trembling, and my speech and my message were not in plausible words of wisdom, but

---

[3] John Stott, *Between Two Worlds* (Grand Rapids: Eerdmans, 1982), 92.

in demonstration of the Spirit and of power, so that your faith might not rest in the wisdom of men but in the power of God. (1 Cor 2:1–5 ESV)

Paul was a highly educated individual, and yet he resolved to know "nothing except Jesus Christ and him crucified" (1 Cor 2:2). At the end of this same letter, he tells the Corinthians that he delivered to them what was of "first importance" (15:3); namely, the crucifixion and resurrection of Christ, which was in "accordance with the Scriptures" (vv. 3–4). In between these two bookends, Paul talks to the Corinthian church about a lot of important matters, but everything was understood in light of the gospel, not abstracted from the gospel nor placed in higher regard than the gospel.

THE HEART OF THE MESSAGE AND THE MESSENGER: CHRIST

Paul made it quite clear what he was most excited about. Have we? We can surely talk about a lot of things. Sometimes we can suggest very helpful things to people. But when people think of your ministry to the world, do they think "gospel" first? Do you think it should be first?

Some have abandoned the centrality of heralding Christ because they have abandoned historic Christianity. Joel Green and Mark Baker say, "We believe the popular fascination with and commitment to penal substitutionary atonement has had ill effects in the life of the church and in the United States and has had little to offer the global church and mission by way of understanding or embodying the message of Jesus Christ."[4] It has had ill effects and has little to offer the world? According to Paul, that is precisely what we hold out to the world, the good news of a substitute! Tim Keller stresses the need to emphasize this central doctrine in ministry, also. While recognizing the beautiful diversity of Scripture, and the diamond-like quality of the gospel, he contends, "At the heart of all of the biblical writers' theology is redemption through substitution."[5] Let the heart of their theology captivate your heart and impress it on the hearts of your listeners.

---

[4] Joel B. Green and Mark D. Baker, *Recovering the Scandal of the Cross* (Downers Grove, IL: InterVarsity, 2000), 220.

[5] Tim Keller, *Center Church* (Grand Rapids: Zondervan, 2012), 40.

Others have abandoned Christ-centered preaching and teaching for pragmatic moralistic instruction, using the Bible merely as a book of virtues to commend to others. Many of these moralistic sermons do not even contain the gospel. So one may hear a children's sermon on Noah's ark conclude by telling the children, "Now, go love animals." The story of Ruth is turned into a sermon on merely loving your mother-in-law. I recently heard a popular evangelical preacher actually open his sermon on pride (from Daniel 4) by saying, "Today I'm going to tell you a really fascinating story from the Old Testament. This is the great news: If you're not a Christian, this is the perfect Sunday for you to be here because we're not going to talk about Jesus—because this is from the Old Testament." There are so many problems with this statement (I listened to the whole sermon, and he fulfilled his objective). Putting his Old Testament understanding aside for now, it is astonishing to think that a Christian preacher would deliberately set out to *not* talk about Jesus in any sermon, and then to consider this approach to be "great news" for the unbeliever in the audience. Such an idea of preaching is foreign to the New Testament. The early church could not stop preaching about the risen Christ. Why would we want to give people anything else? What else do we have to offer? Yet, many are preaching sermons in Christian churches without speaking about the work of Christ and think that they are actually helping people by giving them a gospel substitute.

Christless Pulpits

In *Christless Christianity*, Michael Horton asks the following question: "What would happen if Satan really took control of a city?" He alludes to Donald Grey Barnhouse, who offered his own scenario half a century ago. Barnhouse speculated that if Satan took over Philadelphia all of the bars would be closed, pornography would be banished, and pristine streets would be filled with tidy pedestrians who smiled at each other. There would be no swearing. The children would say, "Yes, sir" and "No, ma'am," and the churches would be full every Sunday. But . . . *Christ would not be preached.*[6]

Whether or not you agree with Barnhouse's whole scenario, you see what he was driving at, right? Satan does not mind a moral improvement plan; what he hates is Christ being proclaimed.

[6] Michael Horton, *Christless Christianity* (Grand Rapids: Baker, 2008), 15.

We have a "Christless Christianity" today because we have too many Christless pulpits, too many Christless youth ministries, too many parents giving their kids Christless instruction. To be clear, I am not against morality. I am not advocating immorality! I only want to point out that mere morality is insufficient. Morality might keep my kids out of jail, but only Jesus can keep them out of hell, and only Jesus can change their hearts presently and permanently.

Today's Christless message is basically, "God created the world. He wants you to be nice and fair. He wants you to be happy. He's not very involved in your life, but He's there in case you have a problem. And if you are basically a good person, then you can go to heaven when you die." Christian Smith calls this *Moralistic, Therapeutic Deism.* It is not the gospel, yet it is believed by far too many. Moralism is insufficient, and it is deceptive.

Furthermore, many moralistic messages, filled with "be good, try harder" exhortations, could be preached by Mormons, Jews, or any other moral teachers. But they are not Christian messages. The Pharisees said a lot of true things about the Bible, and were quite moral (at least in appearance), but they missed Jesus! Jesus reserved his harshest words for them! The focus of the Christian life and Christian teaching must center on Christ himself.

Do You Preach Christ?

I find that when I talk about making exposition explicitly Christ-centered, everyone thinks I am talking about someone else. They never dream that they could possibly be preparing Christless messages. One of my students recently delivered a message on Deuteronomy 6 but said nothing about the gospel. I asked the class, "Was the gospel explicit in this message?" The answer was no. The student received this review humbly, admitting that he failed to do this essential part of sermon preparation. We then talked about how to do this appropriately, and in the next sermon he did a fine job of dealing with both the historical context and the over-arching gospel storyline of the Bible. I try to get students to do just that, to relate their particular text to the overarching redemptive thrust of Scripture.

My friend Charlie realized his own Christless preaching and changed his method.[7] He told me that for his first seven years

---

[7] Pseudonym. Story taken from a recent conversation with him.

as a pastor he mainly created man-centered, moral exhortations from the Bible. He then read Bryan Chapell's wonderful book, *Christ-Centered Preaching*. He said, "It wrecked me. I repented and changed my approach." He said most of what was passing for good exposition when he was a student was someone reading the text and giving a cleverly alliterated outline. But those sermons often had little depth and failed to have a consistent, explicit, gospel focus. He said, "I can tell you that after six years now of constantly making Jesus the hero every week, there's more fruit in my ministry than the previous years. The people are far more generous, more are going overseas on mission, and there's more growth in holiness." He then said, "I have more joy in ministry than I've ever had in my life." His story reflected the same testimony of other pastor friends who have made a similar adjustment in their preaching and ministry and witnessed similar results.

Charlie later shared with me a vivid story that illustrates how his people love Christ-centered exposition. He said, "One day we were unable to meet for corporate worship because of a snow storm, so I told our people to go check on a particular pastor's website and tune in for the live-streamed service." Charlie said, "I knew that this pastor loved Jesus, and the Bible, and that the sermon should be edifying and helpful." However, he was surprised and disappointed. He said to me, "Brother, there was no Jesus in that sermon. Jesus was not even mentioned." Charlie began getting e-mails from members. He then sent an e-mail to the church, apologizing for having them go to the site. Interestingly, that pastor called Charlie a few weeks later! He said, "I heard what you said . . . that I didn't preach Christ." Charlie was a bit taken back by this. Then the pastor said, "I want you to know I went back and watched the sermon, and you were right. I'm embarrassed." I appreciate this pastor's honesty and humility.

Later a similar experience occurred, only this time it was his youth minister. Charlie said that his youth minister is quite a gifted communicator of the gospel. But something happened when he gave him the pulpit one Sunday. He said, "It was a train wreck." Charlie said that one of his senior adult ladies called him and said, "This church has been known for having Jesus as the hero of every sermon. But today the preacher was the hero." Charlie then watched the sermon with the youth minister, and he humbly received correction.

I do not share these stories to be critical of these brothers. I admire their honesty, humility, and repentance. I regretfully admit that I have preached some terrible sermons myself. My singing is embarrassing, but my early preaching was far worse! I once preached an entire sermon on *ants* and failed to mention Christ and the gospel (and was even proud of my knowledge of ants!). So I do not intend to belittle anyone. I come in the spirit of "Let's all examine our teaching and preaching and see if we're proclaiming Christ faithfully, accurately, and explicitly."

If our Sunday morning service was snowed out, and we all watched your sermon, would Christ be preached? I love Spurgeon's reminder, when commenting on Paul's sermon in Acts 13, "The motto of all true servants of God must be, 'We preach Christ; and him crucified.' A sermon without Christ in it is like a loaf of bread without any flour in it. No Christ in your sermon, sir? Then go home, and never preach again until you have something worth preaching."[8]

Even the best of preachers can fall victim to having a weak or absent Christ focus. D. Martyn Lloyd-Jones, one of my heroes, was one of the finest expositors of the previous generation. However, on one occasion, another minister came up to Lloyd-Jones after he had preached and said, "I cannot make up my mind what you are! I cannot decide whether you are a hyper-Calvinist or a Quaker." Lloyd-Jones assured him that he was no hyper-Calvinist, and he asked the man why he would make such a statement. The minister said, "Because you talk of God's action and God's sovereignty like a hyper-Calvinist, and the spiritual experience like a Quaker, *but the cross and the work of Christ have little place in your preaching.*"[9] How would you respond to this statement? "The cross and the work of Christ have little place in your preaching." Lloyd-Jones said, "I was like Whitefield in my early preaching. First I preached regeneration, that all man's own efforts in morality and education are useless, and that we need power from outside ourselves. I *assumed the atonement but did not distinctly preach it* or justification by faith. This man set me thinking and I began to read more fully in theology."[10] He took this minister's statement to heart and began studying the

---

[8] Charles Spurgeon, "To You," sermon online, accessed February 15, 2015, http://www.spurgeongems.org/vols49-51/chs2899.pdf.

[9] Ian Murray, *D. Martyn Lloyd-Jones: The First Forty Years*, 3rd ed. (Carlisle, PA: Banner of Truth Trust, 1982), 190–91, my emphasis.

[10] Ibid., 191, my emphasis.

cross more diligently in order to make the cross more central in his proclamation. That is the type of teachable spirit we need.

The Life-Changer

My concern is not that the Bible is absent in the weekly sermon. My concern is the seeming great lack of gospel clarity in weekly preaching and teaching. I am troubled by the lack of gospel-saturation in weekly messages, even by many who say they believe the gospel.

Today we hear some popular evangelicals calling for the need to preach and teach for "life change." And I am all for life change. The question is, "How are lives changed?" I fear that many think that life change is mainly about behavior modification, rather than transformation through Christ. As I listen to a lot of those who champion "life-changing preaching," their sermons are filled with moralistic instruction devoid of the gospel. We must understand that in order to preach "life-changing sermons," *we must keep the Life-changer at the heart of the sermon.* Keller says, "The main way to avoid moralistic preaching is to be sure that you always preach Jesus as the ultimate point and message of every text."[11] In other words, keep the Life-changer at the heart of the sermon.

Jesus Christ was the all-consuming subject of Paul's ministry because he saw Christ as the grand subject of biblical revelation, and all of human history. His passion to proclaim the Life-changer appears throughout his writings:

> For what we proclaim is not ourselves, but Jesus Christ as Lord, with ourselves as your servants for Jesus' sake. For God, who said, "Let light shine out of darkness," has shone in our hearts to give the light of the knowledge of the glory of God in the face of Jesus Christ. (2 Cor 4:5–6 ESV)

> What then? Only that in every way, whether in pretense or in truth, Christ is proclaimed, and in that I rejoice. (Phil 1:18a ESV)

> Remember Jesus Christ, risen from the dead, the offspring of David, as preached in my gospel. (2 Tim 2:8 ESV)

---

[11] Keller, *Center Church*, 77.

Let us be most excited about proclaiming Christ incarnate in the context of the full sweep of redemptive history. Proclaim Jesus, his person and his work, within the context of the entire Bible. Aim for your hearers to say each week, "What a great Savior!" not "What a great sermon!" Such Christ-centered preaching always offers hope to people. To do this, you need to make your motive consistent with your message. Do you long for people to make much of Jesus or *you* when you deliver the Word? Long for him to be the hero in your heart and your message.

Some fear that constant Christ-exalting preaching will get old and become monotonous. But the riches of Christ are "unsearchable" Paul says (Eph 3:8). This means that as long as we are proclaiming Christ, we will never run out of material! Further, it is wrong to assume that people are not longing to see glory (more in chap. 7). If Christ-centered proclamation gets old, the problem is not with the Savior—it may be a problem with the speaker's heart (or those in the audience), but it is not in the subject matter.

Clarifications

I am not advocating that you merely mention Jesus's name in a sermon, use wild allegory, or leap-frog to the cross during an invitation after preaching a moralistic message. I am calling for something wider and deeper. I want people to see the unity of the Bible and how it points to Jesus, by way of whole-Bible context, theme development, and pattern. I want to see teachers and preachers make appropriate grace-filled, new-covenant applications from their chosen text.

Sometimes students ask about the Trinity when I emphasize Christ-centered exposition. Am I advocating that you neglect the Father and the Spirit? Certainly not! Proclaim Christ within a trinitarian theology. Indeed, we do not understand Christ properly apart from his relationship within the Trinity. Christ humbled himself, relied on the Spirit, and died an atoning death to the glory of God the Father (Phil 2:5–11). At the cross, Jesus absorbed the Father's wrath for sinners like us. To preach Christ rightly is to preach him in view of the Triune nature of God.

I am talking about being Christ-centered because we are called to teach and preach *the Bible*—and the Bible is mainly about Jesus! In the words of one of America's great theologians and pastors,

Jonathan Edwards, "Christ and his redemption are the great subject of the whole Bible."[12] If we are preaching about what is in the Bible, and Jesus is the hero of the Bible, then our exposition should point to him somehow.

Finally, I am not saying we do not get practical and talk about the nitty-gritty stuff of life. I am saying that when you get practical, remain Christ-centered in your application. There is a Christ-centered practicality, seeing all of life through the gospel and living by the Spirit. And there is a "practical application" that involves mere conventional wisdom, felt-need tips, and behavioral suggestions to improve one's life, or legalistic exhortations that go beyond the Bible (but never really change the heart). Resolve to exalt the Savior and give people hope as you challenge them with practical matters such as parenting, vocation, and stewardship.

Take them to their final resting place each week: Christ. Avoid the weekly "do more, try harder" exhortations. When "do more, try harder" becomes your dominant note in preaching and teaching, not only is it missing something, but it also leads to two inevitable responses: pride or despair. Those who think they are keeping the standards will be puffed up, while the more honest types will realize that they are not measuring up and they will be crushed. Only gospel-centered instruction can make a person both humble and happy. The gospel humbles us, showing us that we cannot keep God's law, and that we are desperate for the law-fulfiller. And the gospel makes us happy because we see that Christ is our righteousness, and he has given us his power to live out this Christian life. The irony of reminding people of the good news is that they will actually "do more" by hearing this constantly. How? Gospel-saturated proclamation will cause people to love Jesus more. People who love Jesus passionately will lay down their lives for him gladly.

BACK TO THE CENTER

The Church at Colossae was much like the church today. They needed to know the real Christ. People were "religious" or "spiritual" in Colossae. Quite a blend of theologies had developed, but

---

[12] Jonathan Edwards, *A History of the Work of Redemption*, in *The Works of Jonathan Edwards*, volume I, 6th printing (Peabody: Hendrickson, 2007), 571.

there was massive theological confusion. They needed clarity, particularly clarity regarding the person and work of Jesus.

In this letter, Paul is calling the Colossians back to the center. In Colossians 1, verses 15–23 are about the glorious supremacy of Jesus Christ. Paul exalts Jesus for his lordship over creation (vv. 15–17), his headship over the church (18–19), and his saving work at the cross (19–23). Paul then describes his apostolic ministry in general and his view of proclamation in particular (1:24–2:5). After exalting the greatness of Christ, Paul gets to verse 28 and makes the logical conclusion: preach him. I love how Phillips paraphrases verses 28–29: "So *naturally, we proclaim Christ!*" (my emphasis). If these things are true about Jesus, then naturally you should preach him. Why would you want to proclaim anything or anyone else?

Notice also in verse 28, Paul shifts from the singular to the plural. He has been talking about his own personal ministry, his own suffering, and his responsibility, but he shifts and says, "Him *we* proclaim" (my emphasis). Paul is probably referring to Timothy and Epaphras in particular, but by extension, he is calling for *everyone* who proclaims the message to proclaim Christ. We need an army of Christ-centered teachers and preachers to fill pulpits, homes, and nations.

In this particular text (Col 1:24–29) Paul mentions four ways in which we do the work of Christ-centered exposition in order to make mature followers of Jesus in a diverse, confused, mixed-up world.

> Now I rejoice in my sufferings for your sake, and in my flesh I am filling up what is lacking in Christ's afflictions for the sake of his body, that is, the church, of which I became a minister according to the stewardship from God that was given to me for you, to make the word of God fully known, the mystery hidden for ages and generations but now revealed to his saints. To them God chose to make known how great among the Gentiles are the riches of the glory of this mystery, which is Christ in you, the hope of glory. Him we proclaim, warning everyone and teaching everyone with all wisdom, that we may present everyone mature in Christ. For this I toil, struggling with all his energy that he powerfully works within me. (Col 1:24–29 ESV)

Proclaim Like an Evangelist

Paul uses the term "proclaim" (*kataggellomen*) meaning "to announce throughout," or "to proclaim far and wide." Paul is speaking of announcing the facts. Proclamation involves declaring the good news. This word is used in Acts 13 when Paul and Barnabas went out on their first mission. They went to Salamis and "proclaimed the word of God in the synagogues" (Acts 13:5). They heralded the facts in the synagogue. As faithful expositors, we get to say what God has said and announce what God has done *in Christ*. We are not giving advice. We are declaring the news.

We must proclaim the facts about Jesus because we believe that there is "salvation in no one else, for there is no other name under heaven given among men by which we must be saved" (Acts 4:12). Believe that the gospel contains converting power when you announce it (Rom 1:16). I believe that exposition can be a life-changing, on-the-spot experience when the gospel of Christ is proclaimed. Do not merely preach *about* the gospel. Preach the gospel.

We also need to declare the facts about Jesus and his work to correct popular ideas. We must distinguish between religion, irreligion, and the gospel because people may be lost "younger brothers" (irreligious types) and lost "elder brothers" (religious types, see Luke 15:11–32). It is imperative that the expositor understands the doctrine of Christ and salvation. The expository evangelist recognizes that there is no separation between theology and evangelism. Every evangelist does theology. The only question is whether they are doing good theology. Present the real Jesus to people.

Additionally, as you preach Christ, aim to make the truth *real*, not only *clear*, by exalting the beauty of Christ.[13] Impress the wonders of Christ upon the hearts of people; do not merely give them information about Jesus. Believe that the person and work of Christ is compellingly attractive. Tim Keller shares how a skeptic once told a pastor that he would be happy to believe in Christianity if the pastor could give him a "watertight argument" for its truth. The pastor replied, "What if God hasn't given us a watertight argument, but rather a watertight *person*?"[14] Paul says that the Greeks look for wisdom, the Jews for miracles, but we preach Christ crucified (1

---

[13] Keller, *Center Church*, 77.
[14] Timothy Keller, *The Reason for God* (New York: Dutton, 2008), 232.

Cor 1:22). I think the best way for a skeptic to find Christianity compelling is by simply considering Jesus from his Word. Do not underestimate the power of plainly proclaiming Jesus weekly, and pray for the Spirit to open eyes for people to believe. Tell them to look to Jesus, to come to Jesus, to find their rest in Jesus.

Are you holding up the gospel for people to see and believe? I have always been challenged by Paul's words to the Galatians when he said, "It was before your eyes that Jesus Christ was publicly portrayed as crucified" (3:1b ESV). He did not mean that the Galatians were there at Golgotha, but rather that his preaching was so cross-centered that it was as if they were there! Take them there and urge them to repent and believe.

Warn Like a Prophet

The next action word Paul uses is to "warn," "admonish," or "counsel" (*noutheteo*). This word is often used to warn against wrong conduct (see Acts 20:31; 1 Cor 4:14; 1 Thess 5:12, 14; 2 Thess 3:15). A primary role of the prophet-expositor is to warn people about false teaching and ungodly living.

Paul uses this word for "warn" in writing to the Ephesian elders, saying, "Therefore be alert, remembering that for three years I did not cease night or day to admonish everyone with tears" (Acts 20:31 ESV). I love that Paul says that he did the work of warning with "tears." Prophetic instruction should come from a deep, brokenhearted love for people. Jeremiah was the "weeping prophet." Jesus wept over Jerusalem. Be a brokenhearted prophet. Paul says, "I admonish you as my beloved children" (1 Cor 4:14 ESV). Love your people deeply as you warn them about false gospels, the dangers of sin, God's judgment, and living in futility.

As expositors, we cannot be afraid to warn. Do not be naive or simplistic. Be aware of the dangers and threats and help people stay on the path of truth. A good expositor is like a forest ranger, aware of the landscape, alerting people to dangerous wildlife in the area. If you are not warning people of heresy and ungodliness, then you are not doing your job. Paul was often viewed as a troublemaker because he was not afraid to sound the alarm; he warned of wolves and snakes nearby.

Of course, to warn people is to confront people. This flies in the face of a culture that loves its "autonomy" and "privacy." But that does not matter. We have to confront people with the truth of

Scripture. A good shepherd will love his sheep enough to tell them the truth.

Teach Like a Theologian

The next way the expositor exalts Christ is through "teaching" (*didasko*). This refers to the skill of the teacher in imparting knowledge to the pupil. In proclamation we are announcing the facts, and in teaching we are explaining the facts.

Paul's evangelistic outreach was not devoid of doctrinal instruction. He regularly taught, building up believers. Both are critical for the church's mission. We must reach the unreached people groups, proclaiming Christ where he has not been named, and we must teach and build up the church.

We need a generation of Christ-centered teachers. It takes time for people to understand gospel truths. The shepherd will feed the sheep bite by bite—over time—understanding that sanctification is a slow process.

Do you long for your people to have an "Emmaus Road experience" when they hear the gospel expounded from the text? The Emmaus disciples asked, "Did not our hearts burn within while he talked to us on the road, while he opened to us the Scriptures?" (Luke 24:32 ESV). Exposition is for exaltation. Theology should lead to worship. At some point during dynamic gospel-centered instruction, people put their pens down and forget about notetaking because their hearts are soaring in worship before the Savior.

Apply Christ-Centered Wisdom Like a Pastor

Paul adds that we perform all three of these acts (proclaiming, warning, and teaching) "in all wisdom." This recalls the same phrase in Colossians 1:9, as Paul shares his pastoral heart with the believers in Colossae. He says that he is praying for them to be "filled with the knowledge of his will *in all spiritual wisdom* and understanding" (my emphasis). The goal of this wisdom is so "that we may walk worthy of our calling" (Col 1:10). Later he adds that such wisdom is found in Christ "in whom are all the treasures of wisdom and knowledge" (2:3).

Applying wisdom means to show people how the Word of God relates to all of life. As we expound the Bible, we want to apply it in such a way that people begin to see all of life through the lens of the gospel. Later Paul says, "Christ is your life" (3:4). We want to help our people develop a gospel-centered worldview. That is what Paul does in Colossians 3. He explains ways in which they must "put on Christ" (3:12). He says that racial diversity is a gospel issue (v. 11). Forgiveness is a gospel issue (v. 13). Vocation is a gospel issue (v. 24). Anxiety is a gospel issue (v. 15). How so? Well, once you understand the gospel deeply, and learn to put on Christ, you will see that racial issues aren't acceptable because we are one in Christ. Once you learn to apply the gospel, you will see that you should forgive because the Lord has forgiven you of an infinite offense. As you view life from a gospel-centered worldview, you can rest in the peace of God's gracious provision, most gloriously displayed at the cross (Rom 8:32). When you see all of life through the gospel, even your vocation is different. You realize that you are ultimately serving Christ, anticipating his reward, and not only working for a weekly paycheck.

Elsewhere in the New Testament, we see other examples of ethical demands rooted in the cross. For example, when Paul tells husbands to love their wives, he says that they should do it "as Christ loved the church and gave himself for her" (Eph 5:25). He does not say, "Love your wife because you should" or "because you have to" but "as Christ loved the church and gave himself for her." Marriage is to display the glory of the gospel. When it comes to financial contribution and stewardship, he also roots his exhortation in the cross. He says, "For you know the grace of our Lord Jesus Christ, that though he was rich, yet for your sake he became poor, so that you by his poverty might become rich" (2 Cor 8:9 ESV). Christ-centered exposition does not mean you do not give ethical exhortations; it simply means that we must root them in the cross, reminding people of what Christ has done, of who they now are, and of the power that is now theirs to live out these commands.

One may give all types of wisdom to people: worldly wisdom, conventional wisdom, suggestions from human observation, Chinese proverbs, and religious clichés. But the wisdom we need is the wisdom to know how to live all of life through the lens of the gospel by the power of the gospel. As expositors, we need to show people how this works and teach them to apply Christ-centered wisdom to their lives every day.

We often talk about five-tool players in baseball. These are players who hit for power, hit for average, can steal bases, can field, and can throw. You might say that Paul has laid out a "five-tool expositor" who carries out five communication tasks. He handles the word like a steward (Col 1:24), proclaims like an evangelist (v. 28a), warns like a prophet (v. 28b), teaches like a theologian (v. 28c), and applies wisdom like a sensitive pastor (v. 28d).[15]

Who Needs Christ-Centered Exposition?

Notice Paul's universal audience. He speaks of warning "everyone," teaching "everyone," and presenting "everyone" mature (Col 1:28). Douglas Moo says, "This verse is remarkable for its emphasis on universality."[16] Paul wants everyone, Jew and Gentile, to know Christ. Earlier Paul says that the gospel is bearing fruit and growing in "the whole world" (1:6).

Who's our audience? The nations. We have a global God. We have a global gospel. We have a global audience. What do people need to hear in New York? They need to hear the gospel of Christ. What do they need in China? The gospel of Christ.

This reality struck me on a recent mission trip to Nigeria. Our team of doctors, engineers, and pastors were doing all types of work. One day we went to a leper colony. I had never seen living conditions like that. It was a heartbreaking place for people to live. It was full of men, women, and children. Some of them had no fingers or toes. After visiting with them for a few minutes, the local chaplain said, "Now Pastor Tony will preach." Preach? I did not know I was preaching that day! I had no Bible or notes. So, what do you preach in a Nigerian leper colony? Would you say, "Now, I want to give you five tips on how to manage your finances?" or, "I want to urge you to be like David," or "Ten things they don't teach you in seminary."

To the best of my ability, I quoted Romans 8 and began to explain to them that we are all dying. I told them of the fall, the suffering of the present age, and the hope we all share in Christ. As I preached "For I consider the sufferings of this present age not worth comparing next to the glory that is to be revealed to us" (Rom 8:18), a lady with little nubs for fingers raised her hands to the sky in worship of Christ. We had a powerful time of worship in the middle of a dirt village because *everyone* needs the gospel.

---

[15] Zack Eswine speaks of this homiletical range in *Preaching to a Post-Everything World* (Grand Rapids: Baker, 2008).

[16] Douglas J. Moo, *The Letters to the Colossians and Philemon*, The Pillar New Testament Commentary (Grand Rapids: Eerdmans, 2008), 159.

In his great book, *The Mission of God*, Christopher J. H. Wright says, "The proper way for disciples of the crucified and risen Jesus to read their Scriptures is messianically and missionally."[17] There is a missional thrust to the Bible because there is this messianic thrust to the Bible. Sometimes people ask, "Where do you get your passion for missions?" The Bible. It has been said, "If you take missions out of the Bible, all you are left with is the covers!"

The nations need Christ-centered exposition! And it is through Christ-centered exposition that the nations will gather around the throne in worship one day.

One more thing should be said about doing Christ-centered preaching and teaching to the ends of the earth: it may get you killed. You can probably keep your job if you preach moralism, and you can keep your head if you do not preach Christ. No one is martyred for preaching Christless sermons. Jesus told us that suffering would come. Regarding Christ-centered heralds who proclaim, warn, teach, and apply wisdom, He says, "Therefore I send you *prophets* and *wise men* and *scribes*, some of whom you will kill and crucify, and some you will flog in your synagogues and persecute from town to town" (Matt 23:34 ESV, my emphasis). Christ-centered preaching is dangerous because the cross is offensive. We should not aim to be offensive, but we should not be surprised if the message of a bloody cross offends people and brings persecution.

Proclaiming Jesus for Sanctification, Not Only Evangelization

The purpose of Paul's Christ-exalting exposition is stated with the clause, "that we may present everyone mature in Christ" (Col 1:28b) or "complete" or "perfect" in Christ. This highlights how Christ-centered exposition has a sanctifying purpose, not only an evangelistic purpose. Indeed, Paul, as an evangelist, desired to "preach Christ where he was not named" (Rom 15:20). But it did not stop there. He also sought to bring them to maturity, which meant bringing them into Christlikeness (Gal 4:19; Col 3:10–11). He proclaimed Jesus to make disciples of Jesus.

The idea that people need Jesus for both evangelism and discipleship (growth in Christ) does away with the artificial distinction that is sometimes made about one's purpose in preaching and teaching. The question is often asked, "Do you preach to

---

[17] Christopher J. H. Wright, *The Mission of God* (Downers Grove, IL: InterVarsity, 2006), 30.

seekers or believers?" I think Paul's answer would be "I preach to sinners. They both need Jesus." Notice what he says in Colossians 2:6–7: "Therefore, as you received Christ Jesus the Lord, so walk in him, rooted and built up in him and established in the faith, just as you were taught, abounding in thanksgiving." Did you catch that? Just "as you received Christ," keep walking in him. In other words, you do not move on to something else! You received Jesus by grace through faith; you received him desperately, needily, and as your only hope—keep walking in him like that!

We must remember that we never outgrow Jesus and the need for the gospel. I was moved when I read Eric Metaxas's biography of Dietrich Bonhoeffer recently, particularly the final chapters of the book. He reported how, less than twenty-four hours before Bonhoeffer was martyred, he gathered some prisoners and held a worship service. Think about this. What would you expound if you were leading a Bible study a short while before your death? Bonhoeffer, who never outgrew his need for the gospel, expounded Isaiah 53 (on Christ's substitutionary death) and 1 Peter 1:3ff (our "living hope"). After the study and a prayer, two evil-looking men came and said, "Come with us." Bonheoffer said, "This is the end; but for me, the beginning of life."[18] Did Bonheoffer go looking for deeper mysteries outside of the gospel? No, he went deeper into the gospel!

You will grow people into Christlikeness by continuing to hold up Christ. Has it ever dawned on you that Paul spends eleven chapters in the book of Romans on the gospel before he ever gets to application? These were people who "knew" the gospel. Yet, Paul knew that what they needed was an increased understanding of the nature of salvation for their growth in Christlikeness.

As you continue to edify people with a better understanding of the gospel, a number of things will occur. You will provide a safeguard against heresy. You'll help them see their security in Christ. You will point them to the satisfaction of their soul. You will point them to their source of sustaining power (see Rom 16:25a). You will nurture them in the way that Paul says growth occurs in 2 Corinthians 3:18, "And we all, with unveiled face beholding the glory of the Lord, are being transformed into the same image from

---

[18] Eric Metaxas, *Bonhoeffer* (Nashville: Thomas Nelson, 2010), 527–28.

one degree of glory to another. For this comes from the Lord who is the Spirit" (ESV).

In Colossians 1:28b, Paul also shows that Christ-centered preaching has an eternal purpose, not only a temporal purpose. He has eternity in view. When he says, "Present everyone mature in Christ," the word *present* carries the idea of standing before God. We who lead the flock, who labor in teaching and preaching, will give an account for our teaching (Heb 13:17). Our people are unfinished business (like us); therefore, we must give them what is most important to see them fitted for eternity. What should we be giving them? Here we see it: Christ-centered proclamation, warning, teaching, and wisdom.

Laborious Work, Limitless Energy

Notice Paul's work ethic in verse 29. He says, "For this I toil, struggling. . . ." These two words, *toil* and *struggle*, express the work of authentic ministry. The first word *toil* describes the weariness that comes from being repeatedly struck. Paul knew this both physically as well as emotionally. After describing his physical hardships in 2 Corinthians 11:23–27, he then says, "And apart from other things, there is the daily pressure on me of my anxiety for all the churches" (v. 28). Yes, Paul took a beating in more ways than one—and so will all who seek to minister for God's glory.

His work ethic is further described by the complementary imagery of engaging in an athletic contest. He calls it a "struggle" (see Col 2:1). This term carries the idea of strenuous effort, with all the self-discipline required to achieve a goal.

I've read several biographies of great men, and one thing is common: none of them were lazy. They do not write biographies about lazy people. Martin Luther reportedly fell into the bed some nights because he was so tired. John Wesley and George Whitefield exhaust me just reading about them! It is reported that D. L. Moody's bedtime prayers were sometimes, "Lord, I'm tired, amen."

To be clear, I believe in taking a day off and having vacations. I do not want to die at age forty from being overworked. But the trend I am seeing is not one of dying early deaths because people are working too hard. The trend I see is the tendency to drift, coast, and be lazy. Let us resolve to serve the Lord with diligence. Learn from Paul the principle of hard work. He says, "I worked harder than any of them" (1 Cor 15:10).

Why Preaching and Teaching Is Exhausting

The work of exalting Jesus from his Word is particularly exhausting for several reasons. One of them is that your product is often invisible. You cannot always see the results of your work. That is tough. When you mow the grass, you can see the results. But with preaching and teaching, the results are difficult to measure.

Further, when you teach the Bible, you are doing something that is controversial. God's Word has a divisive effect. It is hardening or softening. The subject matter and the tension that it creates will alone make you tired.

You will also encounter waves of discouragement for various reasons. Conflict is inevitable. You will face betrayal, unjust criticism, grief, loss, doubt, and perhaps depression. Church history also shows us that your body will wear down from preaching and teaching.

Only those who preach know the internal war that goes on as you labor in this ministry. In 2 Corinthians 4:4–6, Paul describes this spiritual war. In verse 4 he says that the "god" of this world is blinding the minds of unbelievers, keeping them from seeing the glory of Christ. Then in verse 6, he says the real God has "shown in our hearts to give the light of the knowledge of the glory of God in the face of Jesus Christ." But what is in between these two verses? It is the proclamation of Christ: "For what we proclaim is not ourselves, but Jesus Christ as Lord" (v. 5a ESV). Do you see this? We proclaim Christ in the middle of a cosmic war! That is why Christ-centered exposition is exhausting (see Acts 26:18).

During some days you may want to check out and find another job. But we must go on. How? Here's what Paul says: "with all his energy that he powerfully works within me" (Col 1:29b). The apostle balances work ethic with God's enabling power. Paul knew that underneath his work was God's work. He could say, "I worked harder than them all" because he knew "though it was not I, but the grace of God that is with me" (1 Cor 15:10b ESV).

Though the work is laborious, Jesus's power is limitless. Paul shows us that Jesus is not only the subject of our proclamation; he is also the source of power behind it. Our strength for proclaiming Jesus is not in how long we have been Christians. It is not in how much we know about the Bible. It is not in how long we have been in ministry. Our strength (this very moment) is in our union with

Jesus Christ. It is in his mighty energy that he so powerfully works within us.

SUMMATION

Charles Spurgeon illustrates this reliance on Christ's energy. Spurgeon's work ethic was incredible. He commented once,

> No one living knows the toil and care I have to bear . . . I have to look after the Orphanage, have charge of a church with four thousand members, sometimes there are marriages and burials to be undertaken, there is the weekly sermon to be revised, The Sword and the Trowel to be edited, and besides all that, a weekly average of five hundred letters to be answered. This, however, is only half my duty, for there are innumerable churches established by friends, with the affairs of which I am closely connected, to say nothing of the cases of difficulty which are constantly being referred to me.[19]

At his fiftieth birthday, a list of sixty-six organizations was read that he founded and conducted. Lord Shaftesbury said, "This list of associations, instituted by his genius, and superintended by his care, were more than enough to occupy the minds and hearts of fifty ordinary men."[20] Amazingly, he typically read six substantial books a week and could remember what he read and where to find it.[21] He produced more than 140 books of his own. He often worked eighteen hours a day. The missionary David Livingstone (who was a worker in his own right) asked him once, "How do you manage to do two men's work in a single day?" I love Spurgeon's reply. He said, "You have forgotten, there are two of us."[22] Amen! We are not on our own!

---

[19] Charles Spurgeon, *Autobiography*, vol. 2 (Edinburgh: Banner of Truth Trust, 1973), 192.

[20] Arnold Dallimore, *Spurgeon* (Chicago: Moody Press, 1984), 173.

[21] Eric W. Hayden, "Did You Know?" The Spurgeon Archive, accessed March 12, 2015, http://www.spurgeon.org/spurgn2.htm.

[22] Ibid. I'm indebted to John Piper's message on Spurgeon for these testimonies. "Charles Spurgeon: Preaching Through Adversity," accessed February 16, 2015, http://www.desiringgod.org/biographies/charles-spurgeon-preaching-through-adversity. Piper's message inspired me to read more of Spurgeon's work.

Spurgeon understood Paul's words, "Christ in you, the hope of glory." This is good news! We do not labor in our own strength. What a privilege to know this Christ! What a privilege to preach this Christ! What a privilege to have the power of the indwelling Christ!

Make disciples of Jesus by proclaiming him like an evangelist, warning like a prophet, teaching like a theologian, and applying wisdom like a sage. Preach Christ until you die! Preach him on earth, until you see him in glory. I promise you on that day, you will not regret having made him the hero of the Bible, the hero of every message you prepare.

QUESTIONS

1. What are you most excited about when you preach/teach?
2. Why have some abandoned a Christ-centered focus in preaching and teaching?
3. How do you preach for "life change"? Explain.
4. In our zeal to herald Christ, what are some dangers to avoid?
5. How does Colossians 1:28–29 (and the surrounding context) provide a model for us to follow?

5

Rely on the Spirit's Power

I came to you in weakness, in fear, and in much trembling. My speech and my proclamation were not with persuasive words of wisdom but with a powerful demonstration by the Spirit, so that your faith might not be based on men's wisdom but on God's power.
—1 Corinthians 2:3–5

Except the Lord endow us with power from on high, our labor must be in vain, and our hopes must end in disappointment.[1]

—C. H. Spurgeon

My friend Landon wrote his doctoral dissertation on the amount of attention given to the Holy Spirit in Southern Baptist preaching books since 1870.[2] After the project was completed, he discovered at least some mention of the Spirit in each of the texts. These references fell under the categories of Spirit and Word, Spirit and delivery, and Spirit and pastor. However, many of the references to the Spirit, in these selected texts, were treated

---

[1] C. H. Spurgeon, *An All-Round Ministry* (Carlisle, PA: Banner of Truth, 2000), 322.
[2] Landon Dowden, "An Examination of Pneumatological Content in Southern Baptist Homiletic Theory Since 1870," PhD diss. (New Orleans Baptist Theological Seminary, 2007).

quite *limitedly* compared to the other rhetorical elements so greatly emphasized.

One would hope that anyone writing a Christian book believes in the work of the Spirit in preaching! What seems to be happening, though, is that books on preaching/teaching do not contain a large emphasis on the matter. It seems the Spirit is often *assumed* in preaching books *and* in homiletics classes, leaving theologians to discuss his person and work. But the subject of preaching falls properly in the area of practical theology and cannot be taught without an emphasis on the work of the Holy Spirit. An overemphasis on the mechanics of preaching has led us to an underemphasis on the means of power for preaching.

If we continue to assume something for a long period of time, eventually it becomes forgotten, ignored, or disbelieved. Some have illustrated this reality with what occurred after the Great Awakening in New England. How could the church go from a Spirit-led, gospel-preaching revival to Deism so quickly? Many began to functionally deny the Spirit's activity before they abandoned their belief in him altogether. They became functional Deists before they became theological Deists. We cannot assume the Spirit's work. We need to understand his work and personally depend on him daily for Spirit-empowered proclamation as the early church did.

Some rightly emphasize the Word in the life of the church, and others rightly emphasize the Spirit's work in the life of the church. But churches and preachers/teachers need *both* for fruitful ministries. It is true: "All Word and no Spirit, the people dry up; all Spirit and no Word, the people blow up; both Spirit and Word, people grow up." We need to emphasize both Spirit and Word. In the book of Acts, we see a vivid example of this need. Jesus trained the disciples for three years, and then they sat under his teaching for forty days (the Word), but they still *lacked* something: power. Education and biblical training are essential but not sufficient. This is why Lloyd-Jones said, "I spend half my time telling Christians to study doctrine, and the other half telling them doctrine is not enough."[3]

In Greg Heisler's helpful book *Spirit-Led Preaching*, he identified at least ten ways in which the second person of the Godhead is at work in the preaching event:

---

[3] D. Martyn Lloyd-Jones, *Life in Christ: Studies in 1 John* (Wheaton, IL: Crossway, 2002), 386.

1. The Spirit's inspiration of the biblical text
2. The conversion of the preacher to faith in Jesus Christ
3. The call of the preacher to preach the Word
4. The character of the preacher to live the Word
5. The illumination of the preacher's heart and mind in study
6. The empowerment of the preacher in proclaiming the Word
7. The testimony to Jesus Christ as Lord and mediator
8. The opening of hearts of those who hear and receive the Word
9. The application of the Word of God to the listener's lives
10. The production of lasting fruit displayed in the lives of Spirit-filled believers.[4]

Indeed, one can see that preaching from beginning to end is a work of the Spirit. In this chapter I will focus my attention on only two activities of the Spirit: *called by the Spirit* and *proclaiming by the Spirit.*

CALLED BY THE SPIRIT

Every Christian is called to be a minister and a missionary in some way. As priests of God, every Christian can take God to people (in witness) and people to God (in prayer). This ministry is not reserved exclusively for those in vocational ministry. Too many church members believe that "professional pastors" should do most of the work of ministry. In Ephesians 4:1, however, Paul uses the word for "call" (*kaleo*), referring to the Christian's calling to Christ and His mission. After proceeding to talk about the character that should mark the Christian, and the need to recognize God's gifts for service, Paul then identifies those who are called and gifted in a unique sense: "And He personally gave some to be apostles, some prophets, some evangelists, some pastors and teachers" (Eph 4:11). God calls these out for the "training of the saints in the work of ministry" (4:12). Therefore, those called to an office of ministry are to equip those called to do other works of ministry.

How, then, do you know if you have been called to an *office* of ministry as a preacher? Have you been called to lead the flock as a pastor, teacher, or evangelist? I do not presume to have the final word for you on this matter, but I can share some realities that seem trustworthy.

---

[4] Greg Heisler, *Spirit-Led Preaching* (Nashville: B&H, 2007), 4.

A first thing to emphasize is *the actual existence of a call to the ministry of the Word*. Throughout the years, many have provided insights on this important subject. In Spurgeon's classic *Lectures to My Students*, he said:

> How may a young man know whether he is called or not? That is a weighty inquiry, and I desire to treat it most solemnly. . . . That hundreds have missed their way, and stumbled against a pulpit is sorrowfully evident from the fruitless ministry and decaying churches which surround us. It is a fearful calamity to a man to miss his calling, and to the church upon whom he imposes himself, his mistake involves an affliction of the most grievous kind.[5]

I cannot help but believe that one of the reasons for so many fruitless ministries is that many have "stumbled into the pulpit" instead of being summoned to it.

The preacher should believe, like Paul, that he has been "appointed to the ministry" (1 Tim 1:12). The work of ministry simply is too demanding to enter it without a sense of calling. It is also so glorious that we should never get over the privilege of it! Lloyd-Jones said, "To me the work of preaching is the highest and the greatest and the most glorious calling to which anyone can ever be called."[6] Years earlier Luther said a similar statement, "If I could today become a king or emperor, I would not give up my office as a preacher."[7]

One's *specific* calling into the general ministry of the Word may become clearer over time. Some start out with the calling to preach and do ministry but are unsure of what form that will take. (This was my experience. I wanted to exposit the Word in some way, but I did not want to be a pastor!) I encourage those in this state to experiment when possible with various ministries to discover gifts and abilities in order to discern the particulars. The specifics may develop progressively rather than suddenly and dramatically. One's calling may also even change slightly from season to season in terms of position and location. And everyone's calling experience will certainly be unique and different from others. However, there

---

[5] Charles Spurgeon, *Lectures to My Students* (Grand Rapids: Baker, 1980), 25.

[6] D. Martyn Lloyd-Jones, *Preaching and Preachers* (Grand Rapids: Zondervan, 1971), 9.

[7] Quoted in Fred W. Meuser, *Luther the Preacher* (Minneapolis: Augsburg, 1983), 39.

seem to be some shared similarities of those who are called into ministry leadership. To help those wrestling through this matter, I use an acronym, CALL, to ask some important questions.

C – Confirmation. Is there internal and external confirmation? The inward call is what Luther understood as "God's voice heard by faith."[8] God, by his Spirit, confirms his calling through an inward drawing. Al Mohler says, "Those whom God has called know this call by a sense of leading, purpose, and growing commitment."[9] A Spirit-called person will have a great sense of God's leading and sense of His providence. Calvin said the inward call is "that secret call of which every minister is conscious before God."[10] Thomas Oden posited that the inward call is "a result of the continued drawing or eliciting power of the Holy Spirit, which in due time brings an individual closer to the church's outward call to ministry."[11] Therefore, one should ask whether there is a sense of this divine drawing.

A second part to confirming the call seems to be overlooked in many cases. The *external* call has to do with the affirmation of spiritually mature Christians. This confirmation is seen in Paul's words to Timothy about "the laying on of hands" (1 Tim 4:14; 2 Tim 1:6), which carries the idea of spiritual affirmation and approval. Spiritual leaders and the congregation have a responsibility to identify and affirm new spiritual leaders (e.g., Acts 16:1–3). Oden said, "The external call is an act of the Christian community that by due process confirms the inward call."[12] We should ask potential ministry leaders: Do other mature Christians acknowledge God's call on your life? Does your ministry bless them? Do they recognize God's gifts in you?

A – Aspiration. Is there an intense, all-absorbing desire for the work? Spurgeon said, "'Do not enter the ministry if you can help it,' was the deeply sage advice of a divine to one who sought his judgment. If any student in this room could be a newspaper editor, or a grocer, or a farmer, or a doctor, or a lawyer, or a senator, or a king, in the

---

[8] Quoted in Albert Mohler, "Has God Called You?" accessed June 30, 2016, www.albert mohler.com/2013/07/19/has-god-called-you-discerning-the-call-to-preach-2.

[9] Ibid.

[10] John Calvin, *Institutes of Christian Religion*, trans. Henry Beveridge (Grand Rapids: Eerdmans, 1957), 2:323.

[11] Thomas C. Oden, *Pastoral Theology: Essentials of Ministry* (San Francisco: HarperOne, 1983), 25.

[12] Ibid.

name of heaven and earth let him go his way."[13] Indeed, the call to ministry is a passion. Paul says, "If anyone *aspires* to be an overseer, he *desires* a noble work" (1 Tim 3:1, my emphasis). Paul relayed his passion for preaching saying, "For if I preach the gospel, I have no reason to boast, because an obligation is placed on me. And woe to me if I do not preach the gospel!" (1 Cor 9:16).

Do you have a fire in your bones to preach and serve the body? Is there a constraining desire for expounding the Scriptures to the flock of God? Can you do anything else and be happy? If you have a passion, then fan it into flame (2 Tim 1:6). Lloyd-Jones stated, "The man who is called by God is a man who realizes what he is called to do, and he so realizes the awfulness of the task that he shrinks from it. Nothing but this overwhelming sense of being called, and of compulsion, should ever lead anyone to preach."[14]

L – Lifestyle. Do you have a lifestyle that is exemplary and above reproach? As Paul identified the marks of an overseer, the striking reality is that all but one qualification (the ability to teach) has to do with character. Therefore, every pastor must first set a godly example. How can one manage the household of God and not manage his own life or his own family? Pastoral leadership is not *lordship* (1 Pet 5:2–3). It involves following Jesus personally and inviting others to follow you as you walk in the ways of the Chief Shepherd. We must then ask potential ministry leaders: Will people follow you? Should people follow you? Are you following Jesus passionately?

L – Leadership Gifts. Has God given you the necessary spiritual gifts for ministry? It should go without saying that anyone who does not have the gift of preaching and teaching should do something else. Certainly, some are more gifted than others. God has gifted his people with different measures of grace (Eph 4:7). If God has given you, however, the ability to teach and preach in some measure, then you must not ignore God's good gifts. It surprises me sometimes when church members say, "I like that pastor; he is a good teacher." To which I say, "He must be a teacher." It is a requirement that the pastor be "an able teacher" (1 Tim 3:2).

In addition, the pastor needs some degree of administrative and shepherding gifts. Ideally, the church will have a plurality of pastors/elders who will complement one another in these areas.

---

[13] Spurgeon, *Lectures to My Students*, 26–27.
[14] Lloyd-Jones, *Preaching and Preachers*, 107.

As we mentioned earlier, godliness makes up for many deficiencies in gifting, but God gifts the people whom he calls to do the work of ministry. Lloyd-Jones makes this point in regard to preaching: "What is a preacher? The first thing, obviously, is that he is a speaker. He is not primarily a writer of books, he is not an essayist or a literary man; the preacher is primarily a speaker. So if the candidate does not have the gift of speech, whatever else he may have, he is not going to make a preacher."[15]

Let us emphasize the need for gifts as we counsel others thinking through their calling (see Rom 12:3–8; 1 Cor 12).

PROCLAIMING BY THE SPIRIT

Certainly, the act of proclamation is not the only spiritual exercise of a church's ministry, but it is one with unusual magnitude. Three issues are important to consider in developing a practical theology of Spirit-empowered proclamation: the need for the Spirit, the nature of the Spirit, and the necessities for obtaining the Spirit.

The Need for the Spirit

A good metaphor for Spirit-empowered preaching is an old one: *heat* and *light*. Often many preachers are too brain oriented, preaching only with *light* (knowledge). Their sermons are loaded with Greek words, chiasms, and background information. While these issues are significant, we should not believe that all we need to do is parse verbs for lives to be changed. The objective source of truth (Scripture) is half of the matter. We need the subjective work of the sovereign Spirit of God (*heat*) in order for the truth to transform individuals.

Why do many of us fail to think much about our need for the Spirit in preaching? In my case, I do not neglect to *believe* in the need for the Spirit's operation. Rather, I often fail to *experientially* depend upon him. I find myself, on too many occasions, spending hours of time analyzing a passage, without giving a prolonged thought to my desperate condition. We need to remind ourselves repeatedly that apart from the branch we can do nothing (John 15:5). Apart from the Spirit of God, we will not see the glory of God (1 Cor 2:9–12).

---

[15] Ibid., 111.

One fundamental reason for preaching in the flesh is this: we do not understand our human inability. Art Azurdia is correct in saying, "The neglect of the ministry of the Spirit in the work of preaching has emerged as a result of a failure to see the full-orbed implications of the nature of sinful humanity. Stated more directly, one's understanding of human depravity will determine the extent to which dependence is placed upon the sovereign Spirit of God."[16] We will not see our desperation until we understand our human insufficiency and sinfulness.

We should remember, then, the presence and particular effects of sin in three groups of people: unbelievers, believers, and ourselves. Concerning *unbelievers*, the unregenerate listener is neither willing nor able to respond to God's truth apart from the Spirit (Rom 3:9–19; Eph 2:1–4; 4:17–18). Further, Paul states that the evil one "has blinded the minds of the unbelievers so they cannot see the light of the gospel of the glory of Christ" (2 Cor 4:4). Spurgeon's words are riveting:

> The Gospel is preached in the ears of everyone; it only comes with power to some. The power that is in the Gospel does not lie in the eloquence of the preacher, otherwise men would be the converters of souls. Nor does it lie in the preacher's education, otherwise it would consist of the wisdom of man. . . . We might preach till our tongues rotted, till we should exhaust our lungs and die, but never would a soul be converted unless there were the mysterious power of the Holy Spirit going with it, changing the will of man. O my friends! we might as well preach to stone walls as preach to humanity unless the Holy Spirit is with the Word, to give it power to convert the soul.[17]

The Christian preacher, then, must plead with God to do what he did for unregenerate Lydia, when he "opened her heart to pay attention to what was spoken by Paul" (Acts 16:14). Apart from this work, we may preach till our tongues rot out, but we will fail to see one convert. Be aware of the condition of the unregenerate. We need God's breath to give life to the dead.

---

[16] Arturo Azurdia III, *Spirit Empowered Preaching* (Ross-shire, Great Britain: Mentor, 1998), 13.

[17] Charles Spurgeon, "Election: Its Defenses and Evidences," accessed July 10, 2008, http://www.biblebb.com/files/spurgeon/2920.htm.

Next, we must be aware of the sinfulness of *believers*. The residue of indwelling sin, the enticements of the evil one, and the rebellion of God's people make it difficult for the Word to stick. The preacher must therefore ask for God's help to preach to rebellious people. Clever communication is not enough in order to see Christ formed in his people. The attendant Spirit must be present.

Finally, we must be mindful of *our own human limitations*. It is easy for the eloquent pastor to preach in the flesh. Paul reminded the Corinthians that his preaching was done "with a demonstration of the Spirit and power" (1 Cor 2:4). While Paul did employ rhetorical elements in his preaching (e.g., Acts 17:16–34), and was himself a highly educated man, he still understood that his ultimate hope was in the powerful work of the Spirit. He actually reveled in these weaknesses (1 Cor 2:3). Regardless of our wit and charisma, like Paul, we are "clay pots" (2 Cor 4:7). We must never lose the *fear* of preaching God's Word (1 Cor 2:2), and we must never lose the feeling of *powerlessness* apart from God's Spirit. A failure to experience these two realities is a glaring reminder of our sickening pride. We are in over our head. Much is at stake. May we preach with a holy fear and a sincere desperation. Like Paul, we must desperately desire to see God transform hearts, instead of desiring to captivate a crowd.

The Nature of the Spirit in Preaching

Describing the work of the Spirit in preaching is difficult. It reminds me of the famous jazz musician Louis Armstrong, who was asked to explain jazz music. He said, "Man if I've got to explain it, you ain't got it!" Indeed, there is a lot of mystery to the work of the Spirit, but there are some clear truths that we can build our ministries upon.

What should we call preaching that is coupled with the transforming effects of the Spirit? A popular term is "anointed." Some, however, believe that anointed preaching does not exist. Is this idea an unnecessary and unbiblical notion that often weighs the preacher down with guilt? Alex Montoya seems to thinks so:

> It is my conclusion that such a thing [the anointing] does not exist. We should be relieved of this unspeakable burden placed upon us by those who teach this about preaching. Every example given of men who preached with unction were men endowed with manifold speaking and intellectual

abilities. Where are the men with no talent or abilities? If unction is all of God, surely we would see the plain, ignorant, untalented yet godly preacher so endowed! Even uneducated Moody was a naturally eloquent speaker![18]

I do not think that "such a thing" *does not* exist. Should we attribute the success of every powerful preacher solely to "manifold speaking and intellectual abilities"? Consider the apostles. They had the greatest education possible. And certainly, some were gifted communicators. But why did Jesus say that they still lacked something; namely, the power of the Spirit (Luke 24:49; Acts 1:4–5, 8)? I believe something such as preaching with "unction" does exist and should be pursued.

However, Montoya is right in encouraging us to reconsider our terminology. Usually the term *anointed*, in the New Testament, refers to the privileges of all who are in Christ (2 Cor 1:21–22; Heb 1:9; 1 John 2:2) or to the person and work of Christ himself (Mark 4:18; Luke 7:46; John 9:11; Acts 4:26; 10:36–38). The only reference that I have identified with the idea of *anointed preaching* is when Jesus quotes Isaiah 61:1–2: "The Spirit of the Lord is on Me, because He has anointed Me to preach good news to the poor" (Luke 4:18). Because this reference is primarily (if not exclusively) reserved for Christ, perhaps a better phrase would clarify the role of the Spirit in preaching.

Biblical Foundation. Many references in the Old Testament related to the work of the Spirit focus specifically on the ministry of proclamation (Num 11:16–30; 2 Sam 23:2; 2 Chr 24:20; Neh 9:30; Ezek 11:5). God empowered the prophets to declare his Word to people. In the New Testament, Jesus preached immediately following the Spirit's descent at his baptism and the Spirit's power at his temptation (Matt 4:17). Of course, Paul, a theologian of the Spirit, wrote frequently about his awareness of his need for the Spirit's work for proclamation (1 Cor 2:1–5; 2 Cor 4:4–6; Eph 6:18–20).

Interestingly, Luke-Acts contains eight specific references to a prophetic type of speaking by the Spirit.[19] In these instances, Luke uses the aorist passive verb, which seemingly denotes a special moment of inspiration.[20] It can be rendered "having been filled

---

[18] Alex Montoya, *Preaching with Passion* (Grand Rapids: Kregel, 2000), 35.
[19] See Azurdia, *Spirit Empowered Preaching*, 105–15.
[20] F. F. Bruce, *Commentary on the Book of Acts* (Grand Rapids: Eerdmans, 1970), 99.

with the Holy Spirit" he "said" or "preached." When Luke uses this aorist passive verb, he describes *the actual event* of speaking by the Spirit's power (Luke 1:13–15, 39–41, 42–45, 67–79; Acts 2:2–4; 4:8, 31; 9:17; 13:8–11). Granted, each of these occasions does not involve the act of preaching as we understand it today. But each time this verb is used, some form of speaking follows it. This verb form is different than the filling of the Sprit that refers to an *abiding state* of fullness elsewhere in Luke-Acts (Luke 4:1; Acts 6:3, 5; 7:55; 11:24; 13:52).[21] This suggests that there was a spontaneous work of the Spirit in proclamation. Whatever one makes of these differing tenses, we must at least conclude that the Spirit is mightily at work in the proclamation of his Word.

Therefore, while the term *anointed* may not be the best word to describe preaching by the power of the Spirit, the biblical rationale for *Spirit-empowered preaching* is still warranted. The prophets, Jesus, Paul, and the examples in Luke-Acts provide a rich understanding of this important reality.

Marks of the Spirit. Before identifying some marks of Spirit-empowered preaching, it may be helpful to begin with what Spirit-empowered preaching is *not*. It is not the act of *trying* to be someone else in the pulpit. Some preachers do an "incredible Hulk" transformation, turning into an entirely different person on the platform. Lack of genuineness is no sign of the Spirit. Another common misunderstanding is the idea that Spirit-empowered preaching involves changing your sermon right before you preach! Sure, there may be times to do just that, but the act in itself is no sign of vitality. "Screaming, yelling, and slinging sweat" is also thought of as Spirit-empowered preaching by some. If the preacher does not lose control, in some traditions, he has "lost the Spirit."

Further, the preacher is often tempted to push the audience's "hot buttons" in order to elicit a response. After doing so, he is often praised as "being anointed." We should avoid such manipulation and deceit. Getting a verbal response is no barometer for the presence of the Spirit. A final misconception is that only those who preach without notes are preaching by the power of the Spirit. If this were the case, then many of the great preachers in our history apparently preached apart from the Spirit—like Jonathan Edwards, John Piper, and thousands more.

---

[21] Azurdia, *Spirit Empowered Preaching*, 114.

In contrast, I believe that there are several key biblical principles for understanding true Spirit-empowered preaching. To start, we must admit that Spirit-empowered proclamation is, in some sense, an indescribable and indefinable aspect of preaching. Lloyd-Jones stated:

> How does one know the unction of the Spirit? It gives clarity of thought, clarity of speech, ease of utterance, a great sense of authority and confidence as you are preaching, an awareness of power not your own thrilling through the whole of your being, and an indescribable sense of joy. You are a man "possessed," you are taken hold of, and taken up. I like to put it like this—and I know of nothing on earth that is comparable to this feeling—that when this happens you have a feeling that you are not actually doing the preaching, you are looking on at yourself in amazement as this is happening. It is not your effort; you are just an instrument, the channel, the vehicle: the Sprit is using you, and you are looking on in great enjoyment and astonishment.[22]

This is an apt description of the mysterious element of biblical preaching.

Spurgeon also recognized the mystery of the Spirit. He said, "What is it? I wonder how long we might beat our brains before we could plainly put into words what is meant by preaching with unction; yet he who preaches knows its presence, and he who hears soon detects its absence."[23] Though we may not be able to define it completely, all who have tasted it want it more and more.

Next, we should note that Spirit-empowered preaching is not simply mystery and emotion. It seems that the Spirit works mightily when Christ is made much of in the pulpit. Spirit-empowered preaching will be God-centered, Christ-exalting preaching because the Spirit glorifies Christ and makes the glory of God known (John 15:26; 16:14; 1 Cor 2:9–11). While the Spirit can and does move through poor sermons, the faithful preacher must determine to exalt Christ, praying for the Spirit to come and draw the hearers' minds to the Savior.

---

[22] Lloyd-Jones, *Preaching and Preachers*, 305.
[23] Spurgeon, *Lectures to My Students*, 50.

In addition, Spirit-empowered preaching will bring conviction of sin and repentance (Acts 2:37–41). While some sermons may stir up emotion, true repentance that leads to fruitfulness and faithfulness is a work of the Spirit. Genuine converts are produced by the Spirit and the Word (1 Pet 1:23–25). Preaching is thus set apart from other modes of secular communication because of the Spirit's presence in the preaching of the inspired text.

Finally, Spirit-empowered preaching will be evidenced in the character of Christ on the preacher (Gal 5:22–23) and in his boldness in preaching the gospel (Acts 4; Eph 6:18–20; 2 Tim 1:6–7). Often we look for other observable effects that are not mentioned in Scripture, such as loudness and body movement. We should pray for the fruit of the Spirit to be present in our preaching and for the Spirit to empower us to preach with a humble and courageous boldness.

The Necessities for Obtaining the Spirit

The Holy Spirit is sovereign and free. He comes like the wind, blowing wherever he wills (John 3:8). Therefore, I cannot offer a how-to type of formula for obtaining the mighty working of the Spirit. However, some practices appear to be present in preachers who consistently preach with spiritual power. Nine interrelated disciplines are especially important (in no particular order).

First, proclaim Christ (John 16:14). Look to see how the Savior is made much of in a passage, and behold his beauty personally first, and then aim to make much of him in the message. Show the ongoing flow of redemptive history. Highlight his person, his teaching, and his work. Remember that the Spirit has a floodlight ministry, magnifying the glory of Jesus. Be Christ-absorbed not self-absorbed in your life and ministry by the Spirit's power.

Second, preach the crucified Christ as a crucified man (1 Cor 2:1–5). When Paul writes to the Corinthians, he shows us, in the words of D. A. Carson, "The cross not only establishes what we are to preach, but how we are to preach."[24] Paul highlights four traits of a crucified preacher: (1) not allowing communication style to rise above or overshadow God's message (1 Cor 2:1–2); (2) a sense of weakness

---

[24] D. A. Carson, *The Cross and Christian Ministry* (Grand Rapids: Baker, 2003), 9. For an excellent treatment on this subject, see also Steven W. Smith's *Dying to Preach* (Grand Rapids: Kregel, 2009).

and humble trembling (v. 3); (3) the renouncing of human manipulation (v. 4); and (4) a total reliance on the Spirit to transform
lives (v. 5). We must die to our love affair with people's applause,
to the feeling that we have arrived, to worldly salesmanship, and
to self-reliance. To preach the cross from the pulpit effectively, we
must walk as people of the cross personally.

Third, beware of ministry professionalism. Before Jesus ascended,
he issued those famous last words to the disciples, "Apart from
me you can do nothing" (John 15:5). Do you believe this? C. J.
Mahaney advises us to begin each day, as we awake, by acknowl-
edging our complete dependence upon God and our need for
him.[25] Let the first thought of your day be a confession of John
15:5 regardless of how "successful" in ministry you have been, or
are currently. Periodic seasons of fasting and prayer for God's
power should be practiced as well in order to increase our level of
desperation. Do not let the professionalism of ministry keep you
from panting after God like a thirsty deer. We are desperate for
him and his vitality.

Fourth, maintain personal holiness (2 Tim 2:21). While God has
used unholy men to change lives throughout history, this does not
give us an excuse not to "watch our lives closely" (1 Tim 4:16a ESV).
God can and does work wonders through men who are absolutely
yielded to him. His Spirit is holy, therefore, let us be holy vessels
through whom he is pleased to work. Spurgeon said, "God will
speak through a fool, if he is but a holy man."[26]

Fifth, pray for God to do a great work through you (John 14:12–14).
In the farewell discourse, Jesus told his disciples that they would do
"greater works" than his own. How? Jesus said, "because I am going
to the Father." When Jesus ascended, he sent the Spirit to empower
his disciples. So what are these greater works? I take this to mean
greater in number and greater in geographical scope, rather than
greater in physical manifestations.[27] Consequently, we see in Acts
that multitudes were drawn to Christ from various places (see Acts
2:41; 4:4; 5:14; 6:1, 7; 9:31, 35, 42; 11:21, 24; 12:24; 13:48; 14:1; 16:5;
17:4, 11–12; 18:8; 19:20). Do you pray for multitudes to be saved
under your ministry? Let us ask God to do great works through us.

---

[25] C. J. Mahaney, *Humility* (Sisters, OR: Multnomah, 2005), 69.
[26] Charles Spurgeon, *The Soulwinner* (New Kensington, PA: Whitaker House, 1995), 41.
[27] Azurdia, *Spirit Empowered Preaching*, 22–28.

Sixth, pray for illumination (Ps 119:18; Acts 16:14). We need spiritual eyes to see "wonderful things from God's Word." The doctrine of illumination teaches that we need the Spirit to overcome the residue of sin in our lives in order for us to adequately understand and be moved by the Scriptures. Illumination in our personal study also will keep the process of preparing sermons, and the act of preaching, from being burdensome. We do not study for sermons like one prepares for a science exam. Heisler said that "whatever the Spirit illumines in the study, he will empower in the pulpit."[28] So let us pray for the Spirit to be our teacher in the study, and the opener of eyes in our preaching.

Seventh, do your own homework (2 Tim 2:15). Ethically, we should never steal someone else's sermon (even though we can utilize their stuff so long as we give credit). This is because we will miss the dynamic of the Spirit that comes in our own preparation. God wants to bless your time of personal study as you lay yourself and your people before him. Remember that the Spirit illuminates his inspired text. Therefore, diligently seek the mind of the Spirit in personal Bible study in order to apply his intended meaning to your particular audience. Begin your study with the text and the Spirit as your only commentary, before rushing to other resources.

Eighth, work to cultivate congregational unity (Eph 4:25–32). The congregation has a role in the preaching event. The Spirit is a person who can be grieved (Eph 4:30) and a fire that can be quenched (1 Thess 5:19). He is sensitive. Whatever is inconsistent with his nature offends him. It is thus necessary for the congregation to understand her role in the preaching event. Unloving attitudes and commonly tolerated sins such as gossip, slander, evil speaking, and jealousy may affect the degree of influence of the Spirit. Sin in the camp offends the Spirit, but holiness and love attracts the Spirit. Azurdia states that "the wounding of the Spirit can and often does, lead to a withdrawal of His influences."[29] Let your people know that their lifestyle and relationships may in fact play a role in the effect of your preaching.

Finally, ask for the prayers of God's people (Eph 6:18–20; 1 Thess 5:25). You need someone to hold up your arms. Spurgeon often said that the success of his preaching had to do with the prayers

---

[28] Heisler, *Spirit-Led Preaching*, 51.
[29] Azurdia, *Spirit Empowered Preaching*, 155.

of his people. The story was passed down that one day five college students came to hear Spurgeon preach at the Metropolitan Tabernacle. While waiting for the doors to open, they were greeted by a gentleman who offered to show them around. He asked if they would like to the see the "heating plant." They were not particularly interested because it was a hot day in July. But they followed down the staircase anyway. The man then opened a door and whispered, "This is our heating plant." The students looked in astonishment at seven hundred people bowed in prayer, interceding for the service that was about to begin upstairs. After shutting the door, the man introduced himself as Charles Spurgeon.[30] Pastor, do you have a heating plant? Prayer is the engine of our ministries. Even the mighty apostle knew the importance of saints interceding for him. Our ministries are too important to avoid this practice.

SUMMATION

From start to finish, preaching is a spiritual activity. Spirit-called preachers should maintain a proper balance of diligent study of the Scriptures and a desperate reliance upon the Spirit. Both elements are critical for seeing lives changed and God glorified. The preacher should do everything that he can for the sovereign Spirit of God to come and empower his proclamation.

QUESTIONS

1. Explain the acronym "CALL" to describe the calling of the minister.
2. Why do we need the Spirit's help in preaching and teaching?
3. What are some misunderstandings about the Spirit's work in preaching?
4. List some practices that appear to be present in Spirit-empowered preaching.
5. Identify some key passages related to the work of the Spirit in preaching?

---

[30] Quoted in David Larsen, *The Anatomy of Preaching* (Grand Rapids: Kregel, 1989), 55.

6

Cultivate a Vibrant Prayer Life

But we will devote ourselves to prayer and to the ministry of the word.

—Acts 6:4 ESV

Of course the preacher is above all others distinguished as a man of prayer. . . . The minister who does not earnestly pray over his work must be a vain and conceited man. He acts as if he thought himself sufficient of himself, and therefore needed not to appeal to God. . . . He limps in his life like a lame man in Proverbs, whose legs are not equal, for his praying is shorter than his preaching.[1]

—C. H. Spurgeon

THE PURPOSE OF THIS chapter is not to lay a religious guilt trip on you for not praying enough. Most Christians that I know, including myself, admit that their prayer life should improve. So even though I am not insinuating major-league performance in the arena of prayer on my part, I do want to remind you of the priority of prayer as a pastor-preacher and encourage you with some biblical and practical insights that I have picked up along the way from

---

[1] C. H. Spurgeon, *Lectures to My Students* (Grand Rapids: Zondervan, 1954), 42, 48.

some seasoned veterans. I share a desire that we have to learn to pray better.[2]

At its core, prayer is conversation with the Father, through the Son, by the Spirit (Eph 2:18). We approach a Holy Father who is wise and good (Matt 6:9; 7:11). We can pray to the Father because of Jesus, not because of our own merit (1 Tim 2:5; Heb 10:19). We may pray at any time because of the Spirit (Eph 6:18), who even helps us pray in our weakness (Rom 8:26). We will spend years meditating on and hopefully applying these glorious truths!

According to the Scriptures, we should seek God daily (Mark 1:35), privately (Matt 6:6), continually (1 Thess 5:17), faithfully (Jas 5:13–18), and publicly (1 Tim 2:1–8). A failure to take these disciplines seriously will lead to spiritual coldness, increased vulnerability to temptation, relational problems, and mechanical ministry activity.

As ministry leaders, we must always remind ourselves that study and sermon delivery are not all that we are required to do. Like the apostles, we must "devote ourselves *to prayer* and to the preaching ministry" (Acts 6:4, my emphasis). Our job description includes both prayer and exposition. Jim Shaddix sometimes asks his classes, "What would happen if we patterned seminaries after Acts 6:4? What if half of our courses were about *prayer* (intercession, supplication, thanksgiving, repentance, etc.), and the other half were on *ministry of the Word?*" His provoking questions lead to lively class discussions because students realize the lack of emphasis on prayer in ministry preparation. Shaddix usually follows by saying that the seminary actually cannot teach a person everything he needs for ministry. Many ministry disciplines are developed personally and through the local church, and cultivating a vibrant prayer life is one of these disciplines (even though seminaries can help). Even so, his point is powerful because Acts 6:4 shows that we have to take both of these responsibilities seriously, and if we are giving way more time to the Word than to prayer, it seems as though we are out of balance.

EXAMPLES OF FAITHFUL PRAYER

In my first preaching class in seminary, we were assigned to read a book on prayer by E. M. Bounds. I had never heard of Bounds

---

[2] See Tim Keller's testimony of personal growth in this area in his book *Prayer* (New York: Dutton, 2014), 9–18.

before, but this book was riveting. Bounds wrote several inspiring books on prayer, challenging Christians and preachers to recognize the significance of seeking God early and often. Bounds said, "The Bible preacher lives by prayer, loves by prayer, and preaches by prayer. His bended knees in the place of secret prayer advertise what kind of preacher he is."[3]

During a class discussion one day, I posed a question in reaction to the topic. We were discussing how men of old got up at 3:00 and 4:00 a.m. to pray. I asked Dr. Shaddix, "Didn't these guys get up early because they didn't have electricity? I mean, I could get up at 4:00 a.m. if I went to bed at 8:00 p.m." Someone then asked Dr. Shaddix what time he arose to pray. He modestly responded, "Guys, I've been getting up at 4:30 a.m. for the past twelve years, in order to spend two hours of unhindered and unhurried time with God. . . . I don't like getting up early, but I realized after I had kids that if I was going to pray without being rushed and distracted, then I needed to get up before they did." I did not ask any follow-up questions. I woke up at 7:54 a.m. to make his 8:00 a.m. class that day! All I had experienced was a two-minute "prayer-walk" to class. I had much to learn.

Every preacher and great servant of Jesus whom I admire emphasizes the importance of fervent prayer. Theologian J. I. Packer says, "I believe that prayer is the measure of the man, spiritually, in a way that nothing else is, so that how we pray is as important a question as we can ever face."[4] Scottish pastor M'Cheyne said, "What a man is alone on his knees before God, that he is, and no more."[5] What if we measured our spiritual maturity not by our position, popularity, and church population but by our praying? Who are you in the secret place?

Prayer is an essential part of homiletics, though it is often neglected. Spurgeon said to his students, "All our libraries and studies are mere emptiness compared with our closets. We grow, we wax mightily, we prevail in private prayer."[6] David Larsen, who

---

[3] E. M. Bounds, *E. M. Bounds on Prayer*, comp. (New Kensington: Whitaker House, 1997), 585.

[4] J. I. Packer, *My Path of Prayer*, ed. David Hanes (Worthing, West Sussex: Henry E. Walter, 1981), 56.

[5] Quote taken from Arturo Azurdia, "Reforming the Church Through Prayer," in *Reforming Pastoral Ministry*, ed. John H. Armstrong (Wheaton, IL: Crossway, 2001), 167.

[6] Spurgeon, *Lectures to My Students*, 43.

is a tremendous teacher of preaching, says, "Strange it is that any discussion of preaching should take place outside the context of believing prayer. We have not prepared until we have prayed. . . . We cannot represent God if we have not stood before God. It is more important for me therefore to teach a student to pray than to preach."[7] Vines and Shaddix say, "No preacher can be used effectively apart from daily time with God."[8]

Therefore, as preachers we must develop a daily routine of time alone with God. In Mark 1:35, the young Gospel writer says of Jesus, "Very early in the morning, while it was still dark, He got up, went out, and made His way to a deserted place. And He was praying there." Jesus, after a full day of ministry (1:32–34), understood the importance of solitude with the Father. Luke records three specific examples of our Lord's pattern. He says, "Yet He often withdrew to deserted places and prayed" (Luke 5:16); "During those days He went out to the mountain to pray and spent all night in prayer to God" (Luke 6:12); "While He was praying in private" (Luke 9:18a). The logic is obvious: if Jesus, the incarnate Word, had to spend time in solitude with the Father, how much more do we?

Of course, the mornings are not the only time to pray. Lloyd-Jones reminded preachers to get to know themselves before setting a program to follow. He reminded them that everyone is different based upon physiological factors, among other things. He said, "I confess freely that I have often found it difficult to start praying in the morning."[9] Lloyd-Jones did not deny the importance of praying in the mornings but tried to emphasize how preachers should consider ways in which to awaken the soul in the morning (i.e., reading) in light of personal differences, and then go on praying throughout the day. What we must all strive for is *unhurried* and *unhindered* time with God. Lloyd-Jones said that we must fight for our life to maintain such solitude.[10]

So make time to seek the Father in the prayer closet. Seek him early; seek him late; seek him without ceasing. E. M. Bounds, pastor and Civil War chaplain, habitually prayed from 4:00 to 7:00 a.m. in the morning. George W. Truett, long-time pastor of First Baptist Dallas, retired to his personal library for prayer and study

---

[7] David Larsen, *The Anatomy of Preaching* (Grand Rapids: Kregel, 1989), 54.
[8] Jerry Vines and Jim Shaddix, *Power in the Pulpit* (Chicago: Moody, 1999), 68.
[9] D. Martyn Lloyd-Jones, *Preaching and Preachers* (Grand Rapids: Zondervan, 1971), 170.
[10] Ibid., 167.

from 7:00 p.m. till midnight.[11] Charles Simeon, influential pastor of Holy Trinity Church, experienced God's grace by meeting with him early. A friend said of him, "Simeon invariably rose every morning, though it was winter season, at four o'clock; and after lighting his fire, he devoted the first four hours of the day to private prayer and the devotional study of the Scriptures. . . . Here was the secret of his great grace and spiritual strength."[12]

Other pastors who prayed specifically for particular needs during the week inspire me. Edward Payson, former pastor in Maine, kept a discipline of twelve hours for study, two for devotion, two for relaxing, two for meals and family devotions, and six for sleep.[13] That is discipline! F. W. Robertson, former pastor in England, prayed for the church and the Spirit's outpouring on Sunday, special devotion on Monday, spread of the gospel on Tuesday, the kingdom of Christ on Wednesday, self-denial on Thursday, special examination and confession on Friday, and intercession on Saturday.[14]

Contemporary examples also remind us to always prepare our sermons by praying in the Spirit. Sinclair Ferguson, Scottish pastor and theology professor, said, "For me, it is of primary importance that all my preparation be done in the context of a praying spirit . . . looking to the Lord and depending on the grace of His illuminating and enlivening Spirit."[15] He added that this study is then punctuated by periods of petition for the explanation and application of the sermon.[16]

John MacArthur provided an explanation of his prayerful study:

> During the week . . . locked up with my books . . . study and . . . communion mingle as I apply the tools of exegesis and exposition in . . . open communion with the Lord. I seek His direction, thank Him for what I discover, plead for wisdom and insight, and desire that He enable me to live

---

[11] J. W. Burton, *Prince of the Pulpit* (Grand Rapids: Zondervan, 1946), 23–24.

[12] H. C. G. Moule, *Charles Simeon* (London: InterVarsity, 1948), 66.

[13] A. Cummings, *A Memoir of the Rev. Edward Payson* (New York: America Tract Society, 1830), 13–14. I am indebted to James E. Rosscup's "The Priority of Prayer and Expository Preaching" in John MacArthur Jr. and the Master's Seminary Faculty, *Rediscovering Expository Preaching* (Dallas: Word, 1992), 63–84, for pointing me to some of these biographies.

[14] S. A. Brooke, *Life and Letters of Frederick W. Robertson* (New York: Harper and Brothers, 1865), 60–61.

[15] Sinclair Ferguson, *Inside the Sermon*, ed. R. A. Bodey (Grand Rapids: Baker, 1990), 82–83.

[16] Ibid.

what I learn and preach. . . . A special burden for prayer begins to grip my heart Saturday evening. Before I go to sleep, I . . . spend one final time going over my notes. That involves an opening line of communication with God as I meditatively and consciously offer my notes up to the Lord for approval, refinement and clarity. . . . I awake Sunday morning in the same spirit of prayer. Arriving at the church early, I spend time . . . in prayer, then join elders who pray with me for the messages. On Sunday afternoon, I go through a similar time of reviewing my evening message prayerfully.[17]

These examples of prayerful preparation illustrate Andrew Blackwood's words: "Start, continue, and end with prayer."[18]

The Content of Faithful Prayer

What should occupy the prayers of pastors and teachers? On the one hand, ministry leaders are simply people who have been redeemed by the blood of Jesus. We should pray like any another Christian. But on the other hand, we have been entrusted with a group of people for which to pray. Spurgeon said, "He [the preacher] prays as an ordinary Christian, else he were a hypocrite. He prays more than ordinary Christians, else he were disqualified for the office which he has undertaken."[19]

Prayer for *illumination* stands out as a primary prayer concern. As expositors of Scripture, we need for God to open up our eyes to behold his wondrous truths (Ps 119:18). Azurdia commented, "Pastors must pray themselves into the marrow of the biblical text if they are to experience its relevance in penetrating fashion. Such Spirit-produced illumination, sought in fervent prayer, will profoundly contribute to preaching that is more than chilling analytical discourse."[20] Prepare your sermons at the throne of grace, asking for divine illumination.

In addition to illumination is the need to *intercede* on behalf of others. The apostle Paul's life and writings magnify the significance

[17] Rosscup, "The Priority of Prayer and Expository Preaching," in MacArthur, *Rediscovering Expository Preaching*, 79.

[18] Andrew W. Blackwood, *The Preparation of Sermons* (New York: Abingdon, 1948), 36.

[19] Spurgeon, *Lectures to My Students*, 42.

[20] Azurdia, "Reforming the Church Through Prayer," in Armstrong, *Reforming Pastoral Ministry*, 174.

of intercession. After explaining the wardrobe and the warfare of a Christian in Ephesians 6:12–17, Paul teaches the Ephesian church about praying for people: "Pray at all times in the Spirit with every prayer and request, and stay alert in this with all perseverance and intercession for all the saints. Pray also for me, that the message may be given to me when I open my mouth to make known with boldness the mystery of the gospel. For this I am an ambassador in chains. Pray that I might be bold enough in Him to speak as I should" (Eph 6:18–20).

In verse 18, Paul shows us the comprehensive nature of intercession. He describes *when we should pray* ("at *all* times"), *how we should pray* ("in the Spirit" and "stay alert"), *how long we should pray* ("with *all* perseverance"), *for whom we should pray* ("*all* the saints"), and *with what forms we should pray* ("with *every* prayer and request"). Paul follows these instructions with a petition for his own need saying, "Pray also for me" (6:19).

The apostle Paul, perhaps the greatest theologian-missionary-preacher who ever lived, understood the necessity of intercession. He did not rely upon his own strengths and abilities, nor did he tell others to do so. Paul led the way, as every pastor should, in the discipline of intercession.

We will never fully embrace the power of intercession unless we believe that God will actually respond. Think about the problems in your church. How should you deal with them? How did Paul deal with the immorality in Corinth, the false teachers in Ephesus, the complainers in Philippi, the mystics in Colossae, the end-times fanatics in Thessalonica, and the weakness of Timothy? Along with personal instruction to deal with the issues, Paul interceded for these people. Think about the amount of time devoted to prayers in the letters of Paul. He was not trying to fill space. He understood that some problems are only solved by prayer, and some problems are avoided through prayer. Remember, pastor, God can do more in response to one prayer than in one hundred years of our plotting and planning.

Paul demonstrates the need for pastors to serve both as prophet and priest. Consider these exemplary supplications:

- "This is why, since I heard about your faith in the Lord Jesus and your love for all the saints, I never stop giving thanks for you as I remember you in my prayers" (Eph 1:15–16).

- "I give thanks to my God for every remembrance of you, always praying with joy for all of you in my every prayer, because of your partnership in the gospel from the first day until now" (Phil 1:3–5).
- "For this reason also, since the day we heard this, we haven't stopped praying for you. We are asking that you may be filled with the knowledge of His will in all wisdom and spiritual understanding, so that you may walk worthy of the Lord, fully pleasing to Him, bearing fruit in every good work and growing in the knowledge of God" (Col 1:9–10).
- "We always thank God for all of you, remembering you constantly in our prayers. We recall, in the presence of our God and Father, your work of faith, labor of love, and endurance of hope in our Lord Jesus Christ" (1 Thess 1:2–3).
- "I thank God, whom I serve with a clear conscience as my forefathers did, when I constantly remember you in my prayers night and day" (2 Tim 1:3).

Similarly, the prophet Samuel said, "As for me, I vow that I will not sin against the Lord by ceasing to pray for you. I will teach you the good and right way" (1 Sam 12:23). Couple your instruction with a regular pattern of intercession. Let your private ministry be as faithful as your public ministry. John Stott reminds us of the tendency to neglect what is unseen. He said, "And only love will make us thus diligent, for prayer is hard work and secret work. . . . Because it is secret and therefore unrewarded by men, we shall only undertake it if we long for their spiritual welfare more than for their thanks."[21]

The godly pastor will develop some practical ways to intercede for his people. Developing prayer lists is a good idea because we are often bombarded with information overload. Prayer lists help us remember the specific needs. Long-time pastor Kent Hughes said that he kept a daily prayer list with the following headings: Family, Staff, Secretaries and Custodians, Ill, Grieving, Important Events, Present Problems, Ministries, Weekly Worship, New Believers, and Missions Lists.[22] In addition to this daily list, he prayed through four other lists, which he tried to pray through once a week.[23] May

---

[21] John Stott, *The Preacher's Portrait* (London: Tyndale, 1961), 88.
[22] R. Kent Hughes, *Disciplines of a Godly Man*, rev. (Wheaton, IL: Crossway, 2001), 102.
[23] Ibid.

we never be guilty of telling someone that we will pray for them and then fail to actually intercede. Developing a pattern of intercession is hard work. We cannot wait until we "feel like praying." By God's grace, train yourself for the discipline of intercession.

Mark Dever, pastor of Capitol Hill Baptist in Washington DC, encourages pastors to pray for the flock by keeping a copy of the church's pictorial directory on hand. Dever says that he mingles daily Bible reading with intercession through the directory. At the elders' meetings, substantive time also is given to pray for each member of the church. The body is also encouraged to pray through the directory, usually about a page per day during their personal time.[24] Our church is organized in the following way. We currently have ten elders. They each oversee three to five small groups in our church. Each elder meets with the small group leaders regularly, participates in the groups in various ways, takes care of shepherding issues within those groups, and most importantly, prays for those in the groups. We also meet weekly as an elder council to pray about various issues in the groups, and for individual needs.

In addition to your own personal prayer life, plead with others to pray for you. Behind every strong preacher and every strong church is a group of intercessors. Spurgeon reminded everyone of where the power of his ministry came from:

> What can we do without your prayers? They link us with the omnipotence of God. Like the lightening rod, they pierce through the clouds and bring down the mighty and mysterious power from on high. . . . The Lord give me a dozen importunate pleaders and lovers of souls, and by his grace we will shake London from end-to-end.[25]

Spurgeon's high view of prayer, as the means of experiencing God's power, also led him to say:

> The condition of the church may be very accurately gauged by its prayer meetings. So is the prayer meeting a grace-ometer, and from it we may judge of the amount of divine working among a people. If God be near a church, it must

---

[24] Mark Dever and Paul Alexander, *The Deliberate Church* (Wheaton, IL: Crossway, 2005), 36.
[25] C. H. Spurgeon, *The Metropolitan Tabernacle Pulpit*, vol. 25 (repr., Pasadena: Pilgrim Publications, 1980), 445.

pray. And if he be not there, one of the first tokens of his absence will be a slothfulness in prayer.[26]

In Acts 12:5, Luke records, "So Peter was kept in prison, but prayer was being made earnestly to God for him by the church." The early church had few human resources, but that did not keep them from shaking the world. They interceded earnestly throughout the book of Acts (e.g., Acts 1:14, 24; 2:42; 4:29–31; 13:1–3).

Intercession is a key to awakening. An interesting note about the first Great Awakening (which peaked 1740–42) was that it was preceded by the imprisonment of many ministers in England. In his biography of George Whitefield, Arnold Dallimore makes a wonderful observation:

> Legislation was enacted which distressed the Puritan conscience, and in 1662, on one of the darkest days in all British history, nearly two thousand ministers—all those who would not submit to the Act of Uniformity—were ejected from their livings. Hundreds of these men suffered throughout the rest of their lives, and a number died in prison. Yet these terrible conditions became the occasion of a great volume of prayer; forbidden to preach under threat of severe penalties—as John Bunyan's Bedford imprisonment bore witness—they yet could pray, and only eternity will reveal the relationship between this burden of supplication and the revival that followed.[27]

Revival follows supplication. Do not neglect the discipline of intercession, pastor, and do not fail to encourage your people to spend time pleading for the power of God on your ministry.

A final matter that should occupy our prayer life is *victory over personal attacks.* As pastors we deal not only with problems inside the church but problems inside our heart. The inevitable trials of ministry include jealousy, bitterness, fear, discouragement/depression, frustration, doubt, and anxiety—to name a few. In light of these weekly interior struggles, we must "fight for our life," as Lloyd-Jones said, and seek God's help in the quiet place in order to overcome.

---

[26] Charles Spurgeon, *Spurgeon at His Best*, comp. Tom Carter (Grand Rapids: Baker, 1988), 155.

[27] Arnold Dallimore, *George Whitefield*, vol. 1 (Edinburgh: The Banner of Truth Trust, 2001), 19–20.

I like to pray through the Psalms and Proverbs every morning, mingled with some daily Bible reading. I also love memorizing and praying the prayers of Paul. Then, other means of prayer have been good for me, like mingling my exercise program with prayer. I find that after a workout, especially in the morning, with my blood flowing, while I am not at a desk, I can experience great prayer times with a cool-down walk. Morning jogs with worship music playing, followed by a prayer walk, are also wonderful times for me. I have discovered that my spiritual life is greatly affected by my physical condition, so I have to care for my body with exercise, nutrition, and rest. Vacations and retreats are also important times to slow down and seek God's presence individually, and with your family (and perhaps your ministry team, if you retreat together).

HINDRANCES TO FAITHFUL PRAYER

We need to deal with two related problems that keep us from having a vibrant prayer life: (1) our common excuses and (2) our sinful actions.

Common Excuses

In D. A. Carson's challenging book *A Call to Spiritual Reformation*, he notes several excuses that Christians often use to justify prayerlessness.[28] Scripture speaks to each of them.

I am too busy to pray. If we believe that our lives and ministries demand so much time that we cannot give a portion of it to unhindered and unhurried prayer, then we need to repent. Luther said that he was so busy that he had to spend the first three hours of the day in prayer! Jesus responded to Martha's business by telling her that "Mary has made the right choice, and it will not be taken away from her" (Luke 10:42). Good things can do great damage. Before you turn on the computer and get to work, remember to choose what is best. Cut something out, but do not neglect time at the feet of Jesus.

I feel too dry to pray. Behind this excuse is the problematic idea that the basis for our prayers is our feelings. Do not wait for joy to pray. Pray for joy in Christ. Like George Mueller, seek to have your soul "happy in God." Our reason for praying in dry times

---

[28] D. A. Carson, *A Call to Spiritual Reformation* (Grand Rapids: Baker, 1992), 113–14.

is because it is there that we meet the all-sufficient Savior. Christ must be the motive of our prayers, not our feelings. Further, Jesus taught us much about persistency in prayer (Luke 11:9–10; 18:1–8), teaching us to ask and keep on asking. Sure there will be days in which our spirits sag, but let us not forget Paul's words, "Rejoice in hope, be patient in tribulation, be constant in prayer" (Rom 12:12 ESV). And get around other Christians who can stir your affections for prayer.

I feel no need to pray. Many Western Christians who think that success is rooted in human ingenuity and gifting use this excuse (though they may not verbalize it). We do well to remember the story in Joshua 9, where the Israelites were deceived by the Gibeonites because they "did not ask counsel from the Lord" (v. 14 ESV). Failure to seek the Lord is an obvious mark of pride and our arrogant self-righteousness.

I am too ashamed to pray. How do you pray after a bad night? We have to remember that the basis of our prayers is in the grace of Jesus. We do not approach a throne of works or performance but a throne of grace (Heb 4:14–16). We need gospel appropriation and application in these moments to couple our prayers.

Prayer is not my gift. Many Christians conveniently use this "gift excuse" to avoid responsibility to commands that are uncomfortable, such as prayer and evangelism. While some people certainly are gifted pray-ers, all Christians are commanded to pray (Eph 6:18–20).

I believe in God's sovereignty. This excuse is used by the hyper-Calvinists who see no need to pray because God is sovereign. Spurgeon, himself a Calvinist (not a hyper-Calvinist), said:

> In God's Word we are over and over again commanded to pray. God's institutions are not folly. Can I believe that the infinitely wise God has ordained for me an exercise that is ineffective and is no more than child's play? Does He tell me to pray, and yet does prayer have no more of a result than if I whistled to the wind or sang to a grove of trees? If there is no answer to prayer, prayer is a monstrous absurdity, and God is the author of it, which is blasphemy.[29]

---

[29] Charles Spurgeon, *The Power in Prayer* (New Kensington: Whitaker House, 1996), 9.

I personally do not understand the mystery of God's providence and Christians' prayers. But I agree with Spurgeon: "God's institutions are not folly." God said to pray and keep on praying. That is what we must do—and leave the results to his sovereign will.

Sinful Actions

Prayer and Bible reading are similar in that sin affects both practices. It is often said, "Sin will keep you from the Bible, and the Bible will keep you from sin." The same can be said of prayer, as well. On the one hand, fervent prayer will guard you from sin. Jesus said, "Pray that you may not enter into temptation" (Luke 22:40). On the other hand, sin will keep you from prayer. What sins are these, specifically?

Peter teaches us three sinful barriers to prayer. In 1 Peter 3:7 he says, "Husbands, in the same way, live with your wives with an understanding of their weaker nature yet showing them honor as co-heirs of the grace of life, *so that your prayers will not be hindered*" (my emphasis). So your relationship with your spouse affects your prayers. Next, when talking about unity in 1 Peter 3:8, Peter quotes Psalm 34, saying that the Lord hears the prayer of the righteous but not of the wicked (1 Pet 3:12). Finally, Peter adds another hindrance, in addition to unhealthy relationships and unrighteousness, saying, "The end of all things is at hand; therefore be self-controlled and sober-minded *for the sake of your prayers*" (4:7 ESV, my emphasis). So, a lack of self-control leads to an interrupted line of communication. The big idea? Do whatever you can do not to hinder the effectiveness of your prayers. Right living leads to right praying.

In addition, James teaches us that praying for selfish purposes hinders prayer. He says, "You ask and don't receive because you ask with wrong motives, so that you may spend it on your evil desires" (4:3). Isaiah shows us that sin and injustice hinder prayer. He told God's rebellious people that "your iniquities have built barriers between you and your God, and your sins have made Him hide [His] face from you so that He does not listen" (Isa 59:2).

Furthermore, two quite practical problems block our communication with God: unconcern for the poor and an unforgiving spirit. I wonder sometimes whether our lack of giving and helping the poor around the world has contributed to the spiritual decline in our land. The author of Proverbs says, "The one who shuts his ears to the cry of the poor will himself also call out and not be answered" (21:13). God hears the prayers of people who give to the poor.

Another great barrier to vibrant prayer is a lack of forgiveness. Our relationships on earth affect our relationship with God. This truth is expressed throughout the Scriptures. Consider the following: "And whenever you stand praying, if you have anything against anyone, forgive him, so that your Father in heaven will also forgive you your wrongdoing" (Mark 11:25). Jesus said in the Lord's Prayer, "And forgive us our debts, as we also have forgiven our debtors," and "For if you forgive people their wrongdoing, your heavenly Father will forgive you as well. But if you don't forgive people, your Father will not forgive your wrongdoing" (6:12, 14–15). Jesus later illustrated this principle (that we should not expect forgiveness if we do not forgive) by telling the parable of the unmerciful servant (Matt 18:21–35). Therefore, we must make sure we are right with our brother and sister if we desire the mercy of God (see Eph 4:32).

I heard of a story about a church in which the stove stopped working and no one knew why. When it was inspected, they discovered that a spider had spun an enormous web and stopped the pipe that went from the stove to the power source. Like this spider, unrepentant sin can do great damage to our lives, and it will hinder us from having a dynamic prayer life. By God's grace, kill the spiders—for the good of your relationship with God and others.

MORE PRACTICAL TIPS ON PRAYER

While I advocate finding your own routine for prayer, as mentioned previously, I suggest ten more ideas for you to consider, which have helped me.[30]

First, plan to pray. If you want to get into physical shape, then you need a plan. You may consult some experts in the field, read a book, or note helpful exercises. The same is true for the spiritual realm. Think about it. What will you do to increase your discipline of prayer? Where will you pray? When will you pray? For what will you pray? Carson seems correct in saying that Paul's many references to his "prayers" (e.g., Rom 1:10; Eph 1:16; 1 Thess 1:2; 2 Tim 1:3) suggest that he set aside designated times for prayer—apparently as

---

[30] Several of these ideas come from D. A. Carson, *A Call to Spiritual Reformation*, 19–38.

Jesus did (Luke 5:16).[31] Plan to pray like you plan to eat or exercise or meet with someone.

Second, find some ways to keep your mind from wandering. You may choose to vocalize your prayers, pray Scripture, or go on a prayer walk. Again, everyone is different. Do something that will keep you alert.

Third, mingle Bible reading with prayer. I believe God has given us a book for which to do this: Psalms. Whereas all Scripture speaks to us, the Psalms have a special way of speaking *for* us. We find ourselves in the Psalms. Our emotions and desires resonate with the cry of the psalmist. Personally, I have found that most mornings I do not rise ready to pray. But after reading the Psalms, my passions are awakened.

In addition to the Psalms, simply praying through passages is quite helpful because it ensures that you are praying in God's will (John 15:7), it brings variety to your requests, and it gives your Bible reading an extra spiritual dynamic.

Fourth, mingle writing with prayer. This practice can be done by writing prayers for people, developing serious prayer lists, or journaling. A lady recently wrote me a prayer based on Colossians 1:9–14, and it was very encouraging. What a great way to focus your prayer time, by writing a prayer for someone by using the text.

Fifth, mingle praise with prayer. As you praise God in the car, on a walk, or at your desk, couple petitions with your worship.

Sixth, work on your public prayers. I think the general rule for public prayer is that it should be both formed and free. You should have some idea as to what you are about to pray but still be free enough to pray somewhat spontaneously. If you want your people to pray for other churches, missionaries, governmental leaders, and so forth, then teach them to intercede for others publicly.

Seventh, develop prayer partner relationships. As a pastor, it is important for you to verbalize prayers with some close friends. Of course, this should occur with your fellow elders/pastors. But hopefully you can find some other brothers to pray with during the week.

Eighth, do not stop praying until you have prayed. Press hard into the presence of God during sessions of prayer with honesty and persistence. Carson says, "To enter the spirit of prayer, we must stick to it for a while. If we, as the Puritans used to say, 'pray until we've

---

[31] Ibid., 20.

prayed,' eventually we come to delight in God's presence, to rest in his love, to cherish his will. Even in dark or agonized praying, we somehow know that we are doing business with God."[32] Do business with God. Do not stop until you know you have communed with the Almighty.

Ninth, fast and pray regularly. Fasting is a wonderful means of grace that Jesus expected his disciples to practice (Matt 6:16). Exchange a meal on a Tuesday for time with God. Perhaps you can take a day per week to fast and pray. Even go longer periods of time, if possible. Food is not the only thing to sacrifice for prayer, but I believe it is the most rewarding thing to say no to, in order to say yes to God. Fasting removes substitutes for God, it reveals what controls us, it increases humility and dependence on God, it assists in fighting temptation, and it gives us more time to pray. Do it privately, wisely, gradually, and faithfully—avoiding spiritual pride.

Finally, develop a routine for praying right before you preach or teach. I use John Piper's "APTAT" because it is simple and biblical.[33] "A" stands for *admit*. Admit that we are helpless apart from Christ (John 15:5). "P" stands for *pray*. Pray a promise from the Scriptures. "T" stands for *trust*. Trust that God answers according to his Word. "A" stands for *act*. Act in confidence, as you ascend to preach, because God is faithful. "T" stands for *thank God*. Thank him after the sermon because he sustained you and helped you preach his Word. Perhaps you can find another way to voice your desperation before preaching, but I challenge you to acknowledge, one more time, that you need God's help as you stand to say, "Thus says the Lord."

SUMMATION

The examples of Scripture and Christian history magnify the importance of a praying minister. Faithful preachers and teachers are more than orators. They are individuals who spend unhurried and unhindered time with God in the prayer closet. Ministers of the Word should seek God for illumination as they study the Scriptures. They should also intercede on behalf of others, while asking for the prayers of people as well. Victory over personal attacks is also a

---

[32] Ibid., 36.
[33] John Piper, *The Supremacy of God in Preaching*, rev. ed. (Grand Rapids: Baker, 2004), 48–49.

matter of prayer, as the ministry leader seeks to overcome the spiritual struggles of leading a church. While many excuses exist when it comes to praying, the preacher must kill them, along with any prayer-blocking sins that hinder communication with God. Finally, the pastor should implement various practical methods for keeping his prayer life fresh and consistent.

QUESTIONS

1. What should ministers pray for regularly—noted under "The Content of Faithful Prayer"?
2. What are some practices that others have used to enjoy a disciplined prayer life?
3. List common excuses that hinder us from praying.
4. List some practical tips on prayer. Which is most helpful or challenging to you?
5. In the spirit of Acts 6:4, what are some changes in your life that you need to make in order to devote yourself to prayer more faithfully?

7

PREACH AND TEACH FOR GOD'S GLORY

As each has received a gift, use it to serve one another, as good stewards of God's varied grace: whoever speaks, as one who speaks oracles of God; whoever serves, as one who serves by the strength that God supplies—in order that in everything God may be glorified through Jesus Christ. To him belong glory and dominion forever and ever. Amen.

—1 Peter 4:10–11 (ESV)

A preacher's call to preach is rooted in his call to Christ, and his call to Christ is rooted in a quest for the glory of God.[1]

—Jim Shaddix

WHEN I WAS A boy, my parents let me purchase an old television from my uncle Eddie for twenty dollars. It was so cheap because the picture on every channel was burnt orange! I played Contra, Mike Tyson's Punch Out, and other video games on this cheap TV. Most enjoyably, I watched my favorite team, the Kentucky Wildcats, play basketball. One day my dad came home with news that he had some

---

[1] Jim Shaddix, *The Passion-Driven Sermon* (Nashville: B&H, 2003), 3–4.

tickets to watch Kentucky at Rupp Arena and asked if I wanted to go with him. Of course I did. But I acted as if it was no big deal. After all, I watched the games on my prehistoric TV all the time. Surely watching the game in Lexington would be quite similar to watching it in my bedroom.

On the day of the game, I put on my fifth-grade satin basketball jacket, my sweat pants, British Knights shoes, and hat (tilted to the side). I was ready to strut into Rupp Arena. After arriving, we first spent some time in the shopping area, and then we eventually decided to make our way to our lower-level seats. I will never forget the experience that followed. After casually walking past the ticket man, I walked through the door to the actual arena . . . and I lost my breath. I stood speechless in the entryway. My three-ounce brain almost crashed, trying to grasp the amazing sights and sounds. The colors were so different than they were on my TV! The players were so big and fast; the crowd was so loud; and Kenny "Sky" Walker could jump so high! I felt small in this big arena. My view of Kentucky basketball and the arena was elevated. I was awestruck. And I wanted to tell everyone about my experience.

Sometimes I compare that experience to corporate worship services and ministry in general. Questions about the glory of God come to mind: Am I in awe of the holiness of God? Am I dazzled by the unspeakable grace of God in Christ? Do I strut into the presence of God? Have I gotten so familiar with the things of God that I no longer view my task with fear and trembling before God? Do I want others to behold the greatness of God and be changed into the image of the Son of God?

A primary role of an expositor is to escort the hearers into the arena of God's Word, so that they may experience God's glory in the face of Jesus Christ (2 Cor 3:18–4:6). Professor Robert Smith calls good biblical preachers "exegetical escorts."[2] They aim to show people the beauty of the Lord in the pages of his Word.

But before we usher the hearers into the arena of God's Word, we need to experience the Triune God's glory personally. In the following pages, I want to challenge you to make God's glory your passionate quest and to examine your heart through a personal test.

---

[2] Robert Smith Jr., *Doctrine That Dances* (Nashville: B&H, 2008), 35.

A PASSIONATE QUEST: TO BEHOLD THE GLORY OF GOD

As Christians, we believe that God is one in *essence* or *nature* and three in *person*.[3] Each member of the Godhead possesses the divine nature equally, eternally, simultaneously, and fully.[4] The Father, Son, and Spirit are thus identical in essence but unique in person. Both unity and diversity are within the glorious Triune God. The persons of the Trinity work in harmony with one another, fulfilling distinct roles. In so doing, the relationship of the Father, Son, and Spirit provides the greatest example in the universe of love, community, beauty, humility, joy, and unity. Only in relationship to God can mankind find peace, joy, meaning, and love as his image bearers.

The Father is the designer of creation, redemption, and consummation.[5] He deserves glory and praise for his matchless grace. Paul says that everyone will confess, "Jesus Christ is Lord, *to the glory of God the Father*" (Phil 2:11, my emphasis). Amazingly, in divine humility, the Father does not seek all the attention, however. Despite his role within the Godhead, the Father chooses to work through his Son and manifest his glory in the Son (John 1:14). The Father gladly rejoices in the glorification of Christ. The Spirit works "in the background," not putting himself forward. Instead, the Spirit purposes to magnify Christ (John 16:14), and the Son seeks to glorify the Father (John 17:2, 4). The Father is glorified through the Son by the Spirit.

Further, as Christians, we believe that the Triune God is the Creator and Sustainer of all that is; consequently, God is the rightful recipient of honor and glory alone. Paul said it like this: "For from Him and through Him and to Him are all things. To Him be the glory forever. Amen" (Rom 11:36). God is not only the Creator and Sustainer, but he is also the Redeemer. Elsewhere, Paul said, "You are not your own, for you were bought with a price. So glorify God in your body" (1 Cor 6:19b–20 ESV). Therefore, we are doubly owned. God possesses us as Creator and Redeemer in order to display his glory.

---

[3] Bruce Ware, *Father, Son, and Spirit: Relationships, Roles, and Relevance* (Wheaton, IL: Crossway, 2005), 41.

[4] Ibid.

[5] Ibid., 51.

The Westminster Confession applies this truth about God's supremacy for us saying: "The chief end of man is to glorify God and enjoy him forever." A God-centered Christian will desire above all things to glorify God the Father, through Jesus Christ, by the Spirit. The Christian's theme will be "whether you eat or drink, or whatever you do, do everything for God's glory" (1 Cor 10:31). It is precisely in this pursuit that we find meaning and lasting joy.

I find no reason to believe that the chief end of preaching should be any different than the chief end of man. In fact, Peter said of those who have speaking gifts, "Whoever speaks, as one who speaks oracles of God; whoever serves, as one who serves by the strength that God supplies—in order that in everything God may be glorified through Jesus Christ. To him belong glory and dominion forever and ever. Amen" (1 Pet 4:11 ESV). According to Peter, if one is to speak, then he should do so from God's Word, by God's power, through God's Son, for God's glory. For Peter, true preaching is therefore Word-driven and trinitarian in nature.

Noted pastors and teachers have reminded us in recent years about this God-glorifying trajectory in preaching. Jim Shaddix stated, "A preacher's call to preach is rooted in his call to Christ, and his call to Christ is rooted in a quest for the glory of God."[6] Similarly, pastor-theologian John Piper captured this high purpose of preaching saying, "Therefore, the goal of preaching is the glory of God reflected in the glad submission of his people."[7] I too believe that being captivated by the God-ness of God and a desire to see him known and worshipped, through Jesus Christ, must remain central to expositors.

Has the glory and greatness of God, displayed most magnificently in the crucified and risen Christ, captured your mind and heart so much that you preach out of an overflow of your knowledge of him? Do you desire to please God with your treatment of his Word more than you desire to impress others? Do you preach by the Spirit, through the Son, to the Father? Do you long to make his majesty known to your generation? Is your passion to "declare his glory among the nations?" (Ps 96:3). Faithful preachers are those who are captivated by the majesty, the reality, and the wonder of God.

---

[6] Shaddix, *The Passion-Driven Sermon*, 3–4.
[7] John Piper, *The Supremacy of God in Preaching*, rev. ed. (Grand Rapids: Baker, 2004), 29.

The Preacher's Quest

Perhaps one of the reasons that God is not declared with great clarity and warmth is that many pastors have lost their vision of God's majesty personally. Prior to standing behind a pulpit, they have not entered the arena of glory themselves. More than forty years ago, A. W. Tozer wrote: "Were we able to extract from any man a complete answer to the question, 'What comes into your mind when you think about God?' we might predict with certainty the spiritual future of that man. Were we able to know exactly what our most influential religious leaders think of God today, we might be able with some precision to foretell where the church will stand tomorrow."[8]

What will people think of God in our culture forty years from now? The answer to that question is dependent largely upon whether thousands of God-centered, Christ-exalting preachers and teachers rise up and proclaim the excellences of God (1 Pet 2:9).

The early disciples were captured by the nature of God and the hope found in the risen Christ. In fact, they had no category through which to understand Jesus. The disciples replied on one occasion like a little child, "What kind of man is this?" (Matt 8:27). In Acts the apostles boldly proclaimed the "name" of Christ, pointing out his absolute authority on earth and his exclusive salvation (4:12). What motivated these disciples? They saw his glory. Consequently, they could not stop speaking of the things that they had seen and heard (4:20).

When computer gadgets, social media, deer hunting, pop-TV shows, sporting events, and worldly comforts excite us more than our Creator and Redeemer, then it should not surprise us when God's greatness is absent in pulpits.

Where should we go to see the glory of God? Psalm 19 teaches that we see the glory of God first in creation but most vividly in the Scriptures. Creation is like the twenty-dollar television, when the Scriptures are like entering the arena itself, where we see the glory of the gospel unfolded and the hero of the Bible exalted.

Writing from prison, the apostle Paul told the Philippian church about his ultimate quest: to know Christ more and become like him (Phil 3:10–11). Knowing the Savior consumed Paul. He

---

[8] A. W. Tozer, *The Knowledge of the Holy* (San Francisco: Harper, 1961), 1–2.

had experienced wonders in his life and ministry, yet there was still more glory to behold, more gospel to enjoy, more awe to experience. Unfortunately, many in ministry start off with such zeal to know Christ more, but excitement gets replaced with the quest for personal fame and financial gain; wonder turns into familiarity and dead religious ritual; and ministry success becomes the goal instead of faithfulness to God.

When I was in seminary, I had a terrific theology teacher named Stan Norman. His classes were so moving that I used to say, "We type on our knees as we take notes in Dr. Norman's class because class becomes a worship service." One particular day, he was teaching on the resurrection of Christ, and we were considering some awesome implications of the empty tomb. But one particular student was obviously uninterested. Dr. Norman, not shy to call people out in class, noticed this student's coldness. When he asked the student about his demeanor, the frustrated student said, "Look, I didn't come here to study this stuff. All I want is to know how to pastor a big church." After a few words, Dr. Norman essentially replied, "You are here to know Jesus Christ."[9] How contrary was this student's quest (and others who quietly hold the same pursuit) to the apostle Paul's quest? Paul considered everything as "dung" compared to the surpassing greatness of knowing Jesus as Lord (Phil 3:7–8).

J. I. Packer put it well: "Once you become aware that the main business that you are here for is to know God, most of life's problems fall into place of their own accord."[10] What is your main business in life? Is it to pastor a big church? Is it to make money? Everything in life flows from the fountain of knowing Christ.

The People's Quest

The quest to behold the greatness of God in Christ is the unconscious cry of every person. Unfortunately, those who preach do not always take this basic truth seriously. In seeking to be *relevant*, it seems, many preachers and teachers actually have become *irrelevant*. It is a tragic misunderstanding to think that our knowledge of God and the gospel is not *practical*. The most fundamental need of humanity is to know God and to know him with ever-increasing

---

[9] Paraphrase of the exchange. Dr. Norman and I recently talked about the details of this unforgettable class moment. I am extremely indebted to faithful teachers like Dr. Norman.
[10] J. I. Packer, *Knowing God* (Downers Grove, IL: InterVarsity, 1973), 34.

clarity and intensity (Phil 3:10). In contrast to the self-help sermons of the seekers, the dialogue messages of the emergents, and the "name-it-and-claim-it" sermons of the prosperity preachers, struggling people need pastors to show them the wonders of God revealed in Scripture.

Indeed, many of your people may not realize that understanding the nature of God is their greatest need. You might have to convince them. I agree with Piper:

> People are starving for the greatness of God. But most of them would not give this diagnosis of their troubled lives. The majesty of God is an unknown cure. There are far more popular prescriptions on the market, but the benefit of any other remedy is brief and shallow. Preaching that does not have the aroma of God's greatness may entertain for a season, but will not touch the hidden cry of the soul: "Show me thy glory!"[11]

It is amazing how you will meet the particular needs and hurts of people by declaring simply who God is. Remember, God is *relevant*! People need to know that they have a rock on which to stand, a Savior who sympathizes with them and provides grace to them, and the Holy Spirit who comforts them. Keller reminds us of the comprehensive relevance of declaring God's gospel: "Most of our problems in life come from a lack of proper orientation to the gospel. Pathologies in the church and sinful patterns in our individual lives ultimately stem from a failure to think through the deep implications of the gospel and to grasp and believe the gospel through and through. Put positively, the gospel transforms our hearts and our thinking and changes our approaches to absolutely everything in life."[12] Keller goes on to quote D. A. Carson, "One of the most urgently needed things today is a careful treatment of how the gospel, biblically and richly understood, ought to shape everything we do in the local church, all of our ethics, all of our priorities."[13] Believe that the gospel is the most relevant thing in the world you could teach people. Beholding the greatness of God and grasping the gospel changes everything. Pointing people to the nature of

---

[11] Piper, *The Supremacy of God in Preaching*, 13.
[12] Tim Keller, *Center Church* (Grand Rapids: Zondervan, 2012), 51.
[13] Ibid.

our great God and the work of our glorious Savior is the job of exegetical escorts. And the reality is, the people are starving for this kind of preaching and teaching. Substitute subjects will ultimately not satisfy nor sustain them.

A PERSONAL TEST: 3 QUESTIONS

Beholding the glory of God is the first step in becoming a God-centered, Christ-exalting preacher. The next step is preaching for the glory of God. How can we expound the Bible as an act of worship to God? We must consider three aspects of each sermon: our *motive*, our *message*, and our *manner*. You should ask yourself about each of these subjects as you prepare to deliver messages.

What Is My Motive?

Paul described the motivation we need, saying:

> In their case, the god of this age has blinded the minds of the unbelievers so they cannot see the light of the gospel of the glory of Christ, who is the image of God. For we are not proclaiming ourselves but Jesus Christ as Lord, and ourselves as your slaves because of Jesus. For God, who said, "Let light shine out of darkness," has shone in our hearts to give the light of the knowledge of God's glory in the face of Jesus Christ. (2 Cor 4:5–6)

He reminded the Corinthians that his motive in preaching did not arise from personal glorification. Instead, he intended to glorify God, whose glory is beautifully magnified in the face of Jesus Christ. Paul's preaching was thus radically God centered and Christ exalting. It was not *about* Paul or *for* Paul; it was *about* Christ and *for* Christ. What then takes preachers and teachers away from such a motive? Four obstacles appear obvious to me.

1. Indwelling Sin. Sin clouds our vision of God and hinders intimacy with God. Consequently, our motive gets distorted when our hearts are not clean. Our motive may end up being popularity, praise, success, or power. Therefore, the primary opponent we have to deal with in preaching motivation is the indwelling residue of sin and the pride that is so interwoven with it. Other problems surface as a result of this fundamental problem. We must seek to kill sin on a daily basis (Rom 8:13). In our daily conduct, we must walk by the

Spirit, not after the lusts of the flesh (Gal 5:16). Our mind will not be captured by God's glory if it is filled with shameful depravity, and our motive will be man centered, not God centered.

2. The Praise of Men and the Fear of Men. A second obstacle to preaching for God's glory is caring too much about the reaction of people. Many times we forget that the primary audience of our sermon is God, not people. If we neglect this reality, we will fall into the trap of either altering the message to please people or not preaching truth because we fear people. Remember, if you do not please God, it really does not matter who you please. The preacher who preaches to please people is not a prophet. We must take a higher road. Paul said, "For am I now trying to win the favor of people, or God? Or am I striving to please people? If I were still trying to please people, I would not be a slave of Christ" (Gal 1:10). Jesus also scolded the religious leaders for practicing their righteousness before other people in order to be seen by them (Matt 6:1). Let us end this love affair with the praise of men and preach for the pleasure of God.

Preachers who fear others would do well to remember the God-centered motivation of the great Reformer John Knox, who preached powerfully in Scotland. He was a frail man with a fiery disposition. After his return to Scotland in 1559 from his exile in Geneva, his biblical preaching was changing lives. One person wrote to Queen Elizabeth saying, "The voice of one man is able in one hour to put more life in us than 500 trumpets continually bursting in our ears." The queen vowed to retaliate. Knox replied to her, "Outside the preaching place, Madam, I think few have occasion to be offended at me; but there, Madam, I am not master of myself, but must obey him who commands me to speak plain, and to flatter no flesh upon the face of the earth." When Knox died in 1572, the regent, Earl of Morton, said at his grave, "Here lies one who never feared the face of man."[14] John Knox, like many other Reformers, turned the world upside down by his courageous preaching. Jesus said, "Do not fear those who kill the body but cannot kill the soul. Rather fear him who can destroy both soul and body in hell" (Matt 10:28 ESV).

3. Competition and Jealousy. Another regrettable problem that we have in maintaining a Christ-honoring motivation is the temptation

---

[14] Quoted in John Stott, *Between Two Worlds* (Grand Rapids: Eerdmans, 1982), 304–5.

to compete with other preachers. Unfortunately, this competition is perpetuated by the contemporary milieu. People now have access to more sermons than ever before. Many preachers tend to get jealous when others are favored as the keynote speaker or receive offers from large churches.

An old story from the fourth century illustrates the weakness we have in giving in to the sin of jealousy. Some inexperienced demons were finding it difficult in tempting a godly hermit. They lured him with every type of temptation, but he could not be enticed. The demons returned to Satan and recited their problem. He responded that they had been far *too hard* on the man. Satan said, "Send him a message that his brother has just been made bishop of Antioch. Bring him *good news*." Baffled by the Devil's advice, the demons returned and reported the wonderful news to the pious hermit. In that very instant, he fell into deep, wicked jealousy.[15] Jealousy can tear down the godliest ministers.

Are you aware of the sin of jealousy in your life? It can destroy us. I long for the heart of Paul who said, "What does it matter? Just that in every way, whether out of false motives or true, Christ is proclaimed. And in this I rejoice" (Phil 1:18). Despite the fact that wrongly motivated preachers were using Paul's imprisonment as a means of tearing him down, Paul humbly said, "Christ is proclaimed. And in this I rejoice." Here is how you overcome your wicked jealousy: Care more for Jesus's glory than your own. Let the glory of Christ be your chief concern.

4. Obsession with Church Growth. Certainly, numbers are important because people are important. In the opening pages of Acts, Luke recounts the large number of converts added to the church. And we do have a book of the Bible entitled (at least in English) *Numbers*! However, an unhealthy obsession with church growth has the power to keep you from preaching for God's glory. The temptation is to do "whatever works" (pragmatism) in order to attract a crowd, keep your job, or get a raise.

Indeed, a faithful expositor has a higher goal than merely putting people in the seat and paying the church's bills. We have a doxological purpose in preaching (glorifying God) before we have a numerical purpose in preaching (increasing attendance).

---

[15] Story taken from Kent and Barbara Hughes, *Liberating Ministry from the Success Syndrome* (Wheaton, IL: Tyndale House, 1988), 100.

At the same time, there is no reason to believe that you *cannot* grow a church through Christ-exalting exposition. We have many modern-day examples of this reality. Longing for converts is healthy. Longing for thousands to behold the glory of God in Christ is right and good, but do not love numbers for the wrong reasons.

Many of God's greatest preachers were not successful in the world's eyes. Isaiah was told that no one would respond positively to his message (Isa 6:8–13). Jesus preached to 5,000-plus after he fed them, and at the end of the sermon many walked away never to return (John 6:66). Great Puritan pastors like John Bunyan and Richard Baxter led relatively small congregations yet made an eternal impact. Measure success by faithfulness to your calling: declare the Word of Christ faithfully for the glory of God supremely. We will do this as we tend to our souls, as we preach for one primary audience, as we avoid competition and jealousy, and as we avoid man-centered pragmatism.

What Is My Message?

After checking the motivation of your heart, check the content of your message. A message that does not highlight the Redeemer from his Word will fail to bring great glory to God. The best approach for exposing the nature of God and his voice is Word-driven preaching and teaching.

When God's voice is exposed through the expositor, then the sermon becomes an offering of worship to God. Worship occurs when we meet with God. In singing, we adore God with glad and humble hearts. In prayer, we look to God with contrite and joyful hearts. In preaching, the hearers listen to God and see his glory in the Word. Unfortunately, many differentiate between "preaching" and "worship." We often say, "After a time of worship, we will hear some preaching." However, what is more God-centered than hearing the voice of God? What if I talked to my wife for thirty minutes and then put my fingers in my ears when it was her turn to talk? I would have to eat Ramen noodles and sleep on the couch! Expository preaching glorifies God because it magnifies God's voice and exalts his Son from the Scriptures. Therefore, if you want to preach for God's glory, then preach sermons that are thoroughly biblical. Ask yourself, "Does this message emphasize God's Word and draw attention to God's Son?"

The importance of exposing God's voice was a priority in the early church's public gatherings. One of those examples is found in Paul's clear words to Timothy: "Until I come, devote yourself to the public reading of Scripture, to exhortation, to teaching" (1 Tim 4:13 ESV). Paul's emphasis on the exposition of Scripture followed the pattern of the synagogue, where one read from the Scriptures and then provided commentary on what was just read (e.g., Luke 4:16–22; Acts 17:1–4). It seems that this pattern was maintained in the early church, giving us the origin of the sermon in worship. There is no reason to believe that this pattern is not meant for today. This appears to be one of the primary ways—if not the primary way—we are to "preach the Word" (2 Tim 4:2 ESV). We should read the Word, explain it, and urge people to obey it.[16]

Regarding Paul's words in 1 Timothy 4:13, and the centrality of the Scriptures in public worship, John Stott commented: "This reading of the Old Testament was taken over by Christians from synagogue to church . . . It was taken for granted from the beginning that Christian preaching would be expository preaching, that is, that all Christian instruction and exhortation would be drawn from the passage which had been read."[17] We follow a great legacy of saints who have gone before us, who prioritized the public reading and exposition of God's Word in the worship assembly. Not all forms of preaching today magnify God's Word in the public gathering. This is a tragedy because a major part of worship is hearing the voice of God. In the book of Nehemiah, Ezra stands up and reads for hours, and the people fall down in worship (Nehemiah 8). We need to recapture this biblical pattern of reading and expounding God's Word in corporate worship.

Young Timothy probably faced many of the pressures that you will face in preaching today. Yet Paul urged him not to cease this necessary activity. Are you pressured to back away from making your message thoroughly biblical and your entire worship service Scripture saturated? Are you practicing 1 Timothy 4:13? Are you exposing God's voice and helping people see Christ's glory

---

[16] It is interesting that some preachers who react negatively to exposition argue that no proposed method for preaching is in the Bible. While there is some truth to this statement, in regard to sermon form, Paul's words cannot be clearer. The general practice was to exposit a passage of Scripture in public worship. Not all methods of preaching today can do this.

[17] John Stott, *Guard the Truth* (Downers Grove, IL: InterVarsity, 1996), 121–22.

revealed in his revealed Word? Like Ezra, open the book, read from the book, and convey the meaning of the book, for the glory of our God who gave us the book.

What Is My Manner?

The character of the preacher is another important issue in preaching for God's glory. It is possible to speak God's Word accurately but to do it in a manner that does not reflect the character of Christ or draw attention to God's majesty. Paul provided various lists of vices to avoid and virtues to pursue (e.g., Gal 5:19–23). He reminded Timothy to set an example "in speech, in conduct, in love, in faith, in purity" (1 Tim 4:12). Later, he urged him to flee from evil practices and to "pursue righteousness, godliness, faith, love, endurance, and gentleness" (6:11). While I do not think that any of these lists are comprehensive, they do show us that our character is critically important. Character matters both in and out of the pulpit.

In *Between Two Worlds,* John Stott identified four character traits that should be embodied by the preacher: *sincerity, earnestness, courage,* and *humility.* I have found these four, plus the virtue of *love* (1 Cor 13:1–3), to be critical points of examination in my ministry. Such virtues are really evidences of the work of the Spirit who produces the character of Christ.

Concerning *sincerity,* Stott stated, "Nothing is more nauseating to contemporary youth than hypocrisy, and nothing is more attractive than sincerity."[18] Indeed, young people want to see authentic preachers. Before entering the pulpit, ask yourself, "Am I being sincere? Do I really care about what I am talking about? Am I really trying to implement this sermon personally?"

Next, we should examine ourselves for the presence of *passion.* Stott says, "To be sincere is to mean what we say and to do what we say; to be earnest is, in addition, to *feel* what we say."[19] Passion is also a means of glorifying God. God is not glorified in the preacher in the pulpit who does not make much of God before the people. My wife is not glorified when I begrudgingly serve her out of duty. She is honored when I display passionate joy as I take her on a date or bring her flowers. Passionless preaching does not call people's

---

[18] Stott, *Between Two Worlds,* 262.
[19] Ibid., 273.

attention godward, and it will not hold the ear of most. Ask yourself before preaching, "Is my heart on fire over this text?"

Courage has already been mentioned. The preacher must be a prophet boldly declaring the good news. This courage, however, should be tempered with *love*. Faithful preachers are to be both prophetic and pastoral in delivery. Through courage, we glorify God as the giver of truth and judge of the universe; through love, we glorify God as the gracious redeemer who is patient and forgiving toward us. Before preaching, ask yourself, "Is my heart moved with compassion over the spiritual needs of my people? Am I prepared to speak the truth in love?"

Finally, *humility* is perhaps the greatest character quality missing in preaching today. Stott commented, "Pride is without doubt the chief occupational hazard of the preacher."[20] God is not glorified in arrogance but by the humility of Christ. He told Isaiah, "I will look favorably on this kind of person: one who is humble, submissive in spirit, and who trembles at My word" (Isa 66:2). Check your manner before preaching. Do you tremble at God's Word? Are you seeking his glory not your own? Lloyd-Jones stated, "The greatest of all temptations that assail the preacher is pride."[21] Know this, and do everything you can to humble yourself "under the mighty hand of God" (1 Pet 5:6), so that you do not oppose God but instead receive grace from God (1 Pet 5:5).

SUMMATION

The glory of God should not only be our passionate quest for Christian living, but it should also be our goal as expositors. In order to preach and teach for God's glory, we must first seek God's glory personally. We must then escort the hearers through God's Word, showing them the nature of God and the glory of the gospel. Some ways for us to maintain a God-centered, Christ-exalting agenda in the pulpit are by checking our motive—to see if it is God centered; by checking our message—to see if it magnifies God's voice; and by checking our manner—to see if it reflects Christ's character.

[20] Ibid., 320.
[21] D. Martyn Lloyd-Jones, *Preaching and Preachers* (Grand Rapids: Zondervan, 1971), 256.

Questions

1. What does it mean to be an "exegetical escort"?
2. What does it mean to preach for the glory of God? How do we pursue this aim?
3. What are some obstacles to preaching for God's glory? Explain.
4. How does the content of our message bring glory to God?
5. How can we glorify God with our manner of preaching?

PART 2:

THE EXPOSITOR'S MESSAGE

Below is a diagram of the five steps of preparing an expositional message, covered in the next five chapters. The final two chapters (13–14) will deal with the delivery of the message.[22]

The Five Steps of Preparing an Expositional Message

Step 1	Step 2	Step 3	Step 4	Step 5
STUDY THE TEXT	UNIFY THE REDEMPTIVE THEME	OUTLINE THE TEXT	DEVELOP THE FUNCTIONAL ELEMENTS	ADD AN INTRODUCTION & CONCLUSION
Obvious Observations: What does the text say?	Identify the main point of the text (MPT).	Choose an approach.	Explanation	Adding the introduction
Responsible Interpretation: What does the text mean?	Determine the main point of the sermon (MPS).	Choose your words.	Application	Adding the conclusion
Redemptive Integration: How is the gospel related to this text?	Add a title that reflects the MPS.		Illustration	Writing the message and praying over it
Concluding Implications: How does this passage apply to us today?				

[22] Thanks to Pastor Kevin Larson for the idea of this visual.

8

STEP 1: STUDY THE TEXT

Do your best to present yourself to God as one approved, a worker who has no need to be ashamed, rightly handling the word of truth.
—2 *Timothy 2:15 (ESV)*

How, then, shall we prepare? This is a very subjective matter. There is no one way to prepare sermons. Every preacher has to work out his own method, which suits his temperament and situation; it is a mistake to copy others uncritically. Nevertheless, we can learn from one another. As Erasmus once rather playfully said, "If elephants can be trained to dance, lions to play, and leopards to hunt, surely preachers can be taught to preach."[1]

—*John Stott*

W HY DO PEOPLE NOT study the Bible? It is the best-selling book in history yet studied infrequently. I suppose that some believe the Bible is sort of a magic book that does not require study. Just open it and you will feel the meaning of it! Others, particularly unbelievers, are pessimistic about the Bible. They think that one simply cannot understand such an ancient book or that it has no real relevance

---

[1] John Stott, *Between Two Worlds* (Grand Rapids: Eerdmans, 1982), 213.

for the modern world. But why do so few *Christians* study the Bible in depth? While laziness and business are common excuses, there is perhaps a more painful reason: no one has modeled expositional study for them. Like it or not, the flock will follow the shepherd's study habits to a large degree.

In this chapter, seven guiding interpretive principles for exposition will be identified, along with a four-phase study for developing Word-driven messages. Hopefully, by your example of diligent study, you will also inspire others to passionately study the Scriptures.

GUIDING PRINCIPLES FOR STUDYING THE TEXT

I love the game of baseball. I had the privilege of playing in high school and college. I am still amazed by the details and nuances of the sport, but nothing is more important than learning the fundamentals. Even MLB all-stars practice the fundamentals daily. You can see them practicing with a batting tee (what four-year-olds use) in order to review hitting basics. When they get in the game, they no longer concentrate as much on hitting mechanics; they simply get in the batter's box and instinctively and skillfully hit the ball. But behind these instincts is the prior practice of the fundamentals.

This pattern is sort of like biblical interpretation. Perhaps you already practice the following principles naturally and effectively as you prepare for a sermon. It is still a good idea for "Major League Expositors" to return to the batting tee for review. If these principles are brand new for you, then you should read slowly and practice them carefully, so that you will develop interpretation instincts and skills that will enable you to open a Bible and practice interpretation without concentrating on a mechanical process.

Our overarching goal in biblical interpretation and expositional teaching is *to minimize our own opinions.* Exposition is about maximizing what God actually said. We need to see what is *really* there in the text, not what we *wish* was there or what we *thought* was there. Only then can we eventually say in a message, "Thus says the Lord."

Principle 1: Read the Bible in an attitude of prayer. While the process for interpreting Scripture is scientific, literary, historical, and theological in method, we must not forget that it is also *spiritual* in nature. Open your study in prayer and remain sensitive to the Spirit during your study. We need the Spirit to open our eyes so that the

Word burns in our heart (Ps 119:18; Luke 24:32). The Holy Spirit is the great Teacher and Guide, leading us into all truth (John 16:13).

Principle 2: Remember that context is king. Always consider the context of the passage that you are studying. Context means "that which goes with the text." Ripping verses out of context and using them in a way that does not represent the intended meaning of the Holy Spirit is irresponsible and inexcusable. Ask yourself, "How does this passage fit within the surrounding context?"

Principle 3: Look for the historical meaning first. The Bible was written during particular epochs of redemptive history; therefore, the historical meaning must be identified before application is made. While a text may have numerous applications, look for the primary meaning of the original author. Always ask, "What did the original author want the original readers to understand about this passage?"

Principle 4: Identify the type of literature in which the verse is found. An oversimplified classification of the genres is (1) Law, (2) Old Testament Narratives, (3) Acts, (4) Prophets, (5) Psalms, (6) Wisdom, (7) Gospels, (8) Parables, and (9) Revelation. We must interpret the text in a manner that is consistent with its literary genre.[2] For example, we should remember that *narratives are not always normative.* In other words, Luke's main purpose in Acts is not to *prescribe* particular actions. His purpose is to *describe* certain events that occurred. After we read about Paul's handkerchief healing people (Acts 19:12), we should not make a one-to-one correlation, leading us to begin our own "handkerchief ministry." Luke is describing, not prescribing. Narratives have application to be sure, but we must apply carefully, reading passages in light of the whole of Scripture.

Further, when expounding the law genre, we must differentiate between Israel's situation and our situation. There are similarities, and there are differences. For the book of Revelation, we must remember that it was written to a particular people at a particular time, before we go rushing after the futuristic elements of the book. The book had to mean something to the original hearers. So, genre keeps us tied to the nature and history of the books of the Bible. For a wonderful resource on reading and teaching with

---

[2] For a good overview of literary genres, see Gordon D. Fee and Douglas Stuart, *How to Read the Bible for All Its Worth*, 3rd ed. (Grand Rapids: Zondervan, 2003).

genre sensitivity, see Steven Smith's book *Recapturing the Voice of God: Shaping Sermons Like Scripture.*[3]

Principle 5: Remember that the whole Bible focuses on God's redeeming work in Jesus. The Old Testament points to Christ, and the New Testament flows from Christ. Therefore, always ask, "What does this passage teach me about salvation history? How does it point to Jesus?" Read with an eye for God's activity and the Christological connection in the text.

Principle 6: Interpret Scripture with Scripture. The Scripture is not only *historical,* but it is also *harmonious.* Always ask, "How is the teaching of this passage consistent with other teachings found elsewhere in Scripture?" Practically, this means that we should look for cross-references and other biblical support for specific teachings.

Principle 7: Because the Bible is a unified testimony, always look for theological themes in the selected passage. Look for where the theme started, how it is developed, and where it culminates. Ask, "What are the biblical themes in this text?" This is one way to look for the redemptive focus of a selected passage with legitimacy.

PREPARING TO PREPARE

Cultivating a hunger for exposition in the hearts of people can be challenging in some settings. Pastors who go into congregations where thorough exposition has not been normative must be *patient.* It may take a long time to develop a "Berean church" or a "Nehemiah 8" congregation. Pastoral wisdom and grace must be applied.

If exposition is new to your audience, then what should you do? One idea is to explain your philosophy of preaching when you begin a new ministry. Tell them why you are committed to exposition and what the benefits are. You should also work strategically at developing a Bible study culture in the church. Create bookstalls in your church that contain helpful theological and practical books. You can do this even with a limited budget. Refer your people to these books during your sermons. Get them studying on their own. You may also give away Bibles, or at least make them available to guests.

Selecting the text is the next preliminary matter. How do you come up with sermon ideas and sermon series? One way is to simply start

---

[3] Steven Smith, *Recapturing the Voice of God: Shaping Sermons Like Scripture* (Nashville: B&H, 2015).

with a Bible book itself. If this is a new idea to you or the church, you might start with a book like Philippians. It is small. It does not contain a ton of controversial doctrines nor hard-to-interpret passages, and it emphasizes unity and joy in Christ. Every congregation will benefit from studying the content of Philippians; and if you do it well, you hopefully will create an appetite for more book studies.

Sermon series through Bible books are advantageous for many reasons. You will hit a variety of issues that you otherwise probably would not select. Sensitive matters are received better when issues simply appear in the weekly passage. People will not feel as though you are shooting at them.

You also will not have to labor over what to preach next! Take the next passage. This will alleviate much sermon stress.

You will save time in exegesis and be able to repeat certain truths because most books have some recurring themes. This repetition should be viewed positively, not negatively. God's truth is worth repeating. Some truths are hard to understand and require more review and further attention. And, the apostles practiced and commended repetition (Phil 3:1; 2 Tim 2:14; 2 Pet 3:1).

Book studies are also good ideas because of the transient nature of congregations. Everyone will not hear each sermon. By going methodically through a book, you can review and catch people up each week.

You will also be able to involve the people through a book series. They can read ahead and discuss the text with others. I recommend that you select a passage that can stand alone each week, yet function within the series. In this way, each sermon is different yet similar.

Various teachers differ in the length of text to take each week. One may consider a small thought block, or one may consider doing a larger unit (we taught through Exodus in large units). I prefer doing larger sections primarily because I want to expose people to multiple Old and New Testament books and multiple genres. I tend to plan a book series in semester length in order to give this exposure (and semester-long series fit the nature of our particular congregation).

Certainly there are times to do alternative types of series that are faithful to the biblical text. Instead of working through an entire book, you could teach through a theme in a book. Preaching a short series drawn from specific congregational questions is another idea. You may also have a particular issue that needs to be addressed (such as evangelism or orphan care), and you may develop a series from various passages to teach on the selected theme. We also should be aware of major events around us. If there is a crisis in the community or in the church, these issues should be handled biblically and pastorally. In considering alternative approaches to verse-by-verse book preaching, we must remember that *a sermon idea is not the same thing as a biblical truth.* You should see if the text addresses some of your ideas before saying, "Thus says the Lord." If you have to twist the text to conform to your idea, *then sacrifice the sermon idea* or *find another text.*[4]

FOUR PHASES OF EXPOSITIONAL STUDY

After selecting the text, the question is, "How do you start preparing for a particular message?" It is helpful to think of the exegetical process in four phases: (1) obvious observations, (2) responsible interpretation, (3) gospel integration, and (4) concluding implications.

Phase 1: Obvious Observations—What Does the Text Say?

Before running to the commentaries for more technical matters of interpretation, start studying your selected text by noting obvious observations. This means that you should first *read* and *reread* the text. If you have the ability, read the text in the original languages. Become intimately familiar with it. Memorize it if possible. Read it slowly and prayerfully along with your devotional reading.

Next, note some of the main features of the text. Consider the surrounding context. How does the passage fit within the book? Look then at how the passage divides. How many parts are in the text? Note the verb tenses also. Are the verbs imperatives or indicatives? Look for the main characters and the big ideas of narratives. What is the obvious point to the story? You should be able to start forming an outline from your obvious observations. A Bible, pen and paper (or computer), and an attitude of prayer are the primary tools in this phase. If possible, I like to do this a week ahead of time in my journal. If Sunday's sermon is ready by Thursday (my goal), then I will start noting observations for the next week.

---

[4] Jerry Vines and Jim Shaddix, *Power in the Pulpit* (Chicago: Moody, 1999), 94.

Another helpful way to think about this phase is to ask the basic questions about any text: Who? What? Where? When? Why? How? You will be surprised at how many notes you will make by answering these questions. To answer some of these questions, you will need to understand some *background* information. Background matters related to particular Bible books include the author, the date, the audience and occasion, and the genre. When you teach through books of the Bible, you will not need to spend as much time on background matters each week.

To emphasize the number of observations one could make about a text, I often tell students to read a passage and make twenty-five observations about it. They often think this is impossible! But soon they realize that many things can be said about a text. I tell them, "It's okay to be Captain Obvious in this phase. The goal is to really see and note what is being said."

Phase 2: Responsible Interpretation — What Does the Text Mean?

After making your initial observations, you still will have some questions. Your goal in the interpretive phase is to answer the questions you do not know. It may be that you have all the answers after your observation, but more often than not, you will need to go deeper in order to understand what a passage actually means (at least in part).

Interpretation later serves as the foundation of our application of the text because the purpose of application is to apply *biblical truth*. I think of the interpretive phase in four parts. I will generally use the same set of notes that I used in making my observations and add to it by considering the following four matters.

First, study the context in greater detail. Review your initial background study. Research unresolved questions. Then look further at the literary context of the passage. Ask the key questions about context. How does this text fit within the book? How are words and concepts used throughout the entire book? What did the author intend by penning this passage?

Many false interpretations of texts are caused by a failure to study the text within the entire context of the Bible book. For instance, Acts 2:38 is often used to promote baptismal regeneration. However, a careful reading of Acts in its entirety teaches no such thing. By reading the whole narrative, other passages show that what is consistent in Acts is repentance and faith for the forgiveness of sins (see Acts 2:21; 3:19; 13:38–39; 15:9; 16:31; 20:20–21).

Baptism is an outer expression of this spiritual reality. Some well-meaning Christians also cite Matthew 18:20 to refer to the assurance of God's presence when only a small group is assembled. While this is wonderfully true, the text is primarily about church discipline, not poor corporate worship attendance, as the rest of the passage clearly shows (18:15–20). Further, I have heard pastors cite Matthew 10:19–20 to excuse themselves from diligent sermon preparation, claiming, "The Holy Spirit will give us words to say." However, the context is not talking about sermon preparation. It is about the Spirit's help when you are brought before authorities when persecuted (which actually happens in the book of Acts). We could go on with examples. Study the context!

Second, dissect the passage. After you are sure of the context, break down your particular text in more detail. Begin by noting clauses. Look also for conjunctions that show contrasts (e.g., "But God," Eph 2:4). Consider the poetic structure if applicable. For narratives, note recurring ideas, characters, and contrasts. For Wisdom literature, look for themes. By analyzing these parts of the passage, you will observe the unique emphasis of the text.

To assist you in dissecting the text, consider diagramming the passage. A structural diagram is a phrase-by-phrase chart that shows the relationship of various ideas in a graphic form.[5] The overall idea is simple, but it can become quite technical. For prose (like Epistles), write independent clauses as your starting point, to the left of the page. An independent clause contains a subject and a verb and does not need other phrases to express a complete idea. Next, place supporting phrases, clauses, and words under the words that they support. You may also line up any series of words, phrases, or thoughts directly under one another. Some teachers also instruct you to place connecting words in brackets in order to set them apart from the main ideas.[6] Some great resources, such as those found in Logos Bible software, can do sentence diagramming for you, as will particular commentaries like the Zondervan Exegetical Series. These tools can help you think through this process. It is truly amazing what you can learn from only analyzing how a sentence is structured. You should be able to see main points and

---

[5] Wayne McDill, *The 12 Essential Skills for Great Preaching* (Nashville: B&H, 1994), 27.
[6] For help in tracing an argument, doing sentence diagramming, and understanding the nature of epistles, see Thomas R. Schreiner, *Interpreting the Pauline Epistles*, 2nd ed. (Grand Rapids: Baker, 2011).

supporting points immediately by looking at it. Consider the following example:[7]

Figure 1: Diagramming the Passage

1a	assertion/temporal	Now **I say, as long as an heir is a minor he is no different from a slave.**
b	concessive	even though he is master of all.
2a	contract *(to 1a–b)*	But **he is under guardians and managers**
b	temporal *(to 2a)*	until the appointed time of the father.
3	comparison *(to 1–2)*	Thus also when we were minors, **we were enslaved under the elements of the world.**
4a	event/contract *(to 3)*	But **when the fullness of time came, God sent forth his Son,**
b	description	who was born of a woman,
c	description	who was born under law,
5a	purpose *(of 4a–c)*	to redeem those under law,
b	purpose *(of 5a)*	so that we should receive adoption as sons.
6a	basis *(for 6b)*	And
		because you are sons,
b	event	**God sent forth the Spirit of his Son into our hearts crying, "Abba, Father."**
7a	inference from 6a–b	Therefore, **you are no longer a slave but a son.**
b	condition	And if you are son, **you are also an heir through God.**

For narratives, you need to begin each verse of the story at the left margin. Underline and label the major components of the

[7] Thomas R. Schreiner, *Galatians*, Zondervan Exegetical Commentary on the New Testament (Grand Rapids: Zondervan, 2010), 263–64.

story, such as the setting, scenes, conflict, characteristics, and plot. Circle key transitional statements, such as *and*, *then*, or *but*. End by dividing the text according to the movements in the plot (life situation, conflict, climax, resolution).[8]

While this process may seem difficult and scientific, there are many benefits. The structural diagram will show you the natural divisions of the passage. You should then be able to develop an outline that reflects the nature of the text. So, take a stab at it. Remember to use a literal translation for this process. If you can use the languages, that's even better. (If not, use some language tools to help you.)

After noting particular clauses and supporting phrases, identify *key words* in the text to dissect the passage further. Look for important doctrinal terms and words that need explanation. Also identify the verbs and their tenses. To assist you, consult lexicons, critical commentaries, and word-study books.[9] Indeed, the meanings of words make a great difference (e.g., Isa 7:14; Matt 16:18; Rom 8:29; 1 Thess 4:17; 1 Tim 3:11). For Romans 12:1–2 (NKJV), you may highlight the following words for further study:

Figure 2: Identifying Key Words

I beseech you   therefore, brethren
     by the mercies of God
   that you present your bodies a   sacrifice,
        living,
        holy,
        acceptable to God
     which is your reasonable service.
And do not be conformed
     to this world
but be transformed
     by the renewing of your mind,
    that you may prove what is that   will of God
       good
       and acceptable
       and perfect.

---

[8] Vines and Shaddix, *Power in the Pulpit*, 111.
[9] I highly recommend Logos Bible Software for careful Bible study.

Third, look at cross-references. Cross-references serve many wonderful purposes in exposition. Overall, it is best to allow Scripture to interpret Scripture. It will also enable you to teach doctrine within verse-by-verse exposition. If your passage mentions a particular doctrine, such as the deity of Christ (e.g., John 1:1), then it is helpful to see what other texts say about the subject (e.g., John 8:58). You can also show the ongoing flow of redemptive history by pointing out where a text's theme is found throughout the story line of Scripture (e.g., "kingdom"). Most practically, by looking at cross-references you will better interpret hard texts by looking at texts with similar words, ideas, and concepts. Remember, however, that word studies are not always fully reliable. Sometimes similar themes and patterns are taught throughout the biblical text *without* using the same terms. And sometimes two authors could use the same word but use it differently; so always consider the author's context.

To use cross-references for interpreting the meaning of a particular text, look first at the *immediate context* of the passage. Is the same word or concept used? After this step, look next at references by the *same author* in the same book. Next, consider *other books of the Bible by the same author.* After considering these verses, look at the *larger biblical text* for the same words, themes, and concepts. It is best to consider the same testament of your passage first. If you still need help, you may choose to look carefully at *extrabiblical sources,* such as background books or classical Greek texts that use a particular word. The following visual illustrates the process:[10]

---

[10] Chart modified from the one in Stephen F. Olford with David Olford, *Anointed Expository Preaching* (Nashville: B&H, 1998), 121.

Figure 3: Using Cross-References

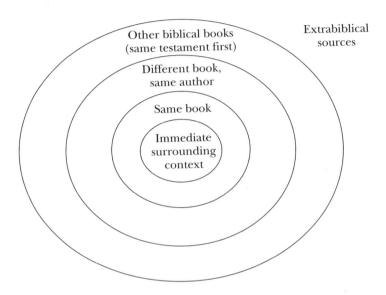

Fourth, consult commentaries and other tools for remaining unresolved issues. If you have not considered commentaries up to this point, this is the time to read them. I like to go to the commentaries last, as a way to check my interpretation. See where the weight of the evidence lies for difficult texts, and make your judgment. I recommend D. A. Carson's *New Testament Commentary Survey* and Tremper Longman's *Old Testament Commentary Survey* for choosing commentaries on particular Bible books.[11] Build your commentary sets initially by authors, not complete series if possible. By studying the context in detail, dissecting the passage, doing word studies, and tracing cross-references, you should have a good grasp on the text and the author's intended meaning.

Finally, summarize your findings. At this point, you should have a good understanding of the text *as a whole*, and you should be able to explain, in your own words, *the individual verses (or paragraphs)* that you are covering in the sermon. So you set out to do a verse-by-verse or paragraph-by-paragraph (for longer texts) summary of

---

[11] D. A. Carson, *New Testament Commentary Survey*, 6th ed. (Grand Rapids: Baker, 2007); Tremper Longman III, *Old Testament Commentary Survey*, 4th ed. (Grand Rapids: Baker, 2007).

the text based on all of your observation/interpretation notes. You simply write the verse(s) out to the side and begin making summary statements about each. Also, you will make an overarching summary about the whole text, and these summaries of the whole and the parts are what will later go into your sermon.

The next two phases are theological and practical. You need to consider how the text relates to the gospel and what the implications are.

Phase 3: Redemptive Integration—How Is the Gospel Related to This Text?

This redemptive step is often left out of books on biblical interpretation. It is theological, exegetical, and applicational. As mentioned, the study of redemptive history is often called biblical theology. The purpose of integrating biblical theology with exegesis is to look for redemptive themes and Christological connections that display the unity of the Bible. Jesus said that the Scriptures testify about him in some way (Luke 24:27). To miss the redemptive connection is to miss an important piece in interpretation. So, we must change lenses from a microscope (considering the immediate passage in detail) to a wide-angle lens (considering where your passage fits within the entire story line of Scripture).[12] The grace of God in Christ should be integrated naturally, not artificially in exegesis, and woven throughout in the application of your sermon. For a helpful book on incorporating a Christ-centered focus from the Old Testament responsibly, see Sidney Greidanus's *Preaching Christ from the Old Testament.*

If we fail to use this step, not only will we possibly miss the meaning or an important aspect of a particular text; we will make some erroneous implications/applications. For example, we cannot always make a one-to-one correlation of Old Testament laws and stories without first going through biblical theology. Otherwise, we would do things like follow our teaching on Solomon's temple with the application that we need to build an opulent temple too. But because biblical theology shows us the progressive nature of redemptive history, we know that we have something better than a temple; namely, Christ. So then, we should make a new-covenant application of such concepts. In other words, biblical theology is *a*

---

[12] Bryan Chapell, *Christ-Centered Preaching* (Grand Rapids: Baker, 2005), 275.

bridge from the Old Testament text to our applications for contemporary believers.

Many times the redemptive focus of the text is obvious. If you are preaching through a Gospel or an epistle, you should always find a redemptive focus. If you are preaching through an Old Testament book, it can be more obscure at times. We do not want to insert Jesus where he is not. But we do want to keep in mind that a passage or a book does not exist in isolation. Therefore, every text is part of the larger story.

Several questions may assist you in legitimately showing the Christ connection. Perhaps the most natural question is, *Where does this text stand in relation to Christ?* If you are preaching through Nehemiah, you know that it is before Christ. Therefore, we know that God was preserving his people in order to bring about the Messiah; that is a legitimate connection.

Another question is, *Does this text speak directly of Christ?* If so, how? In the Gospels, the writers show the person, works, and teachings of Jesus. In prophetic literature, sometimes there is an obvious statement of Jesus's person and work, such as Isaiah 53. In the other parts of the Old Testament, some passages may be used later in the New Testament in Jesus's teaching. Show your people these verses in the New Testament. Interpret the text first in its historical setting and then move to the New Testament to show the Christological features.

When expounding the Old Testament, you may also simply ask, *Does the New Testament speak about this subject?* In other words, pair your Old Testament teaching with New Testament references. It is really remarkable how often the New Testament writers, as well as Jesus, expound on Old Testament concepts and ideas. Good commentaries will point this out, as will books such as *Commentary on the New Testament Use of the Old Testament*[13] and biblical-theological dictionaries (like the *New Dictionary of Biblical Theology*).[14]

We should also remember that ethical matters in the New Testament are always related to the gospel. Ask, *How do the implications of the gospel make these commands possible?* These implications include our access to God through Christ, the presence of the

[13] G. K. Beale and D. A. Carson, eds., *Commentary on the New Testament Use of the Old Testament* (Grand Rapids: Baker, 2007).

[14] T. Desmond Alexander, Brian S. Rosner, D. A. Carson, and Graeme Goldsworthy, eds., *New Dictionary of Biblical Theology* (Downers Grove: InterVarsity, 2000).

indwelling Spirit, and the continual offer of forgiveness. When preaching to believers, remind them of these grace-oriented privileges of Christians. By considering these implications, we will remind believers of the results of being in Christ, and we can also preach the gospel week after week to unbelievers regardless of the passage.

Sometimes the text in the Old Testament is typological. Ask the question, *Does this text reveal a type of Christ?* A type is a correspondence between person, events, and things embedded within the historical framework of the Bible. If the New Testament writers refer to Old Testament characters, institutions, or offices as types of Christ, then keep this in mind when you are preaching from the Old Testament. Allegory makes unfounded leaps to Christ. True typology considers patterns, linguistic correspondences, and interbiblical themes. Typology shows escalation—that Jesus is the better Adam, the priest greater than Melchizedek, a prophet with more glory than Moses, and David's ultimate Son, our final sacrifice, and much more.

Related to this previous question, also ask, *Does the passage reveal a biblical theme that points to Christ?* Themes such as the kingdom of God, the presence of God, the sacrificial system, the covenants, and the Word of God will all point us to Christ. Look for where the theme started and how it will end.

Often in the Old Testament, promises are made about the coming of Christ. Ask, *Does the passage show a promise of God that points us to Christ?* Jesus kept the promises that God made in the Old Testament. For example, all nations will one day worship because of Christ. The Gentiles will hear of God's salvation in Christ. Jesus will be with us forever.

Other times the text predicts the person and work of Christ. Point this matter out. Ask, *How is this passage predictive of Christ?* Does it speak of his coming, his death, or his return? Obviously, this will occur more in prophetic literature, but sometimes it will come in Old Testament narratives, such as a statement on the scepter not departing from Judah (Gen 49:10) or Jesus crushing Satan's head (Gen 3:15—a most important passage for seeing the whole Bible as one redemptive drama!).

A natural way to find the redemptive focus is to ask, *How does this passage show us mankind's need for Christ?*[15] If a passage is from the

---

[15] Chappell, *Christ-Centered Preaching*, 283–84.

Law genre, then be ready to discuss how no one can keep the law fully. Talk about how the law shows our need for a Savior.

Similarly, a natural way to look for redemptive features in the Old Testament is by looking for the attributes of God in the text. Ask the question, *How does this passage reveal the nature of the God who provides redemption?*[16] Statements about God's mercy, grace, justice, and power will point us to Christ, who demonstrated these qualities. This connection is more applicatory than exegetical.

These questions are faithful ways to prepare Christ-exalting, expositional sermons. Add the redemptive summaries to your observation/interpretation notes. I usually place these biblical-theological notes under each verse that I have just summarized. These redemptive comments will consider the whole of Scripture and will include answers to a few of these questions.

When you construct an outline and add the functional elements later in your actual sermon manuscript, you may choose to point out the Christological connections in the introduction, in exegesis, and in application. I believe you should always do it in the closing of your message. Make Jesus the hero in your sermons. Graeme Goldsworthy rightly says that the way you evaluate a sermon is to ask, "How did the sermon testify to Christ?"[17] By showing people the glory of Christ in his Word, they will grow spiritually—and treasure Christ as the Author and Finisher of their faith. This will also keep your preaching from being a lecture. Preaching is preaching when it has the aroma of Christ present.

Often students ask, "How can I grow in my effectiveness in Christ-centered preaching?" My response is threefold. First, read the Bible a whole lot. You cannot substitute anything for reading and rereading the biblical text. You will begin to see correspondences and Christological connections the more you read the Bible. Second, listen to really good Christ-centered preachers, like Sinclair Ferguson, D. A. Carson, Art Azurdia, Russell Moore, Tim Keller, and others. You will learn much by sitting under their instruction. I show several sermons in my class to illustrate effective Christ-centered exposition. I also encourage students to listen to entire sermon series from men like these, especially from the

---

[16] Ibid., 284.
[17] Graeme Goldsworthy, *Preaching the Whole Bible as Christian Scripture* (Grand Rapids: Eerdmans, 2000), 62.

Old Testament, in order to catch how they do week-by-week Christ-centered preaching. Finally, as already mentioned, study biblical theology. Fortunately, a host of good resources have emerged on this subject. They will help you see connections and themes.[18]

Phase 4: Concluding Implications—How Does This Passage Apply to Us Today?

By the time you get to the implications of your study, you may put away your books and summarize the main ideas. This step is the bridge between Bible study and the following sermonic elements. Implications do not include new information. They simply ask, *So what? What does it matter that the text means this and shows Christ in this way?*

Implications move from then-and-there to here-and-now. They may be broken down into two parts. The first is *theological significance.* Some questions to ask include: What does this passage teach us about God? What does it teach us about ourselves? What does it teach us about Christ? What principles are timeless for us? What does the passage teach us about particular doctrines?

Another part of implications deals with *personal application.* Questions include: Are there examples to follow? Are there commands to keep? Are there errors to avoid? Are there sins to forsake? Are there gospel promises to claim? Are there new thoughts about God to gain? Are there truths or doctrines to further explore? Are there convictions to be lived by?[19]

After adding these implications to your notes, I recommend that you back away from your study and marinate on everything. Ponder the meaning of the text, the redemptive features of the text, and the present implications of the text. When you return to your study, you should be ready to start crafting the sermon.

SUMMATION

The first step in preparing an expository sermon is to study the text in detail. Principles for interpreting the text will keep the preacher

---

[18] I recommend *New Studies in Biblical Theology* edited by D. A. Carson, *New Dictionary of Biblical Theology* edited by D. A. Carson et al., and *Kingdom through Covenant* by Peter J. Gentry and Stephen J. Wellum.

[19] John MacArthur Jr., "Rightly Dividing the Word of Truth," in *Preach the Word,* ed. Leland Ryken and Todd A. Wilson (Wheaton, IL: Crossway, 2007), 85.

tied to the intended meaning of the author. A disciplined study method that involves observations, interpretation, redemptive integration, and timeless implications should steer our sermon development. The next steps move us from this science of exegesis to the art of preparing the sermon.

STUDY OF 1–2 TIMOTHY

1. Read 1 Timothy 2:1–7. Note some observations about this text.
2. Circle keywords and phrases that are important.
3. Note any interpretive questions that you have.
4. Identify the redemptive elements of the passage.
5. Identify some implications for your congregation.

9

STEP 2: UNIFY THE REDEMPTIVE THEME

They read from the book, from the Law of God, clearly, and they gave the sense, so that the people understood the reading.
—*Nehemiah 8:8 (ESV)*

A sermon should be a bullet, not a buckshot. Ideally, each sermon is the explanation, interpretation, or application of a single dominant idea supported by other ideas, all drawn from one passage or several passages of Scripture.[1]
—*Haddon Robinson*

IN ANDY STANLEY AND Lane Jones's *Communicating for a Change*, the authors emphasize the need to preach a "one point" sermon.[2] The book provides some helpful ideas for preparing easy-to-remember sermons. The idea of a one-point sermon is not a new idea, however. At the heart of classical expository preaching theory is the conviction that the sermon is mainly about one big idea or theme.[3]

---

[1] Haddon Robinson, *Biblical Preaching* (Grand Rapids: Baker, 2001), 35.
[2] Andy Stanley and Lane Jones, *Communicating for a Change* (Colorado Springs: Multnomah, 2006), 39.
[3] Robinson, *Biblical Preaching*, 33–46.

The theme includes the primary meaning of the text and the primary application of the text. The key questions are these: What is the text about? And what do I want the hearers to do, believe, or change in light of this text?

While there will be numerous supporting ideas in Word-driven sermons, the essence of the sermon should flow from one dominant thought that emerges from the text clearly and naturally. John Stott argues that identifying the dominant theme is essential for two reasons: every text has a theme, and one of the ways a sermon differs from a lecture is that it attempts to persuade the hearers about one primary message.[4] Therefore, after we study the text (step 1), we should then try to identify the main idea of the text and sermon in order to drill this truth into the minds of the hearers.

Two essential stages are involved in unifying the theme of an expository sermon. We first should identify *the main point of the text* (MPT). The MPT is determined through careful exegesis of the selected passage, described in Step 1: Study the Text. Next, we should develop the *main point of the sermon* (MPS)—in view of the meaning of the text, the redemptive elements in the text, in light of our particular audience and occasion.

I have included a third non-essential stage for unifying the theme as well: *the title*. While the title is not an essential element of unifying the theme, it could serve as a way to reinforce the MPT and the MPS.

I will offer some ideas about these three stages in this chapter. It should be noted that I have verse-by-verse preaching through a Bible book in mind primarily. You could also apply these principles, however, to an alternative form of expositional preaching.

IDENTIFY THE MAIN POINT OF THE TEXT

The MPT is *a past tense statement about what the text meant in its historical context*. This is the first step in moving from exegetical study to the process of developing the actual sermon. After doing the hard work of exegesis, you should be able to summarize the passage in a single sentence. This sentence is the foundation for your exhortation. Therefore, the goal is to state the intended meaning

---

[4] John Stott, *Between Two Worlds* (Grand Rapids: Eerdmans, 1982), 224–25.

of the author in the *past tense*, using historical names, dates, cultural nuances, and places.

At first glance, this process may seem a bit oversimplified. What if the text seems to have many points or themes? If this is the case, then you should make sure you have selected a single unit of thought for the sermon. Selecting a thought block is essential for determining the MPT. In addition, sometimes the main point of the text will include two ideas that complement each other. This is well and good. Highlight both of them. On other occasions, if you select a large text, then you will have to state the MPT *more broadly*. For instance, if you wanted to preach the entire narrative about Cornelius (Acts 10:1–11:19), then the MPT will be something general such as "Luke recorded how the gospel reached the Gentiles by describing the meeting between Peter and Cornelius."

Here are some examples of the MPT based on smaller passages:[5]

- Paul instructed the Christians in Ephesus to stop living like the unbelieving Gentiles and start living out their new identity in Christ (Eph 4:17–24).
- Paul charged Timothy to hand off the gospel, by God's grace, to the next generation by teaching those who will teach others also (2 Tim 2:1–7).
- James told the scattered Christians to show mercy, not favoritism, in order to fulfill the Great Commandment and reflect the mercy of God (Jas 2:1–13).
- God encouraged Joshua to be strong and courageous in leading the Israelites into Canaan by relying upon his presence and meditating upon his Word (Josh 1:1–9).

Each example contains a sentence in the past tense, interpreting what the text meant in its historical context. Each example also includes proper names, people, cultural features, and places.

Why an MPT?

Five reasons stand out for identifying the MPT. *First, to preach with authority you need to know first what God intended to say in a particular*

---

[5] For numerous examples of unifying the main idea of a text/sermon (and for constructing an outline), see the *Christ-Centered Exposition* commentary series. Each exposition opens with a main idea and an outline of the passage.

text. Remember that a sermon idea is not the same thing as biblical truth inspired by the Holy Spirit. Our first goal, then, is to discern God's mind in the text for the purpose of resaying what he said.

Second, interpreting the selected text and stating it in a sentence is often the hardest part of preparing an expository sermon.[6] Developing the rest of the sermon is much easier after you identify the MPT. The supporting ideas should flow from the main idea. Of course, there are times when the MPT is obvious, but it is harder to identify for difficult texts.

Third, until the main idea has been identified, you cannot develop the sermon. Expository preaching means that we let the text drive the sermon. We have nowhere to drive apart from the meaning of the text!

Fourth, most pastors are quite busy.[7] If you can determine the main point of the text early in the week (or even before the week begins), then it will help with the development of the sermon when you have time later. One of my pastor friends, Matt Carter, goes away on a retreat each year with other pastors at Austin Stone Community Church, and they plan out a year's worth of sermons, trying to do a rough draft of the MPT and MPS of each sermon.

Finally, pastors are often very tired and weary. Hopefully, determining the MPT will be a dynamic spiritual experience. The discipline of identifying the MPT will cause the text to get inside of you. Then this theme will be on your mind all week, as you meditate upon its truth. As you reflect on the text and the MPT, you can then discuss it with other pastors, friends, family members, and so on.

How Do You Identify the MPT?

To identify the MPT, begin by looking for *explicit statements* in the text itself. Sometimes the big idea is obvious. For instance, James 2:1–13 contains the main point of the text in the very first sentence, "My brothers, hold your faith in our glorious Lord Jesus Christ without showing favoritism" (v. 1). James develops this idea by giving an example of favoritism (vv. 2–4). Then he discusses the folly of favoritism (vv. 5–7). Finally, he gives a seriousness warning about favoritism (vv. 8–13). Therefore, the main point is clear in this unit of the thought.

---

[6] Jerry Vines and Jim Shaddix, *Power in the Pulpit* (Chicago: Moody, 1999), 129.
[7] Ibid.

Another way to identify the MPT is by considering the *surrounding context.*[8] For example, in 2 Timothy 1:3–2:13, Paul urges Timothy to continue handing off the truth that has been passed down to him from his family and from Paul himself (1:3–14). In 2:2, Paul tells Timothy to hand it off to others who will do the same. Therefore, when preaching from one of these paragraphs within 2 Timothy 1:3–2:13, the MPT should include something referring to spiritual multiplication.

You may look also for *recurring ideas* in the text.[9] In 1 Timothy 5:3–6:2, Paul mentions the idea of "honor" three times (5:3, 17; 6:1), referring to three groups of people (widows, elders, slaves). His goal is to instruct the church on how they should treat one another. In Joshua 1:1–9, the recurring ideas are being *strong* and *courageous* (1:6–7, 9). The MPT obviously should include these recurring ideas.

Over time, identifying the MPT will be second nature to the seasoned expositor. You will begin detecting recurring ideas, explicit statements, and contextual matters naturally as you mine the text carefully each week. The MPT will then help you as you build the outline of the sermon. It will also help your hearers follow you as you move through the text.

DEVELOP THE MAIN POINT OF THE SERMON

The main point of the sermon is referred to often as the *proposition* or the *essence of the sermon in a sentence.*[10] I prefer the phrase *main point of the sermon* because I like the simplified language. I actually use this phrase when preaching.

The MPS is *a present or future tense application of the MPT stated in a single sentence.* The difference between the MPS and the MPT is that the MPS is crafted in the present tense (instead of the past), and it does not include proper names, dates, cultural idioms, and places. It is derived, however, directly from the MPT. You cannot develop the MPS apart from the text. Isolate the dominant theme from the text and then state the dominant implication of it.

Consider the following examples of a MPS:

---

[8] Ibid., 131.

[9] Ibid.

[10] Harold T. Bryson and James C. Taylor, *Building Sermons to Meet People's Needs* (Nashville: Broadman, 1980), 63.

- We should not live like unbelievers because we are new people in Christ (Eph 4:17–24).
- We must faithfully hand off the gospel, by God's grace, to the next generation (2 Tim 2:2).
- We must not show favoritism because God has shown us amazing mercy and told us to do the same (Jas 2:1–13).
- We can have strength and courage to serve God because of his presence and his abiding Word (Josh 1:1–9).

Observe how each statement reflects the MPT. Note also how the sentences are in the present tense. They also do not involve historical elements but instead are written in an applicatory manner with personal pronouns (*you* and *we*).

The MPS is the one big idea that people should take away. Unfortunately, many expository sermons are left in the past tense. They include alliterated points about the details of the text. While the details are important, we must seek to apply them to our hearers. Our goal in exposition is not merely to transfer information but to apply biblical truth to real people. By having a good MPS, the sermon will contain application throughout the sermon, not only periodically.

Certainly, there is flexibility in how one chooses to articulate the MPS. We should work very hard at crafting a good statement. All of us have room to grow in our articulation but also be challenged to spend considerable time drafting a well-written proposition. Stanley says that we need a "sticky statement," that is, one that our hearers can remember.[11]

You should state the sticky statement in different places in the sermon. In fact, one common feature among effective communicators is that they repeat their main point/idea often. Pastor Art Azurdia does a masterful job of developing a clear summary statement within his sermons. For Acts 4:32–37, he repeated this phrase as he unpacked the text: "The simplicity of unity turns on generosity." In a sermon on Acts 5:1–11, he stated this one repeatedly: "A dangerous holiness is God's response to a determined hypocrisy."[12]

As you are working through your outline (which supports the MPS), you will have an occasion to restate the MPS in transitions

---

[11] Stanley and Jones, *Communicating for a Change*, 111.
[12] One can listen to these sermons and many others from Azurdia online: http://trinity portland.com/resources/trinity-portland-sermons.

from one part of the outline to the next. And you may also find other places to include it in the body of the sermon. In *Why Johnny Can't Preach*, T. David Gordon expresses his modest desire for preachers to include a discernable main point. This is what he says:

> I've really desired something fairly simple for my family: to be able to talk intelligently about the sermon on Sunday afternoon or throughout the week. And to do this, all I really desire is the ability to answer three questions: What was the point or thrust of the sermon [MPS]? Was this point adequately established in the text that was read [MPT]? Were the applications legitimate applications of the point, from which we can have further fruitful conversations about other possible applications? Frequently, indeed more commonly than not, I have heard sermons about which my family cannot even answer the first question.[13]

Sadly, his experience is not uncommon. Many others are frustrated with poor, unclear preaching. Let us aspire to clearly articulate our main point for the sermon, established from the main point of the text, so that people can think and apply God's Word all week long.

Developing a Redemptive MPS

Another important matter concerning the MPS is that we should seek to make it redemptive, in order for the sermon to focus upon Christ. Bryan Chapell wonderfully describes this aspect of sermon development in *Christ-Centered Preaching*. He calls the concept of identifying a redemptive theme the "fallen condition focus" (FCF). Chapell defines the FCF as "the mutual human condition that contemporary believers share with those to or about whom the text was written that requires the grace of the passage for God's people to glorify and enjoy him."[14] By considering "the mutual human condition" of the original audience and your audience, you will be able to state a redemptive solution that adequately reflects the text and ensures the Christ-centeredness of your sermon.

By saying that we should make the main point redemptive, I do not mean that we should look for something that is not there in the text, but rather, we should look for the reason *why the text is there.*

---

[13] T. David Gordon, *Why Johnny Can't Preach* (Phillipsburg, NJ: P&R, 2009), 19.
[14] Bryan Chapell, *Christ-Centered Preaching* (Grand Rapids: Baker, 2005), 50.

Ask yourself: Why was this text written? Why do my people need to know the thrust of this text? How does the text apply? There is flexibility with the MPS, unlike the MPT, because the text has many applications. Seek to make a grace-filled application of the historical meaning of the text.

The grounds for looking for the "why" or the "how" of the text is based on the idea that Scripture is given to us not merely to inform us but to complete us. Second Timothy 3:16–17 is a foundational passage on the redemptive nature of Scripture. Paul says, "All Scripture is inspired by God and is profitable for teaching, for rebuking, for correcting, for training in righteousness, so that the man of God may be *complete*, equipped for every good work."[15] Notice how Paul states that all of Scripture completes us. In other words, we are incomplete without the truths of the Bible. Consequently, Chapell says that when you preach think of your people as "Swiss cheese."[16] They all have "spiritual holes" that can only be filled by the truths of your particular text. God's redemptive nature is observed in his refusal to leave fallen people where they are apart from divine revelation. Therefore, when you state your MPS, think about doing it in such a way as to highlight the reason that your hearers need to know what you are about to tell them. Think about the hearers' present condition, then think on the truths of the text, and finally state a concise proposition that highlights the relevance of the text.

Developing your main point with a redemptive thrust will keep your sermons from being filled with mere moral principles that say nothing about the transforming work of God in Christ. How many sermons have you heard that tell people to "be like this" or "just do this" or "don't do these things"? While moral instruction is important in preaching, we need to remember that we should show people *how* they are to obey God's standards. Moralistic sermons are often sub-Christian. So, think about stating the MPS in a way that draws your hearers' attention to their identity in Christ, the power of the Holy Spirit, the enabling grace of God, the implications of

---

[15] While Paul is referring primarily to Timothy's work as a minister here, rather than the sanctification of believers, the issue of the need for Scripture remains. Bryan Chapell correctly says, "This interpretation does not undermine the conclusion that God intends 'all Scripture' to 'complete' believers, since a minister's duties of 'teaching, rebuking, correcting, and training in righteousness,' from 'all Scripture' will convey God's perspective on the hearers' inherent need for the scope of biblical truth." Ibid., 49–50.

[16] Ibid., 52.

the gospel, or the particular attributes of God that encourage and empower Christian obedience.

Practically, you may ask three questions (in any order) before you articulate an MPS with a redemptive focus: (1) Why is this text important and needed for fallen people? (2) What concerns do my listeners share in common with the original audience?[17] (3) How is the redemptive nature of God displayed in the text?

The first question is about the human problem. What solution does the text give for fallen people? Sometimes the problem may not be a specific sin. Chapell says, "Grief, illness, longing for the Lord's return, the need to know how to share the gospel, and the desire to be a better parent are not sins, but they are needs that our fallen condition imposes that Scripture addresses."[18] Look to see what the problem is, and how the text provides solution.

The second question keeps your audience in view. For example, you might ask, "What does Corinth have to do with New Orleans? Why do my people need to understand James's words about the sin of partiality?" By asking this question, you will maintain both biblical authority and contemporary relevance.

An additional matter to consider regarding this second question is that the MPS may be tweaked depending upon your hearers. For example, you could insert phrases such as "Students," "Christian leaders," or "As the people of God" in order to focus in on your crowd. Thus, if you were preaching to a young audience on Ephesians 4:17–24, you might state the proposition saying, "Students, because you are new creations in Christ, you should live differently than your unbelieving friends." If you were preaching to a group of leaders from 2 Timothy 2:1–7, you could say, "As Christian leaders, we must invest in future leaders, by God's grace, in order to pass on the gospel to the next generations" (2 Tim 2:2). By considering the audience, you will establish a more precise application of the MPT.

The third question reminds us to look for the God-centered and Christological emphasis in the text. Because the truths about God are timeless, this is the surest way to apply the truths of the text, and it is the surest way to maintain the redemptive focus of the sermon. Perhaps the text highlights the implications of the gospel,

---

[17] Ibid.
[18] Ibid., 51.

the work of the Spirit, or the love of the Father. If so, then make sure these redemptive truths are woven into your MPS. In this way, your people will leave not only with a big idea, but they leave with a Christ-centered idea.

Consider the redemptive elements in the previous examples. The first example (Eph 4:17–24) has a redemptive application because it highlights new life in Christ that believers possess, which makes obedience possible. By highlighting the regenerating work of God, you can offer some solution for how your people should not act like the pagan culture. The second example (2 Tim 2:1–7) is redemptive because it highlights Paul's words to Timothy about relying upon *God's grace* in order to hand off the gospel (another redemptive element). The third example (James 2:1–13) highlights the mercy of God, found in verse 13, in order to talk about loving others apart from partiality. The final example (Joshua 1:1–9) points to our source of courage and strength: God's presence and his Word.

The Benefits of an MPS

An MPS is helpful for several reasons. As mentioned, it *ties us to the biblical text.* By noting the mutual condition between the original audience and the contemporary audience, you will ensure biblical authority. In each of our examples in this chapter, we simply are calling the people to obey God's Word, not our own.

A good MPS also provides *unity* to the sermon. All of our points in the sermon should flow from the text and should be built around the MPS. The MPS helps us determine what to include and what to cut out of the sermon in order to make it a coherent whole.

Additionally, the MPS provides *purpose* to the sermon. As expositors, we are not merely giving a historical lecture about a passage of Scripture. We intend to have people *respond* to the text in some way. So, we should submit to them a purpose or goal in hearing the sermon. For example, if preaching from James 2:1–13, my purpose would be for the church to repent of their prejudices and start loving all types of people.

Finally, an MPS with a redemptive thrust provides *hope.* It points the hearers to the nature and work of our glorious Savior. This type of MPS is best stated early and often in the sermon, so that the hearers' minds are taken upward to God's redeeming grace found ultimately in Christ. A gospel-centered focus will keep preaching from becoming moralistic and will make fallen people eager to listen for the redemptive solution in the text.

ADD A TITLE THAT REFLECTS THE MPS

After thinking through the MPT and the MPS in view of your audience, you may consider adding a title. The title is the final element for unifying the redemptive theme. It serves as a way to pull everything together. The title is one of the most disputed aspects of preaching theory. Some are fans of outrageous titles, or titles that always have a "how to." Others do not even bother with the title.

Indeed, the title is quite subjective, but I think it can serve a really important purpose of reflecting the main subject and theme of the text and sermon. If we want people to leave with "one point," then we should reflect that point in the title. In addition, the title draws attention to the sermon. Certainly, there is room for creativity in the title. We should work to make the title not only a means of reinforcing the MPS but also as a way to make the MPS memorable.

Consider the following titles. Each reinforces the MPS:

- *Living Like a New Creation* (Eph 4:17–24)
- *Making Disciples Who Make Disciples* (2 Tim 2:1–2)
- *Yes to Mercy, No to Partiality* (Jas 2:1–13)
- *Where to Find Strength and Courage* (Josh 1:1–9)

The other purpose of a title has to do with the larger process of preparing for corporate worship. If the title reflects the redemptive theme of the sermon, then it will help with the selection of music, readings, and other corporate elements in worship. In this way, the title will help with advanced worship planning.

To test yourself on understanding the redemptive theme of your sermon, consider what Chapell refers to as the "3 AM test."[19] Imagine that someone wakes you up at 3:00 a.m. and asks, "What's the sermon about, preacher?" What would you tell them? Could you offer a simple, present- or future-tense application of the main point of the text? If so, then you have understood the idea of developing a one-point sermon. Perhaps, if our *title* reflects our MPS, then we can at least tell them that!

---

[19] Ibid., 47.

Summation

Effective expository sermons should reflect the primary theme of the selected text. The theme is based on the main point of the text and the main point of the sermon. In order to maintain the Christ-centered nature of the sermon, the expositor should look for the redemptive elements in the text and highlight these elements in the MPS. An effective MPS ensures biblical authority, unity, application, purpose, and hope. The title of the sermon is a good way to feature the MPS, reinforcing the one dominant point that the hearers should know and live out.

Study of 1–2 Timothy

Read 2 Timothy 2:14–26. Try to complete the following elements:
    MPT:
    MPS:
    Title:

10

STEP 3: CONSTRUCT AN OUTLINE

And what you have heard from me in the presence of many witnesses, commit to faithful men who will be able to teach others also.
—*2 Timothy 2:2*

If preachers were interested in only describing a text, then messages on identical passages might sound similar, since all would follow nearly identical exegetical outlines. Preachers, however, have greater obligations than simply reporting a text's features. To expound a passage, a preacher must explain context, establish meaning, and demonstrate implications in a way that a specific group of listeners will find interesting, understandable, and applicable. To accomplish these goals, an expositor designs a homiletical outline to create a sermon faithful to the truths of the text and relevant to the needs of the congregation.[1]

—*Bryan Chapell*

THE GOAL IN STEP 3 of the preparation process is to develop an outline that both reflects the structure of the text and supports the main point of the sermon. Some argue for the need to do away with

---

[1] Bryan Chapell, *Christ-Centered Preaching* (Grand Rapids: Baker, 2005), 129.

supporting points and subpoints, claiming that it dilutes the main point of the sermon, and that it is not the most effective approach for "life change."[2] While I am in favor of developing a clear MPS, and repeating it throughout the message, I do not think that we need to reduce our sermon to the MPS *alone*. Rather, I think the goal of the supporting points is to serve the MPS by highlighting particular truths about the text and making relevant applications. Besides this, those who argue for no-structure sermons end up having some type of structure anyway. Generally, these critics react to poorly structured messages from poor communicators. So, we should not throw the baby out with the bathwater. We should simply improve on our approach to outlining, so that it aids in teaching and communicating.

Further, the problem with reducing our sermon completely to a "one-point takeaway" is the assumption that our goal in preaching is for people to remember our sermon and go do something immediately. While we certainly want people to act on God's Word, application involves more than "action steps." Sometimes application includes *believing* something different or *knowing* something important. I believe that people experience a greater, more genuine, and more lasting sense of "life change" by developing a more mature gospel-centered worldview than by having one behavior to go home and implement. The fact is you cannot develop someone's worldview by offering one action step per week. It takes a thorough presentation of gospel truth over the long haul through careful, patient Christ-centered exposition.

Additionally, I do not think that our primary goal is for everyone to remember "everything" about the sermon. Instead, I view preaching as the act of feeding people week by week and helping them encounter God through the Word. In order to feed them the living and active Word of God, some meat will need to be in the sermon. Therefore, I am a fan of *dense* sermons. I generally preach for about forty-five minutes. However, I think our material should always serve the MPS, and if anything is remembered on Wednesday of next week, then hopefully it is the dominant truth.

---

[2] Andy Stanley and Lane Jones, *Communicating for a Change* (Colorado Springs: Multnomah, 2006), 102–3.

Therefore, supporting points are not unimportant; they provide many helpful benefits. I will mention three additional benefits regarding discipleship and two benefits regarding communication.

THE BENEFITS OF A SERMON OUTLINE

Discipleship Benefit 1: Biblical Teaching

While you can state the points of the sermon in different ways, a sermon outline that reflects your exegesis of the text is at the heart of expositional preaching. The sermon outline will help you take your people on a journey through the text, stopping off at important phrases, words, and concepts for explanation and application. Sometimes the outline will help you point out not only critical matters in the text but also matters that are overlooked or ignored. In other words, a well-drafted outline will help you teach the Bible.

The sermon outline will also teach your people how to study the Bible on their own, as they see how your points relate to the text at hand. I even encourage my people to outline books of the Bible as they read them on their own, looking for the intent of the author and the major ideas in the text. We need congregations filled with "expositional students."

Discipleship Benefit 2: Doctrinal Instruction

Another benefit of an outline is that it is helpful for teaching doctrine, as it emerges from the selected text. Sometimes doctrinal truths are treated easily as subpoints within the larger structure of the sermon. In a day in which doctrinal instruction is absent in many places, helpful sermon points will promote doctrinal literacy. The pulpit is the primary place for doctrinal instruction because the pastor is generally the most qualified teacher.

One of the reasons that I frown on the "felt-need" approach to preaching is that it will seldom, if ever, take up particular doctrinal matters. How many people wake up and desire for you to teach them about the Trinity? But nothing is more relevant than understanding doctrine because it shapes our worldview. Certainly doctrine can be quite complex at times, and we can lose our hearers. Carefully crafted points will help us stay on track and speak plainly.

In addition, because much of doctrinal teaching involves transferring information (before it becomes God-honoring adoration), an outline will help you transfer doctrinal truth. Many doctrines require precision in our explanation. In AD 325, Athanasius argued against Arius over one letter, related to the Trinity and Christology. One view was Christian (represented by the Latin term *homoousia*, meaning "of the same essence"), and the other was heretical (*homoiousia*, "of similar essence"). Obviously, clarity and exactness is critical for doctrinal instruction. An outline will help you with precision.

Discipleship Benefit 3: Multiplication

Many pastors/teachers provide an outline to the congregation for each message. I use the screen on Sunday morning gatherings and usually both screen and paper for classroom settings. A clear outline accomplishes several purposes. It can clarify the MPS. It can show people the connections in the text and within the sermon. It can provide the congregation with more details for further study. And an effective outline is also useful for reteaching the material.

We must remember the importance of multiplication. After going through the book of Acts, giving outlines every week, members should be able to "teach others also" (2 Tim 2:2). If a group of your people heard your teaching through a book of the Bible, could they teach that book of the Bible on a mission trip to Sudan? Could parents reteach your material to their children? Our goal as expositors is to make disciples who can make disciples—by *teaching* others to obey *all* that he commanded. An outline can assist in multiplication.

Communication Benefit 1: Guidance

A communication benefit of sermon structure is that it gives guidance and pace to both the listener and the preacher. If I have four points that support the MPS, then I know that I have a certain amount of time for each point. This helps me with the pace of my message. One of the most challenging aspects to preaching to youth, particularly, is keeping an effective pace. A carefully crafted outline helps me guide them through the sermon without putting them to sleep or overwhelming them with too much material.

The outline will also help the audience know where I am going and when the plane is landing. This is one of the reasons I ordinarily state the outline in the introduction before getting into it. I want them to know what to expect and how to follow along. This old advice still works: "Tell them what you're going to tell them; then tell them; and then tell them what you told them."

Communication Benefit 2: Unity

Finally, sermon structure helps us preach "one sermon," not "four sermons." Here is the criticism of those who are against sermon outlines: you are preaching more than one sermon. You can present multiple points and only preach one sermon. Simply avoid including matters that do not serve the MPS. Our goal should be to preach a sermon that is a coherent whole. This does not mean that the sermon cannot include a lot of teaching and application. It simply means that we need to cut out unnecessary material in order to maintain unity. Stott rightly says, "We have to be ruthless in discarding the irrelevant."[3] By thinking through the structure of the sermon, irrelevant matters become obvious.

PRINCIPLES FOR DEVELOPING SERMON OUTLINES

Before we discuss some ways to craft an outline, bear in mind a few general principles. Consider three problems to avoid and two ideas to consider.

Problems to Avoid

First, we should avoid distracting outlines that take away from the main thrust of the sermon. If our points serve the sermon's dominant point, then we should state them plainly so that they keep people's minds off of the form of the sermon and more on its essence. This means that we should avoid overly clever outlines (e.g., triple alliteration).

Second, we should avoid imposing an outline on a text. Sometimes preachers build outlines that do not reflect the meaning of the text, nor give any support to the MPS. Outlines that have stretched alliteration or three points when two will do come across as artificial and end up muddying the water.[4]

Third, we should avoid predictability. Of course, this problem is not present only in outlining. But, perhaps nowhere is predictability more present than in the way the pastor outlines the message, using

---

[3] John Stott, *Between Two Worlds* (Grand Rapids: Eerdmans, 1982), 228.
[4] Ibid., 229.

the same number of points, stated in the same manner. You can craft your points in a way that is faithful to the text, while varying your rhetorical elements.

Ideas to Consider

Consider developing your outline in an oral style. Although pure exegetical outlines are fine and good at times, I favor outlines written for the hearer, not the reader. Even if you provide a written outline to your congregation, usually the outline itself is best written in a conversational style. Therefore, I like to offer sentences, as opposed to headings or divisions.

For example, when preaching on Paul's prayer in Ephesians 3:14–21, you could outline the text exegetically: (1) Paul's posture (v. 14), (2) Paul's petitions (vv. 15–19), and (3) Paul's perspective (vv. 20–21). Or you could say it more conversationally:

Since we pray to the God who is sovereign and gracious,

1. Pray with humility (14).
2. Pray for the fullness of his love and power (15–19).
3. Pray with great expectations (20–21).

"Praying to a Sovereign God" is an appropriate title for this text. The MPS might be "We need to remember that we pray to a sovereign God."

Another idea is reflected in this example. *Consider developing your points not only in an oral style but also in a personal application style.* My friend David Platt does an extraordinary job of developing outlines like this. When his hearers write something down, or fill in a blank, they do not simply write down exegetical headings. They write understandable application based on the text. Consequently, he is able to teach and exhort throughout the message in a way that is clear and reproducible.

To draft application-style points, it is helpful to develop an exegetical outline first, based upon your Bible study and your structural diagrams. From these major divisions, think through the application of these details and write the application of the text as the supporting points. However, *try to keep the mood of the text*, with some of its specific language and in keeping with its genre, so that the hearers can see where your points come from and also feel the nature of the text. In short, develop your points in a way that reflects the text and is suitable for your given audience.

How to Construct an Expository Outline

While preachers may treat the same passage of Scripture, the approach to presenting the material normally differs. Therefore, the issue of sermon structure is a bit subjective and flexible. The main obligations of the outline are to reflect the meaning of the text, to support the MPS, and to communicate effectively to a given audience. To provide some examples of possible ways to construct an outline, I will offer nine approaches. After you choose an approach, you should choose your words and the number of points/divisions carefully.

Nine Approaches

A first option to consider is the key-word approach. After the introduction, in the body of the sermon, you may look for a key word that provides structure for the sermon. These key words are parallel ideas within the text, which support the MPS. These ideas generally are plural nouns that characterize the main divisions. Examples of key words include *reasons, truths, characteristics, objectives, marks, ways, steps,* or *phases.* To think about the best word, ask *why, how,* or *what.* For example, when preaching from James 2:1–13, you might say that four *reasons* exist to avoid partiality. In James 2:14–26, you could say that the three *types* of faith are dead faith, demonic faith, and dynamic faith.

Second, the exegetical approach is practiced by many contemporary expositors. This approach will include an MPS and a strong introduction and conclusion but does not employ the key-word approach or outlines with application-based language. The outline is more like an exegetical commentary than an oral style sermon. In a sermon on the nature of the tongue from James 3:1–12, the outline could be: (1) The Directive Nature of the Tongue, (2) The Destructive Nature of the Tongue, and (3) The Deceptive Nature of the Tongue.[5] In this approach, the outline will look almost identical to the structural diagram and the initial exegetical outline.

Third, the preacher/teacher may use a pure exposition approach. This is more of a verse-by-verse explanation and application of the text, which includes little if any structure at all (no real introduction, points/subpoints, or conclusion). Sometimes this is referred to as a

---

[5] Jerry Vines and Jim Shaddix, *Power in the Pulpit* (Chicago: Moody, 1999), 158.

homily, or a running commentary. John Calvin and other Reformers were known for this type of approach. Just read, explain, and apply; read, explain, and apply—until you get finished with the passage. You may find this useful in small-group Bible studies, prayer meetings, or for wedding and funeral messages, when an occasion calls for less formal sermonic structure.

Fourth, one could employ the hybrid homily approach. Here, the preacher/teacher may have some rhetorical elements but instead chooses to move methodically through a passage, giving some running thoughts and applications. The hybrid could consist of a strong introduction (with a dominant point) and conclusion, but the body of the sermon may be more of a running commentary. This approach is good for longer narratives, such as sermons from Acts.

Fifth, the Puritan approach is another application-based way to build an expository sermon. Disciples of William Perkins were taught to identify the main doctrine in the text and then provide several applications of it.[6] It is similar to the one-point sermon idea used by some contemporary preachers, except that the Puritan approach has a greater number of applications and the one point is always doctrinal. In this model, the sermon might be built around a small passage of Scripture, highlighting one dominant theological point but then will include numerous applications for the hearers. These applications are not only action steps, however. Many of the applications are arguments. (The Puritans were wonderful at anticipating the objections of the hearers and responding to them through logical arguments.) Such sermons require a great amount of meditation on the text and require a thorough knowledge of both theology and the particular audience.

Sixth, the question-answer approach is also a good way to teach some passages. In my opening sermon from a recent sermon series on Micah 1:1, my outline contained three questions: (1) Who was Micah? (2) When did Micah minister? (3) What did Micah say?

John Piper has asked questions within his sermons throughout his ministry. One need only survey a few of his sermons to find numerous examples of this approach. In his excellent book *Brothers, We Are Not Professionals,* Piper also stresses the importance of this discipline:

---

[6] William Perkins, *The Art of Prophesying,* repr. (Carlisle, PA: Banner of Truth Trust, 1996), 79.

> We must relentlessly query the text. . . . Therefore, reverence for God's Word demands that we ask questions and pose problems and that we believe there are answers and solutions which will reward our labor with treasures new and old (Matt 13:52). We must train our people that it is not irreverent to see difficulties in the biblical text and to think hard about how they can be resolved. Preaching should model this for them week after week.[7]

Let us show them how to ask questions and find answers.

Seventh, the problem-solution approach is a good way to preach redemptive sermons. While this approach can be incorporated in some of the previous approaches, the main idea is to introduce a problem in the beginning of the sermon and show how the text answers that problem. Another way to do the problem-solution approach is to show the actual problem in the text and then spend the rest of the time unraveling the problem. This approach is helpful in making the hearers read and think critically. You may ask the question in James 2:14–16, "Did Paul contradict James?" The sermon could start off by explaining Paul's teaching on justification by faith and then proceed to explain the relationship to James's teaching.

Eighth, the inductive approach is a good idea for narrative texts. Inductive sermons generally hold the main point for the end of the sermon, whereas the deductive approach begins with the main point and then supports it throughout the sermon. Most expository sermons fall under the deductive method, even though one could faithfully explain and apply the text with an inductive approach. The parables are great texts for implementing the inductive approach. Often, Jesus's main point in the parable comes at the end. Why not let your main point come at the end as well? To get to the point, the preacher could explain the details of the story and offer additional applications and illustrations as the story unfolds. But the main point would come at the end. You could then offer some more application after the point is given.

Finally, the sermonic plot approach also works well for narrative passages. Eugene Lowry popularized this approach in 1980. Lowry says that sermons from narrative passages can follow a five-part

---

[7] John Piper, *Brothers, We Are Not Professionals* (Nashville: B&H, 2013), 95.

sequence effectively: (1) *Oops!*—introduce the problem; (2) *Ugh!*—analyze the problem; (3) *Aha!*—introduce the solution; (4) *Whee!*—bring the gospel to bear on the problem; and (5) *Yeah!*—apply the resolution to contemporary life.[8]

With this approach you develop the MPS through a plot. You treat the passage like a typical narrative, identifying the characters, plot, setting, conflict, climax, and resolution. For example, in a sermon on Mark 4:35–41, the "Oops!" is that Jesus is asleep and the disciples are in a storm. For the "Ugh!" you would analyze the problem, asking probing questions: "Why is Jesus asleep? Does he not care about the disciples? Have you ever felt as if Jesus did not care about your problems?" Next, the "Aha!" is found in Jesus's silencing of the wind. The "Whee!" is found in Jesus's question, "Why do you have so little faith?" (4:40). The "Yeah!" would include applying the disciples' realization of Jesus's deity, "What sort of man is this?" (4:41). This approach is an interesting way to move through a narrative without imposing an outline that does not keep with the narrative nature of the text.

Choose Your Words

After selecting a method that best fits the occasion, work hard at articulating your points in the best possible form. One key to remember is to make the points *mutually exclusive*. If you have three points, then use three, but if there are less or more, then adjust. Next, make your points *understandable and plain*. I favor the application-based form in order to communicate clearly. Complete sentences or independent phrases are important for clarity.

In addition, consider making your points *progressive*. If the points build on each other, with the final idea serving as a climactic point, then you can end strongly (similarly to the inductive method). If possible, I usually prefer to end with a clear, redemptive point about Christ. Tim Keller is a master at making his points progressive, with the last point emphasizing the power of the gospel.

Another helpful style tip is to consider using *reiteration*. Some possible ways to reiterate include: *alliteration* (same letters or first syllable); *assonance* (similar endings, e.g., "mysticism, legalism, ritualism"); *repetition* (repeating parts of each point), and *parallelism* (providing unity and balance with the points). I am not a huge

---

[8] Eugene Lowry, *The Homiletical Plot* (Louisville: John Knox, 1980), 25.

fan of alliteration because it often takes a lot of time, it may lead to arrogance, and it can override the MPS. So I use it sparingly. A friend of mine says that "alliteration is like spice, a little bit is okay but too much makes you sick." Assonance can also make the hearers sick if it is overused or stretched. Use it only if it is appropriate. Parallelism keeps us from having an unbalanced outline like: (1) Paul wrote to the Philippians to humbly consider others more than themselves; (2) Jesus was humble; (3) the Greek word for "emptying" in Philippians 2:7 is the word *kenoō*. These points are true, but they lack any kind of unity.

Of all the ways to reiterate your points, repetition is my personal favorite. I find that repetition is generally a more natural way to construct an outline, and it provides an effective way to repeat the MPS. For example, for a sermon on James 1:18–27, concerning obedience to the Word, you could repeat "Word": value the Word, hear the Word, and do the Word. In addition to teaching purposes, repetition, like these other practices, will help you internalize the sermon and remember it.

A final word about words is to think through your transitional phrases. I generally do not talk through my sermon, but I do practice my introduction and some of my transitional statements. General guidelines for the transitions include making them inconspicuous, simple (i.e., *again, next, additionally*), varied, smooth, and brief.[9]

Summation

After developing the main point of the sermon, the expositor should develop an outline that reflects the meaning of the text, supports the MPS, and is suitable for the given audience. An effective outline helps the preacher teach the Bible and sound doctrine clearly. It also serves the purpose of helping others reteach material. Because substantive teaching shapes people's worldview and feeds their souls, the supporting material in the sermon is quite important. Sermon structure also assists the preacher in maintaining a fluid pace and avoiding irrelevant matters. The possible ways to develop supporting material vary. Nine possible approaches are worth considering for selected sermons. After choosing an approach, the preacher should consider developing the points to the sermon in

---

[9] Vines and Shaddix, *Power in the Pulpit*, 170.

an oral form, with personal application-style points. To articulate the points effectively, the preacher should consider the use of repetition in order to reinforce the big idea of the sermon.

STUDY OF 1–2 TIMOTHY

Read 1 Timothy 4:11–16. Try to complete the following elements:
MPT:
MPS:
Title:
Outline:

11

STEP 4: DEVELOP THE FUNCTIONAL ELEMENTS

*Let the elders who rule well be considered worthy of double honor,
especially those who labor in preaching and teaching.*

—1 Timothy 5:17 (ESV)

The expositor must be intentional about what he lets into his sermon. Every word, sentence, and paragraph must have a purpose for being there. Time constraints, short attention spans, demands for relevance, and other factors call on the modern preacher to be saying something every time he opens his mouth. The use of certain functional elements in the construction of the sermon will ensure intentional content.[1]

—Jerry Vines and Jim Shaddix

PREPARING A SERMON IS hard work. So far, we have discussed the need to study the text, unify the redemptive theme, and construct an outline that supports the MPS. The work, however, is only half finished at this point. The rest of the time involves putting meat to

---

[1] Jerry Vines and Jim Shaddix, *Power in the Pulpit* (Chicago: Moody, 1999), 174.

the outline (functional elements) and adding an introduction and
a conclusion.

From the initial point of the text selection to the completion
of the notes/manuscript, John Stott said that beginning preachers
need at least twelve hours to prepare one sermon.[2] But even this
does not take into consideration the amount of time for meditating late at night, thinking in the car, talking to other preachers,
or doing outside reading. Biblical preaching is therefore an all-
consuming task. Couple this with the other demands of the pastor's ministry, and it makes for a laborious process. No wonder Paul
told Timothy to give double honor to pastors who work like an ox
at "preaching and teaching" (1 Tim 5:17–18).

In this chapter, we will continue plowing through the next
phase of developing the sermon by describing the functional elements. The functional elements include *explanation, illustration,*
and *application.* While you may use these elements at various places
within the sermon (i.e., in the introduction or conclusion), the
functional elements are used normally within the main points of
the outline. Consider the following example of how to use the functional elements:

Because we pray to the God who is sovereign and gracious,

1. Pray with humility (Eph 3:14)
    Explanation:
    Application:
    Illustration:
2. Pray for the fullness of God's love and power (3:15–19)
    Explanation:
    Application:
    Illustration:
3. Pray with great expectations (3:20–21)
    Explanation:
    Application:
    Illustration:

Some teachers include a fourth element: *argumentation.* I defi-
nitely believe that we need persuasive argumentation in our sermons, but I prefer to talk about this mainly in the application
section. You might include argumentation in the explanation and

---

[2] John Stott, *Between Two Worlds* (Grand Rapids: Eerdmans, 1982), 259.

illustration sections as well. In fact, the whole sermon, if it proposes something, is an argument.

The two functional elements that are necessary for expository sermons are *explanation* and *application*. Every point does not necessarily need an illustration. The goal of exposition is to bridge the ancient world with the modern world by explaining and applying biblical truth. Generally, most preachers will use one of the three elements exceptionally well but struggle at the other elements. Striking a good balance is difficult. Allow me to point out some key aspects of these three functional elements.

EXPLANATION

Explanation is the process of making a particular issue clear and understandable. It is the appropriate element to begin with because the other functional elements are servants of explanation. You never just apply; you apply something. You never just illustrate; you illustrate something![3] We can only develop application and illustration after we determine the particular truth that we want people to understand.

After completing the Bible study and the outline, you should understand your passage well. In light of this, the difficult part of explanation is trying to discern the *most* important matters to explain within each point. The key question to ask is: What does my audience *really* need to understand about this passage? You will not always use all of your Bible study notes, but you should keep them somewhere for future projects.

What to Explain

As you move through the text, as it corresponds with the outline, you should first think about explaining *key words or phrases*. Because of your initial Bible study, you should know which words your audience needs to understand. For example, in the book of Ruth, Boaz is identified as a "family redeemer" (Ruth 3:12). This concept has a rich Old Testament background and provides many wonderful gospel-related implications. The expositor would want to explain this idea because it is so important.

---

[3] Vines and Shaddix, *Power in the Pulpit*, 176.

Next, consider explaining the *context* of a passage. Remember the hearers have not spent six previous days thinking through the geography of the passage, the historical figures in the passage, the literary structure of the passage, or the theological purpose of the selected biblical author. Sometimes shining a light upon these matters will help them understand a passage well. For example, the *Colossian heresy* serves as a backdrop to Paul's letter to the church. He is responding, as he normally does in his letters, to a particular problem. In this case, it was a strange combination of theologies that was not consistent with sound Christology. As you explain various parts of this letter, you should teach the hearers about Paul's arguments.

Sometimes a *single verse* is ambiguous or loaded with meaning, and therefore is not fully understood by the hearers. If this is the case, you will need to slow down and have the audience think slowly upon the verse. John 1:1 is an example of a "hot verse." This verse not only affirms the deity of Christ but also the unique relationship of Jesus within the Trinity. Furthermore, it is misused by various cults, who do not keep with the original text of Scripture. In these cases, the expositor should unfold the necessary material in order to properly explain the text.

In addition to unpacking important verses, remember to point out *key doctrines* that emerge in the passage. When expounding 2 Corinthians 5:16–21, the expositor has a wonderful opportunity to explain the doctrines of regeneration, reconciliation, and substitutionary atonement. Sometimes, you may want to simply explain a doctrine in passing if the biblical author did not intend to primarily emphasize a doctrine. Sometimes the author may simply allude to a major truth within the flow of the text. For example, in the story on Ananias and Sapphira, Luke's primary intent is not to teach about the deity of the Spirit. However, this is a great opportunity for highlighting this doctrine as you move through the narrative (Acts 5:3–4).

At other times, readers simply overlook clear trinitarian passages. Sometimes it is because the preacher does not emphasize this great doctrine. Ephesians 1:1–14 is one of the clearest texts for showing the doctrine of the Trinity. But I have heard many sermons that do not even mention the relationship of the Father, Son, and Spirit in the text. Jesus's baptism also includes a clear trinitarian emphasis, and so does the oft-quoted Great Commission. Look for key doctrines and instruct and inspire your audience with these great truths.

How to Explain

Most pastor-teachers, who are gifted in teaching and proclamation, do not need a lot of help on *how* to explain the text. Many of them could make "teaching others how to rake leaves" enjoyable and inspiring. So, as I mention some key ways to explain the text, I assume that many of you already practice these skills naturally. Nevertheless, even the best can improve.

The first way to explain the text is simply to *present the facts.*[4] For example, if preaching on James 1:27, you might say, "When James says 'visit orphans,' the word *visit* means more than drop by for a chat. It comes from the same word that is translated 'overseer,' describing the work of the pastor. In other words, James is saying love the orphan, look out for the orphan, and meet the needs of the orphan."

Next, you can cross-reference other verses in order to *explain Scripture with Scripture.* In a sermon from 1 Timothy 3:1–7, you may point out that Paul uses *overseer* and *elder* interchangeably in Acts 20:17, 28 and Titus 1:5, 7. Therefore, Paul is speaking of the same office when he uses these terms. "Elder" basically refers to his position, and "overseer" has more to do with his function. In addition to articulating particular truths, effective cross-referencing is a great way to show the harmony of Scripture and some of its major themes.

Another way to explain the text is by using *contemporary concepts.* For example, not everyone understands the phrase "jot and tittle" today (Matt 5:18). But you could explain this phrase by comparing it to one dotted *i* and one crossed *t.* You also may explain other cultural nuances by using contemporary concepts such as monetary units or distances.

Further, *theological affirmations* are effective ways to explain the text. After explaining some of the language in John 1:1, you might say, "Jesus Christ is God." After noting a few phrases in 2 Timothy 3:16–17, you might say, "The Bible is God's Word!" You may want to consider explaining passages by quoting respected theologians, as well.

For narrative passages, an effective way to explain the text is by *retelling the story.* After a long Old Testament narrative, such as Elijah confronting the prophets of Baal (1 Kings 18:1–40), you may then

---

[4] Ibid., 177.

simply retell the story in simple and understandable language. In longer narratives, you might want to narrate previous passages and then read and explain your selected part of the story.

Visual aids are useful for explanation at times. In Ephesians 4:24, Paul speaks of taking off an old garment and putting on a new one.[5] You actually could demonstrate this as you explain the text. Multimedia tools are also ways to explain the text. I often use pictures from biblical sites to explain things such as the "wilderness of Judea." Visual aids actually serve as ways to illustrate, explain, and apply.

A final way to explain the text is by *reading the text with emphasis.* You can highlight phrases and nuances that are important for interpreting the text by stressing them orally. Purpose clauses are important phrases to stress. By putting emphasis on the "in order that" or "so that," the reader can see the purpose of the argument. Stressing Jesus's words about himself also highlights important interpretive matters. Jesus said, "*I* am the way, the truth, and the life. No one comes to the Father except through *Me*" (John 14:6).

The overall truth to remember in explaining is to avoid overly academic language. Luther said that when he preached he aimed at the youth in the church, not the highly educated. Refrain from trying to impress people with your personal study. Make the text plain and understandable, so that you teach the text to all of the listeners.

APPLICATION

Faithful expositors not only articulate the meaning of the text clearly, but they also apply the text to people. From your initial Bible study, you will probably already have some applications in mind. But now you can begin to think more carefully about application in light of your explanation and in view of the flow of your sermon.

Understanding Application

Application basically means putting something to use. The tendency, however, is to view only behavioral steps as useful. I use the

---

[5] Ibid., 178.

categories *specific* and *transformative* to describe the nature of biblical application.

Specific application is when you apply the text to particular situations that will have immediate impact. For example, if you are explaining Psalm 119:11, you may immediately challenge the hearers to memorize Romans 8 over the next month. Or, you may be working through Proverbs and give the hearers specific directives to avoid laziness and to work hard by changing some of their daily habits (like not sleeping all day!). Or, you may be preaching on James 1:27 and challenge the hearers to *do something* this month to care for orphans. Or, if you are talking about the nations, by praying, giving, and going, you could immediately challenge them to work at a fund-raiser or be part of a prayer meeting in order to support an upcoming mission trip. Specific application is direct and usually immediate.

I do not mean to imply that specific application cannot *transform* a person. Surely, memorizing Romans 8 or obeying the specific call to care for orphans brings change. I am only using it as a category to describe the simple, direct application in the text. One could get beneath the issue of meditating on Scripture or caring for orphans through transformative application by pointing out why we do not memorize Scripture or why we fail to care for orphans. These deeper questions have the ability to get to the heart level of a person. But we should not shy away from giving the simple, direct application that is plain in the text.

When specifically applying the text, it is quite important to do so with integrity. Haddon Robinson wrote a helpful article called "The Heresy of Application" emphasizing application integrity. Robinson said, "More heresy is preached in application than in Bible exegesis."[6] Often pastors have trouble knowing where to start and stop with specific application. We must stay tied to the meaning of the passage, otherwise we lose authority and may apply the text like a Pharisee.

For example, how would you specifically apply Exodus 20:14: "Do not commit adultery." Robinson encourages these categories: *necessary, probable, possible, improbable,* and *impossible.* He explains:

---

[6] Haddon Robinson, "The Heresy of Application," *Leadership* (Fall 1997): 21.

For example, a *necessary* implication of "You shall not commit adultery" is you cannot have a sexual relationship with a person who is not your spouse. A *probable* implication is you ought to be very careful of strong bonding friendships with a person who is not your spouse. A *possible* implication is you ought not travel regularly to conventions or other places with a person who is not your spouse. An *improbable* conclusion is you should not at any time have lunch with someone who is not your spouse. An *impossible* implication is you ought not have dinner with another couple because you are at the same table with a person who is not your spouse. Too often preachers give to a possible implication all the authority of a necessary implication, which is at the level of obedience. Only with necessary implications can you preach, "Thus saith the Lord."[7]

These categories are helpful at least in getting us thinking about applying with integrity. Do not confuse a suggestion with the clear, specific (and necessary) application of the text.

On this particular text (Exod 20:14), you would want to use Jesus's own words in Matthew 5 about adultery and the rest of the Bible also to address the gospel and the heart of the matter. Addressing the heart, the sin beneath the sin, is *transformative* application.

Transformative application includes theological/gospel implications that hit the *hearts* and *minds* of the hearers. Theological implications are timeless biblical truths that apply to every hearer. These flow from the text and are always relevant for modern hearers. Truths pertaining to God, Christ, man, and salvation have broad implications for the hearers. While the hearers may not put to use particular truths about God's sovereignty the same way that they use specific application steps, theological implications are applicatory because one's view of theological truths touches every area of their life.

For instance, if I were to ask you to give me one sentence that has changed the way you live your whole life, could you rattle off a quote or two? I remember reading, as a new Christian, "God is most

---

[7] "The Heresy of Application: An Interview with Haddon Robinson," accessed February 24, 2015, http://www.christianitytoday.com/le/1997/fall/7l4020.html?start=4.

glorified in us when we are most satisfied in him" by John Piper. This concept changed the way I lived. It was not a "specific application," but it was worldview shaping and heart transforming.

Transformative application will also show people the gospel solutions underneath their problems. It will show them *the beauty of Christ* who fulfilled God's Word perfectly and now empowers their obedience. It will capture *the affections* and *the imagination*. For example, Paul directs the Corinthians to the powerful image of Christ's incarnation in his appeal for generosity. He does not stop by telling the church to be generous. He fires their imagination and stirs their affections by highlighting the grace of Jesus (2 Cor 8:9).[8]

Tim Keller describes how Thomas Chalmers helped him understand the need to apply the text to affections. Chalmers (1780–1847) wrote a powerful piece entitled "The Expulsive Power of a New Affection." The old divine said, "The only way to dispossess the heart of an old affection is by the expulsive power of a new one."[9] Misplaced affections must be replaced by a far greater affection found in the gospel for transforming life change to happen.

As Keller reflected on these (and other related) concepts for preaching, he adjusted his approach to application. He says his former approach went something like this:

- Here is what the text says
- Here is how we must live in light of that text
- Now go and live that way, and God will help you.[10]

This is a pretty common way people apply the text. Upon reflecting on gospel application, however, Keller says, "I have come to realize that my sermons need to follow a different outline."[11] Here is the usual flow of Keller's application (not necessarily his sermon outline):

- Here is what the text says

---

[8] Tim Keller, "Preaching in a Secular Culture," accessed February 25, 2015, https://static1.squarespace.com/static/5315f2e5e4b04a00bc148f24/t/537a728fe4b0d45559686e07/1400533647273/Preaching_in_a_Secular_Culture.pdf.

[9] Thomas Chalmers, "The Expulsive Power of a New Affection," accessed February 25, 2015, http://manna.mycpanel.princeton.edu/rubberdoc/c8618ef3f4a7b5424f710c5fb61cf281.pdf.

[10] Keller, "Preaching in a Secular Culture."

[11] Ibid.

- Here is how we must live in light of it
- But we simply cannot do it
- Ah—but there is One who did!
- Now, through faith in him, you can begin to live this way.[12]

Do you see how this slight change makes a world of difference? This has the power to change a person dramatically, not merely alter someone's behavior for a few days. It also allows you to preach the richness of the gospel each week, while dealing with the demands of a particular text, and it also enables you to hit both the unbeliever and believer every week. Keller explains the difference:

> In nearly every text of Scripture a moral principle can be found, shown through the character of God or Christ, displayed in the good or bad examples of characters in the text, or provided as explicit commands, promises, and warnings. This moral principle is important and must be distilled clearly. But then a crisis is created in the hearers as they understand that this moral principle creates insurmountable problems. I describe in my sermons how this practical and moral obligation is impossible to meet. The hearers are led to a seemingly dead end, but then a hidden door opens and light comes in. Our sermons must show how the person and work of Jesus Christ bears on the subject. First we show how our inability to live as we ought stems from our forgetting or rejecting the work of Christ. Then we show that only by repenting and rejoicing in Christ can we then live as we know we ought.[13]

In order to do this type of deep application that addresses the hearts and minds of people with the gospel, I recommend that you read good gospel-driven counselors such as Paul Tripp and others. Those who apply the Bible well—who articulate the nature of sin and idolatry, holiness and grace, repentance and joy in Christ, are often found in the counseling areas of discipleship. Preachers have much to learn from them. We have all of our interns read *How People Change* by Timothy Lane and Paul Tripp, and I often tell them, "This is a very good book on understanding how we should addresses the mind and heart in preaching."

---

[12] Ibid.
[13] Ibid.

Growing in Application

Over the past five years or so, people like Keller have really helped me grow in my understanding of application. We should all be growing *personally* in gospel application because the gospel is endlessly rich, and we need it every day. But we should also be growing *homiletically* in our use of running and collected application. People should hear the gospel *throughout our sermons,* and we should apply it to a *wide range of people.* Allow me to summarize six related ways that we can grow in effective, gospel-saturated, transformative application.

First, remember to go deeper than only behavioral steps when talking about how people change. Consider the idols of the heart that underlie one's behavior. Try to get at the heart issues of people and call them to repentance. In addition to the counselors just mentioned, I highly recommend Keller's *Counterfeit Gods* for every expositor. Each semester I am tempted to require it as a textbook for preaching because Keller helps us understand what is beneath behavior.

Second, edify while you evangelize and evangelize while you edify.[14] When giving a moral exhortation to people, remind them that they cannot do it perfectly; but Christ *has* done it perfectly, and He died on behalf of those who broke God's commands—and now through Christ, by his power, they can live it out. And when they fail as Christians, the Father will not crush them because he already crushed Christ in their place. Many sermons follow the pattern: The text says, "Do not lie." Application: Stop lying. That is not wrong to say. We must say this. But what is often lacking is a Christ-centered focus to the application. By showing people how Christ fulfills God's demands, we can emphasize both the imperatives of the text, as well as the gospel every week.

Third, remember to apply the text to both individuals and the corporate body. Obviously, we should want to apply the text to individual lives (their hopes, fears, vocations, etc.). But much of the Bible addresses the people of God *corporately.* So it should not be difficult to find the corporate application for the church. We often read the Bible (at least in the West) quite individualistically. Learn to apply the gospel to your local congregation.

---

[14] Keller, *Center Church* (Grand Rapids: Zondervan, 2012), 79.

Further, let the gospel vision of your church drip in your sermons so that they hear it regularly. This is how you lead from the pulpit. A once-a-year vision sermon will only accomplish so much. This drip approach allows people to always hear it.

Fourth, engage the prodigal and the older brother. This means learn to apply the message to the (lost) *irreligious* person and the (lost) *religious* person. Show each of them how the text addresses them. Usually, when people think about applying the text to a lost person, they think younger brother (the hedonist). But we must also learn to apply it to the elder brother (the moralist). Congregations usually have both in attendance. In so doing, you will follow the way of Jesus, who is addressing both types of people as He gives His sermon on the two sons (Luke 15:1–2, 11–32). The gospel powerfully addresses the legalistic Galatians and the hedonistic Corinthians.

Fifth, do the work of an evangelist from the pulpit and in your everyday life. Regarding the pulpit, remember that if you address the non-Christian in your messages, *they will show up!* Eventually, unbelievers will show up for one of two reasons. (1) Some will come because *they know you will address them* and deal with their questions. (2) Others will come *because their friends will bring them*—because the friends know that you will address the unbeliever. Your sermon does not have to be geared at the skeptic exclusively, but you should address them in the introduction and then you should plan to have certain "asides" where you speak to them directly in application.[15]

Here is what happens when you begin addressing the unbeliever. You will begin to create an evangelistic culture in the church. Friends start bringing unbelievers, and believers learn indirectly how to speak to unbelievers by watching you do it.

But what if you know everyone in attendance and they are all Christians? I get this question often. I agree with Keller who essentially says, "Do it anyway." It may be awkward at first, but you may experience what a pastor friend in Illinois experienced when he implemented this practice. People asked him, "Who are you talking to? I noticed you are speaking to non-Christians more often?" He did not really have anyone in mind specifically; he was trying to establish this culture and expectation. Soon, however, an entire Muslim family began attending. No one asked him this question

---

[15] Keller has taught me about the value of this point. Mark Dever also addresses the unbeliever directly in the introduction. I have benefited from Dever's example as well.

anymore. And over time, more and more unbelievers began attending. You should also remember that in almost every crowd, even if you think everyone is a Christian, both sheep and goats are likely present. It should not be too difficult to imagine that unbelievers are in the room each week.

So how can we prepare to do good evangelistic application? One place to start is by *diversifying your people context in your everyday life*.[16] Do not simply hang out with Christians, read Christian books/blogs, and listen to Christian radio, avoiding outsiders at all cost. Instead, read widely. And spend time with unbelievers. For example, coach little league, volunteer at schools, start a board game night, go for walks, and have people over to your house. You tend to apply the text to the people you talk with each week. It is amazing how coaching little league and talking to parents helps me in application. All of life is sermon preparation! If you only hang out with other Christians, your sermon will probably make an outsider feel as if "This is for the Christian subculture." By regularly engaging with the unbeliever, you will also learn the art of listening and responding to them with sound arguments and, in turn, better address them from the pulpit. You will learn how to be truthful and gracious, not rude or ridiculing.

To improve in our evangelistic skills, we must *think about different types of people as we prepare*. The tendency for preachers is to preach to other preachers or only believers. But when you diversify your people context, you will more naturally prepare with various people in mind, and you will more skillfully address the unbeliever from the pulpit.

Finally, aim for adoration, not only information. The goal of explaining and applying the text is for people to behold Christ and change. Pray and work toward this end. Show them the beauty of Christ, and the sermon will be both relevant and life changing. Jonathan Edwards stated that the religious person may find Christ *useful*, but a disciple of Jesus finds him *beautiful*.[17] The need to make the truth *real*, not only *clear*, affected how Edwards viewed preaching, as it did Lloyd-Jones who said the following:

---

[16] Tim Keller, "Applying Christ to the Heart in Preaching," accessed February 24, 2015, http://static1.squarespace.com/static/5315f2e5e4b04a00bc148f24/t/5410791ae4b0c1ca62ec04a0/1410365722378/Applying+Christ+to+the+Heart+in+Preaching.pdf.

[17] Jonathan Edwards, quoted in Keller, "Preaching in a Secular Culture."

The first and primary object of preaching is not only to give information. It is, as Edwards says, to produce *an impression.* It is the impression at the time that matters, even more than what you can remember subsequently. In this respect Edwards is, in a sense, critical of what was a prominent Puritan custom and practice. The Puritan father would catechize and question the children as to what the preacher had said. Edwards, in my opinion, has the true notion of preaching. It is not primarily to impart information; and while you are writing your notes you may be missing something of the impact of the Spirit. As preachers we must not forget this. We should tell our people to read certain books themselves and get the information there. The business of preaching is to make such knowledge live."[18]

As people behold the glory of God in the face of Christ, the Spirit will transform them from one degree of glory to another (2 Cor 3:18). Aim for worship, not simply for people to take notes on your sermon. This type of "on the spot" adoration is truly transforming.

Placing the Application

When should you do application in the sermon? When application is understood mainly as a functional element, then naturally the place of it is within each point of the outline. However, the MPS should include the main application for the sermon, which should then be woven throughout the message. You may also choose to put some application points at the end of the sermon after the exposition. For example, after teaching on the parable of the unmerciful servant, you might choose to apply the text by answering the question in a Christ-centered way: "Why do people find it hard to forgive?"

So I prefer to give both *running* and *collected* application. I prefer to make application in all three places: the introduction, within the body of the sermon, and at the conclusion.

A tendency of some expositors is to not do application until the end of the sermon. But I think it is important to develop a strong MPS that includes a relevant reason for the people to listen in the *introduction.* In other words, try to front the application. Consider

---

[18] D. Martyn Lloyd-Jones, quoted in Keller, "Preaching in a Secular Culture."

doing something like providing reasons everyone needs to understand the selected passage at the beginning of the message.

Each week in the introduction I give some general application for both believers and unbelievers. I work hard to "get everyone on the bus" in the beginning. I generally say something like, "If you are a believer, here's why we need this text . . ." And "If you are not a Christian, this is a great week for you to be here because . . ." My hope is that everyone will then see that the entire sermon applies to him or her.

Further, I like to make application in *the body* of the sermon because if you save it for the end *only*, the people may "duck." Presenting application as you go along allows you to hit people as you go along! This type of running application also retains a great deal of authority because it is tied to the immediate explanation. Application within the body of the sermon also helps the hearers learn how to read and apply on their own. Few of them will read the text and then stop and write down ten ways to apply it.

Having said that, collected application at the end of the sermon is beneficial because it does two things: it reinforces previous ideas, and it leads into a response time. To apply the text at the end, I like to ask questions about issues that were raised earlier in the sermon. Further, this is the time to drop everyone off at the cross. Take everyone to the gospel for transformation. Show them Christ's obedience, his substitutionary death, and the power that we have in Christ to live out the passage.

Therefore, *give careful attention in preparation to gospel-centered, wide-ranging application.* Mark Dever summarizes how he intentionally prepares to apply the text to a wide range of people:

> Each of us has different ways of meditating on how a text applies to our churches. I (Mark) use a tool I call an "Application Grid." Once I've settled on a sermon outline, I create a grid with those points down the side and a number of categories across the top. Those categories ask various questions:
>
> • How does the teaching in this point fit into the salvation-historical progression of the biblical storyline?
> • What does this text say to the non-Christian?
> • What does it say to the larger society and to policy makers?

- What does it say about Jesus?
- How does it apply to the individual Christian?
- Does it say anything in particular about issues of work or family?
- What does it say to my own local church, Capitol Hill Baptist Church?[19]

This idea of using an application grid may be helpful for you. An application grid will help you think through the various ways to apply the text to various people. Following is a grid based on Dever's model that includes some additional sections that you should consider as you prepare your sermon. The goal is not to apply in each category for each point but, rather, to aid in helping you hit several of the categories at some point in your sermon.[20]

You may consider your own grid, adding to or modifying this one (perhaps creating subcategories or new categories from transformative application). Whether you use it or not, it illustrates the multifaceted ways we do application. Do not merely think about individuals; do not merely think about Christians. Be careful and intentional in application preparation.

Stating the Application

The way to state your application varies. One natural way is to use *personal pronouns*. Young preachers sometimes wonder if they should always include themselves in the application. Is it appropriate to say, "Some of *you* need to . . ." or "*You* should . . ."? Certainly, there are times to say, "*We* need to . . ." but my advice is that if you apply the text to yourself during the week, as you should, then you have earned the right to say "you." In fact, we should not preach to anyone until we have first internalized it personally. Just remember to be affectionate, not only forceful, in your direct application.

You should also make the application *decisive* and *appealing*. Call the hearers to act. If you are preaching on caring for the orphan in James 1:27, then call the hearers to give to an orphan ministry or pray about adopting some orphans personally. Do not assume that

---

[19] Mark Dever and Greg Gilbert, *Preach* (Nashville: B&H, 2012), 93.

[20] I am indebted to fellow pastor Seth Brown for helping me develop this grid. The categories are mostly self-explanatory. "Doxological" has to do with preaching to the affections (i.e., "How does this text cause us to adore Jesus?"). For a sample of what Dever describes, see Michael Lawrence's *Biblical Theology* (Wheaton, IL: Crossway, 2010), 184.

Figure 4: Sermon
Application Grid

SERMON APPLICATION GRID

SERMON TITLE

MAIN POINT OF SERMON

TEXT

MAIN POINT OF TEXT

| UNIQUE HISTORICAL | JESUS' LIFE & WORK | INDIVIDUAL | GENDER & FAMILY | VOCATION | PUBLIC SPHERE | LOCAL CHURCH | UNITY & DIVERSITY | NON-CHRISTIANS | NEXT GENERATION | DOXO-LOGICAL |

DATE

PREACHER

TEXTS AND POINTS

Adapted from Mark Dever's "Application Grid."

they will hear the explanation and ponder it for themselves. Call them to something great.

Questions are good ways to state your application, especially as you seek to get to the root of problems. Crafting penetrating questions is a wonderful tool for applying truth. Simply turn the text back on the people and ask the question that flows from it. Ask further questions related to the heart. This is a natural and effective way to apply the text. Further, anticipate objections and raise questions, and then answer them. Probe with self-examination questions. As you ask such questions, give people a moment to ponder it and then proceed.

Finally, *present your application in a powerful, carefully worded sentence.* Piper states, "Books don't change people, paragraphs do—sometimes sentences."[21] Distill what you want to say in a single, powerful, gospel-filled sentence. Consider alerting them to the sentence before giving it and then give them time to ponder it.

The faithful preacher will work hard at applying the text responsibly and appropriately. We must also do this work of application in a spirit of dependent prayer because the Holy Spirit transforms people's lives as the gospel is internalized.

ILLUSTRATION

As you explain the text and apply it within the body of the sermon, the question to ask is, Does this truth need additional light? The way to cast light on the truth is through an illustration. In fact, the word *illustration* actually means to enlighten or make clear.[22] An illustration is that which brings light and life to biblical truth. We all know that good sermons are turned into great sermons with vivid illustrations.

The Purpose of Illustrations

Illustrations are servants of both explanation and application. Therefore, they support the sermon. They should not dominate the sermon. In jest, I have said, "I have a great illustration; so now all that I need is a text!" Sharing a great illustration, by itself, is never

---

[21] John Piper, "Books Don't Change People; Paragraphs Do," accessed February 25, 2015, http://www.desiringgod.org/articles/books-don-t-change-people-paragraphs-do.

[22] R. L. Mayhue, "Introductions, Illustrations, and Conclusions," in John MacArthur Jr. and the Master's Seminary Faculty, *Rediscovering Expository Preaching* (Dallas: Word, 1992), 247.

the expositor's goal. We must illustrate in order to help *explain* and illustrate to help *apply* biblical truth.

In addition, illustrations also help the expositor *intensify* the meaning of a particular truth. For example, a story of a great missionary such as William Carey is a fitting illustration when preaching on Matthew 28:16–20 because this text had such a profound impact on the father of modern missions. A powerful story will show the listeners why your point is important.

Illustrations also help the expositor *argue* for a particular issue. Illustrations can show the validity of one contention and the fallacy of another.[23] Quotations from authorities or statistics and research are examples of illustrations that can help you contend for a point.

Finally, illustrations *inspire* or motivate the hearers. In fact, Bryan Chapell believes that the primary purpose of illustrations is "not to clarify but to motivate."[24] I agree with Chapell's rationale: "Preachers who fail to understand this [purpose] will assume that when the point they are making is clear, they do not need an illustration. Preachers who grasp the true power and purposes of illustration know that *the most clear points often deserve the best illustrations* to make the truth as significant to the hearer as it is in Scripture."[25]

The most effective preachers whom I know can touch the heart and mind with an illustration that explains, applies, argues, or intensifies biblical truth, in such a way as to inspire and motivate the hearers to respond. Tony Evans, Bryan Chapell, Robert Smith, Chuck Swindoll, Tim Keller, and Kent Hughes are only a few examples of those who do it exceptionally well. These communicators follow after the way of Jesus, the master Illustrator.

How to Illustrate

The first tip in learning to illustrate well is to *read widely*. Most of the preachers that I just mentioned are readers. Learn to illustrate not only from biblical examples but also from other types of literature. Read history, fables, fiction, allegories, newspapers, magazines, popular mainstream books, websites, and even books in which you have little interest. It is amazing how many illustrations you will find as you read naturally. I bookmark several particular websites and read

---

[23] Vines and Shaddix, *Power in the Pulpit*, 191.
[24] Bryan Chapell, *Christ-Centered Preaching*, 2nd ed. (Grand Rapids: Baker, 2005), 186.
[25] Ibid., my emphasis.

them regularly for pleasure and potential illustrations. Biographies are also tremendous resources for illustrations. Books that I disagree with also provide me with sermon fodder. I have friends who also send me stories that they think I may use in sermons. (Others send me video clips of movies, events, or interviews that are illustrative). Illustrations from a variety of sources will help you connect with a variety of people. Of course, reading will also help you become a better communicator and a more rounded scholar.

Second, *keep your eyes open.* Illustrations that are taken from life experiences attract the audience and serve as fresh ways to illustrate concepts. Conversations, observations from nature, shopping experiences, hospital visits, trips, parental experiences, sporting events, recreational outings, or current news events are all examples of slices of life that can possibly illustrate important points. Sometimes even the most familiar concepts are the most powerful illustrations because of the shared experience of listeners. A word of caution is to remember not to use too many family illustrations. Your family, especially your wife, will probably even thank you for ceasing to tell everything that happened in the previous week. Your family does not need to think that everything they do is going to end up in next week's sermon.

A third tip is related to these first two: *know how to tell a good story.* It is one thing to find a great story, but it is another to share it effectively and concisely in the sermon. Illustrative stories should include characters, descriptive details, conflict, movement, suspense, and a climax. After sharing the story, relate it to the rest of the sermon smoothly. Avoid the awkward disconnect between the illustration and the next functional element. I often write out a clear sentence that I will say after using an illustration, in order to establish the relevance of the illustration. Bryan Chapell uses a helpful image called *expositional rain* to describe the process of maintaining a tight connection between the illustration and the explanation, by echoing the same terminology within the functional elements.[26] Verbal clues will help the listeners follow along and benefit from the illustration.

Fourth, *remember to use illustrations at various places in the sermon.* In this chapter, I have in mind illustrations as a functional element

---

[26] Ibid., 197. For an excellent study on illustrations, see Bryan Chapell, *Using Illustrations to Preach with Power*, rev. ed. (Wheaton, IL: Crossway, 2001).

primarily. However, you may also consider using an illustration in the introduction (see next chapter). Illustrations also help to summarize the material, reinforce the MPS, and lead to a call for action.

Finally, *bring some creative people into the study process.* Many preachers are analytical types and thus struggle with innovative ways to present content. Church members who are gifted in the arts, media, or production can help augment your message. Use some of their ideas from time to time if it is appropriate and legitimate.

Hopefully, the longer you preach the better illustrator you will become. Listen to great illustrators. Develop a file for illustrations. Have a wise critic (like your spouse). Most of all, seek excellence in this area of exposition.

Cautions Regarding Illustrations

Because illustrations are so moving, the preacher often overuses them. The first caution, then, is to use illustrations *sensibly.* Our goal is to explain and apply biblical truth, not tell a bunch of stories. When you do this, you lose credibility from many hearers, and you end up diluting the thrust of the message. A better approach is to work at maintaining a balance between explanation, illustration, and application. Think about the amount of time that you are spending on each functional element. Are you spending a similar amount of time for each?

The next caution is to use illustrations *ethically.* Never misrepresent the person that you are trying to refute. Be fair and charitable. Also, avoid stretching personal stories to make a point. People will not take you seriously if you do this regularly. Misquoting someone or using the wrong dates also diminishes credibility. (The audience can now fact-check you on the spot with their mobile devices!).

Additionally, illustrate *authentically.* Preachers who only use illustrations from great saints come across as overly pietistic. Be real in your preaching. Occasional illustrations from the Puritans is a good idea, but too many illustrations from George Mueller, Augustine, and other great saints will distance the hearer from the preacher.[27]

Remember to illustrate *humbly,* as well. Do not make yourself the hero in every story. In fact, it is a good idea to poke fun at yourself and confess your own sin from time to time. Let others have the spotlight.

---

[27] Chapell, *Christ-Centered Preaching,* 203.

Finally, use illustrations *respectfully*. Avoid being the shock-jock with crude language. Spare the gore when you can. Be mindful of children in the room when illustrating.

SUMMATION

The key functional elements are explanation, application, and illustration. Explanation and application are the two essential elements because expository preaching purposes to present and apply biblical truth. Illustrations are servants of explanation and application. Effective expositors should explain key words, doctrines, important verses, and contextual issues. The main question to answer is: "What does my audience *really* need to know?" Application may be more specific or transformative. Specific application is that which requires immediate action. Transformative application is that which shapes one's worldview and appeals to the heart through gospel-centered application, thus impacting all areas of life. We need to constantly grow in effective application and our ability to touch the various groups of listeners in the room. Illustration is the act of shining additional light on biblical truth. Illustrations help instruct, inspire, intensify, apply, and argue. After developing the functional elements, the faithful preacher is ready to add an introduction and a conclusion.

STUDY OF 1–2 TIMOTHY

Go back to the outline on 1 Timothy 4:11–16. What would you say for each of the three functional elements within this particular outline?

OUTLINE: 4 CHALLENGES FOR YOUNG MINISTERS

1. Exemplify Your Teaching Personally (v. 12)
   Explanation:
   Application:
   Illustration:
2. Expose the Scriptures Publicly (v. 13)
   Explanation:
   Application:
   Illustration:

3. Exercise Your Gift Passionately (vv. 14–15)
   Explanation:
   Application:
   Illustration:
4. Examine Your Life and Teaching Persistently (v. 16)
   Explanation:
   Application:
   Illustration:

12

STEP 5: ADD AN INTRODUCTION AND A CONCLUSION

Men of Athens, I perceive that in every way you are very religious.
For as I passed along and observed the objects of your worship, I
found also an altar with this inscription, "To the unknown god."
What therefore you worship as unknown, this I proclaim to you.
—Acts 17:22b–23 (ESV)

A good introduction serves two purposes. First, it arouses
interest, stimulates curiosity, and whets the appetite for
more. Secondly, it genuinely "introduces" the theme
by leading the hearers to it. . . . Conclusions are more
difficult than introductions. Some preachers seem to be
constitutionally incapable of concluding anything, let alone
their sermons.[1]

—John Stott

THE LAST STEP IN the preparation process is to add an introduction and a conclusion. The conclusion probably seems appropriate
here, but it may seem strange to add an introduction last. Though

---

[1] John Stott, *Between Two Worlds* (Grand Rapids: Eerdmans, 1982), 244–45.

the MPT and MPS are developed early in the process, you still should consider developing the "opener" or "sermon starter" (what some refer to as the introduction) *last* because you cannot introduce something that you know nothing about. After identifying the MPT and MPS, and the substance of the message, you can then determine an effective opener. Having said this, if I find an opener early in the week, I take it! But I simply do not worry about it if I have no opener early in the week. I save it for later when everything else is finished.

Further, if you prepare an exciting opener, with no text or substance, then you will be tempted later to twist the text to fit your clever sermon starter. We must never sacrifice faithful exegesis on the altar of cleverness.

The conclusion should not only summarize the material but also include a call for response. Therefore, both the introduction and conclusion should add to, not take away from, the overall thrust of the message. Here is a skeleton of a complete expository sermon, after the five-step preparation process is finished:

    I.   INTRODUCTION
        Opener
        MPT
        MPS
   II. BODY (OR EXPOSITION)
        Point 1
           Explanation:
           Application:
           Illustration:
        Point 2
           Explanation:
           Application:
           Illustration:
        Point 3
           Explanation:
           Application:
           Illustration:
  III. CONCLUSION
        Summation
        Response

In the following pages, I will discuss some ways to develop a fitting introduction and conclusion, as well as some thoughts on writing the sermon and the need to pray for God's help.

ADDING THE INTRODUCTION

Some theologically minded pastors frown on introductions. "Just start with the text!" they say. While the introduction can be overdone, I believe that you normally need some type of introduction or "opener" to your sermon. An introduction is like a porch on a house, the prelude to a song, a preface to a book, or the slow rising of the sun in the morning. It is inviting, gradual, easy on the mind, and aesthetically pleasing. Most people dislike abruptness but "delight in a somewhat gradual approach."[2] Obviously, a tiny house with a huge porch is silly, and a fifty-page preface to a five-page book is ridiculous. The goal of the porch is to get you in the house, and the goal of the preface is to escort the readers into the following chapters. So it is with the introduction of the sermon. It should not dominate the sermon; it should simply invite the hearers inside.

Purposes and Qualities of Introductions

With that said, the introduction has several additional purposes. The introduction first should *incite interest for both the believer and unbeliever.*

You may incite interest in a variety of ways, such as a contemporary story, a striking quote, a penetrating question, and so forth. The problem that I have with those who do not see the point to introductions is that they assume interest on the part of the hearer. While many of the Sunday listeners are "ready for the Word," some are ready to go to sleep. They need to be alerted to the gravity of the message. Some assume the sermon is for Christians only. Let the unbeliever know that you are aware of their presence and their questions. Give them a reason to listen. Some guests feel like they are too behind in the series to understand things. We need to bring them up to speed. Therefore, it is important to establish relevancy and incite interest in the first five minutes.

---

[2] Ibid., 244.

Not only should the introduction capture interest, but it should also *introduce the text, MPT, and the MPS.* You need to transition smoothly from the opening story, quote, poem, question, or other type of introduction into the thrust of the message. Use "exposi-tional rain" to rain down key terms that you used in the opener to introduce the subject of the message and the MPS.

Additionally, the introduction should *include a redemptive qual-ity.* Show the hearers why they need to hear this sermon. Promise them a redemptive solution to their fallen problem. Create ten-sion and let the rest of the sermon unravel the tension, pointing to Christ. Do not have a passionless introduction with no conviction. Come with a *burden.* Strike the match early, and let the heat burn throughout the sermon.

The introduction should also *include your expectations.*[3] Here is where the conclusion and the introduction fit together. Know what you are going to call the people to do and include that in the introduction.

Finally, *open up with variety.* Avoid being predictable in the nature of your openers. The consistent elements in the introduc-tion are the main points of the text and sermon. You can vary your sermon starters by utilizing one of the following options.

Types of Introductions

The most common type of introduction is *the story.* A contemporary event that people are familiar with is an effective way to rise into your subject. Keep your eyes open for current news events, sporting events, or stories from popular books. (Paul was certainly aware of the Athenian context.)

Personal stories are useful as well. Andy Stanley puts forward the Me-We-God-You-We approach, illustrating the flow of the intro-duction and sermon.[4] You start with a personal story (Me), relate it to the congregation (We), to the text (God), and back to the hearers (You, We). This progressive journey is a natural way to com-municate. Long-time pastor Adrian Rogers provided a similar for-mula: Hey! You! Look! Do![5]

---

[3] Jerry Vines and Jim Shaddix, *Power in the Pulpit* (Chicago: Moody, 1999), 221.
[4] Andy Stanley and Lane Jones, *Communicating for a Change* (Colorado Springs: Multnomah, 2006), 119–30.
[5] Taken from Vines and Shaddix, *Power in the Pulpit,* 220.

Another approach is to *ask a probing question* or *create a problem*. This approach is my personal favorite. I prefer to put the story and problem approach together. In a sermon on partiality, based on James 2:1–13, I began with a contemporary example of prejudice, and then I asked the question, "Do you love *all* of your neighbors as yourself or only those who look like you?" From that opener, I proceeded to tell the hearers why they needed to understand James's words about keeping the royal commandment.

Multimedia provides many striking ways to introduce the message as well. Consider the following ideas:

- "Man on the Street" interviews related to the message
- A clip that supports or denies your thesis
- Pictures related to the message (one of my favorite ways to introduce the message)
- A popular song that incites interest and leads into the sermon (another favorite)
- Video testimonies from church members who have experienced some aspect of the message
- Maps and other biblical background helps
- Visual aids that illustrate the theme of the message
- Graphs or statistical breakdowns
- Phone/video chat conversations with a missionary oversees
- Website presentations that relate to the message (e.g., missions agencies, online libraries)
- Interviews with those who disagree with you

This list is not exhaustive, but it shows that there are many ways to provoke interest through the world of technology. Remember to use such media wisely and avoid allowing it to overshadow the actual message.

Is there ever a time to not have an opener? Sure! You do not have to do this for the sermon to be expositional. Include the text and the MPS and MPT? Yes. Have a great sermon starter? Not necessarily. For example, for the second part of a two-part message you might just overview the previous week. You might also have so much important content that you need to reduce the introduction to only the MPT and the MPS. I certainly leave room for this approach and practice it myself. However, if possible, I think it is generally good and wise to have some type of opener in addition to the MPT and the MPS.

ADDING THE CONCLUSION

A conclusion generally has two important parts: *a summation* and a *response*. The conclusion is generally the least prepared part of the Sunday sermon. So much time is devoted to constructing an effective outline, developing strong functional elements, and adding a wonderful introduction that the conclusion often is given little thought. The conclusion, though, is quite important. Sometimes it is the most memorable portion of the sermon. It usually carries the strongest sense of burden (by the preacher). It also leads into a call for response, which drives home the MPS.

Summation

The summation, as I prefer to call it, reinforces the MPS and recaps the content of the message. It should never include new information, though some summaries may employ a story or quote or some added dimension. These elements should never take away from the thrust of the sermon but should reinforce it.

Make the summation brief and clear. It should not be like another sermon.

Set up your response in the summation. Remind the audience why your sermon was relevant and why they need to consider acting on it.

Of course, you do not have to just repeat the outline in the summation. There are several ways to summarize the material in a powerful way. Again, a story is a great way. If you come across a story that summarizes the sermon well, then you may sprinkle in key terms from the outline in the story. Sometimes, I think about using my best story at the summation, instead of in the opener, provided that I have another way of opening up the sermon. The caution here is to avoid any type of emotional manipulation (especially with students). Calling them to notice a real-life example that followed the thrust of your text is one thing; playing on their emotions is another. Choose your story wisely and responsibly.

You may also try to use your opening story *again* in the summation. You might tell part of the story in the beginning, for instance, and then finish it in the summation. Or you may simply refer to part of the opening story in the summation. Another alternative is to offer some application questions. Though you should not introduce new material, you may phrase some of your key ideas into self-examination questions.

You may also consider stating your outline differently in the summation without preaching a different sermon. John Stott was a master at repackaging what he previously said in the outline in a way that was both summative and provoking. He often used a more general outline in the summary than he did in the body of the sermon. Often I will have two or three possible ways to give my outline, and I will choose one to use in the summation that will recap, bring variety, and lead into self-examination. A final summation idea is to use a quotation. If you come across a quote that summarizes the heart of the sermon, then use it, and then consider highlighting the key points with some of the language of the quote.

Response

The response (or *invitation* in some circles) is the call to act upon God's Word. Because of the abuses of the "altar call," many do not practice any type of invitation for a public response. In Scripture, however, people responded to God's Word publicly in some way (e.g., Genesis 12–13; Joshua 4; Ezra 9–10; Nehemiah 8–9; Acts 2:38). Do not let the abuses keep you from calling your hearers to respond to the truth. The preaching of the Word demands response. We should always be calling people to repentance and faith. It is not manipulation if you are persuading them to act on God's Word. Persuade with integrity based upon the authority of God's truth.

Clarity. It is essential that we are clear during the response time. Tell your hearers exactly what you want them to do. Make the necessary preparations for specific response times. Anticipate response.

Unity. Remember that effective responses are matched with the message. Think about your thesis and how you want people to respond to it. For example, if you preach on prayer, you might plan some type of prayer experience at the close of the message or later that week.

Variety. Allow me to offer seven ways you may call people to respond. First, you may consider making a simple verbal appeal.[6]

---

[6] The first five examples were adapted from Vines and Shaddix, *Power in the Pulpit*, 213–15.

Call the hearers to "go and do likewise." If the sermon is on evangelism, appeal to them to share the gospel or at least pray for one unbeliever during the upcoming week.

Second, think about calling people to physically move. This traditionally means to "come forward," which was popularized by preachers during the nineteenth and twentieth century. However, you can call people to kneel at their pew, go reconcile with a brother or sister, put their hand on the person next to them, or walk to the front for prayer.

Third, a postmeeting response is wise and good. I am wary of any public response that does not include a postmeeting follow-up. Spurgeon used to have the inquiry room for people who wanted to meet after the service. Tell people clearly how to meet with you or your pastoral team for follow-up. We currently use a "Next Steps" table for prayer, further gospel explanation, membership information, and prayer.

Fourth, a written response is another good idea. Allow the hearers to respond privately by indicating what is going on in their spiritual life. Give them freedom to ask questions or make a request to see a pastor. You may also have the hearers write down people they want the church to pray for or have them journal a response to your sermon.

Fifth, consider doing a question-and-answer session after your sermon. You may do this by allowing people to text questions that you can then answer right after the sermon. You may host a luncheon for unbelievers following the sermon to hear their questions. You may also simply finish and say, "I have time for a few questions." Or, you may have people submit questions during the week regarding your sermon, and you could post a video answering them. This type of engagement with the listener has many wonderful benefits. You get to hear what people are hearing. You get to understand the nature of your audience. It will allow you to clarify unclear statements and points. And overall, it will improve your preparation and delivery.

Sixth, use the Lord's Supper as a time for response. This is my personal favorite—which we use every week.[7] The Lord's Supper is a natural way for Christians to examine their lives, and to repent of

---

[7] See chap. 4, "Proclaiming Jesus to the Ear and the Eye," in my e-book *Proclaiming Jesus* (Gospel-Centered Discipleship, 2012).

sin, and come to the table rejoicing that there is One who is worthy of worship and praise. The Lord's Table enables you to draw everyone to Christ in the conclusion of your sermon, and it allows people to *see* not only *hear* the Gospel. It also enables you to draw a distinction between believers and unbelievers and gives you a natural opportunity to urge the Christian to embrace the Savior. We usually say something like this, "If you are not a Christian, the Table is not for you. But we offer you something greater. We offer you Christ himself. We would love to talk with you during this time, as people move to get the elements, or we can talk after the service about what it means to become a Christian." During this time we sing several songs and lead the people in taking the bread and the cup together.

Finally, consider using multiple approaches. Give the hearers several ways to respond. Use the written record, the physical relocation, the question-and-answer, the "go and do likewise," the Table, and the postmeeting response.

WRITING THE MESSAGE AND PRAYING OVER IT

Preachers vary on what they take to the pulpit. I do not think one is more spiritual or gifted if he takes nothing or an entire manuscript. The important thing to remember is that you must prepare thoroughly. I love the blog series from Joshua Harris on "Preaching Notes" in which he posted what several well-known pastors take to the pulpit, including David Platt, Matt Chandler, Tim Keller, and more.[8]

Obviously, in my five-step process you should have a lot of notes by the time you get to the introduction and conclusion. I recommend (especially for young preachers) writing a *sermon manuscript* each week. The manuscript does not need to look like a commentary nor an exegetical paper. Prepare your manuscript for *the hearer*, not the reader. You may also prepare it with bullet points and choose unique formatting that helps you think and remember your message. No two preachers usually have the same-looking manuscript. So, in preparing a manuscript, do not feel the pressure of submitting your manuscript to a book publisher! The goal is to help you think through the material and draft in a way that is impactful.

---

[8] You can see the variety in each of the examples here: joshharris.com/2011/09/preaching_notes_round_two.php.

The manuscript includes a word-for-word description of how you *plan* on communicating the message. Of course, no one says exactly what is in front of them, unless they read it. I do not advocate reading your sermon like you are reading a book. Simply prepare it, if possible, in a completed manuscript form. You may choose to take an abbreviated version of it to the pulpit, but preparing a manuscript has two major advantages, one related to content and the other related to delivery.

The manuscript will help you with content in that you can see how things relate together exactly. You will benefit by reading through your manuscript and discerning what to keep and what to throw away. In addition, the manuscript will allow you to get the maximum mileage out of your preparation time. If you spend twenty hours preparing a sermon, then you should have some quality material for some other project or sermon later. If all you write down are some Bible study notes, and then a few Post-it notes, then you may not retain some of the wonderful nuggets of thought. Many pastors who write books simply take their manuscripts and rework them into some type of book. Manuscripts are useful for later work.

The manuscript will help with delivery because it helps you choose words wisely. Jonathan Edwards and others moved people through word choice and images. The manuscript will help you use different words, picture words, and powerful words. It also will help you when you teach difficult doctrines, ensuring precision.

Another option is the *sermon brief.* The brief includes a word-for-word introduction and conclusion but just contains some key paragraphs within the body of the sermon under each point. In this form, busy pastors may choose not to write out their illustrations. Instead, they may choose to include well-written exegesis and application. If you are preaching numerous times per week, the brief is a good approach because you can still get some of the manuscript benefits without investing the time needed to prepare a full manuscript.

An *extended outline* is similar to a brief. It contains some key sentences and thoughts, such as the MPS and particular word studies, but it may not include a completely written introduction or body. Different preachers who use a thorough outline usually write out different elements, depending on style and preference. A good idea is to write a manuscript and then transfer it to an extended outline for the pulpit.

In the delivery portion of the book, I will discuss more matters pertaining to communication ideas, but the final word to mention is to remember that the entire sermon process is a prayerful event. Pray before you prepare, pray while you prepare, and pray after you complete your notes. Spend some time on Saturday reviewing your notes and praying for God to use your message. Rise early on Sunday and spend considerable time asking for God's grace and power. Pray as you sing and prepare to stand and declare God's Word. One preacher quipped, "First I reads myself full, next I thinks myself clear, next I prays myself hot, and then I lets go."[9] Do not forget to pray yourself hot before you let go!

If possible, I really like to finish my sermon by Thursday. I then take Friday and Saturday to edit, internalize, and pray. This way I need little if any notes because I have been marinating on it for a few days. If someone asks me on Friday, "What is your sermon about?" I want to be able to at least state the essence of my sermon without looking at any notes.

SUMMATION

The introduction and conclusion are the last parts to prepare for an expositional sermon. The introduction should incite interest for both the believer and the unbeliever and introduce the MPT and the MPS. It should also contain a redemptive quality and the expectations of the expositor. You may introduce the sermon in a variety of ways, such as a story, quote, a problem, a question, or with a multimedia presentation. The conclusion should summarize the sermon and lead into the response. The expositor should call the hearers to respond to the message with integrity. A variety of methods are possible for the response such as a verbal appeal, a physical relocation, a written response, multiple approach, question-and-answer, or using the Lord's Supper. After preparing the introduction and the conclusion, the expositor may choose to write out the sermon in manuscript form, or prepare a sermon brief, which highlights the key points within the sermon. After finishing the notes, the expositor should internalize the message and pray for God's help.

---

[9] Quoted in Stott, *Between Two Worlds*, 258.

STUDY OF 1–2 TIMOTHY

Study 2 Timothy 2:1–10. Sketch out how you might complete the following parts of the sermon, following the instructions in the brackets.

I. INTRODUCTION
   Opener: [*give a two-sentence introduction*]
   MPT: [*state what seems to be the main point of the text*]
   MPS: [*state what may be your main point of the sermon*]
   Title:
II. BODY [*sketch an outline that supports the MPS; include a two-sentence description of each functional element for each point*]
III. CONCLUSION
   Summation [*give a way to recap*]
   Response [*list the type of response that you may give*]

13

DELIVER THE WORD

*At the same time, pray also for us, that God may open to us a door for
the word, to declare the mystery of Christ, on account of which I am
in prison—that I may make it clear, which is how I ought to speak.*
                                        —Colossians 4:3–4 (ESV)

Exposition is not complete until the sermon is preached.
The preaching event culminates in the actual presentation
of the exposition.[1]
                                        —Jerry Vines and Jim Shaddix

THE PURPOSE OF THIS chapter is to discuss the issue of *style* and
persuasion. To do so, I want to point out several qualities that are
needed for preaching the Word clearly and winsomely. I am not
encouraging you to "perform" nor do something that is out of
character with your personality. If God wanted you to preach like
Billy Graham or Rick Warren, he would have called them and not
you to your particular church. We must be comfortable in our own
skin. Our aim is to present the Word authentically and passionately
in a way that connects with people. Bryan Chapell articulates this
well, saying:

---

[1] Jerry Vines and Jim Shaddix, *Power in the Pulpit* (Chicago, Moody, 1999), 313.

The preachers that are most respected are those most able to sound like themselves when they are deeply interested in a subject. Bombast and oratorical flourishes remind one of pulpit caricatures; they do not stimulate pastoral respect. At the same time, staid, unenthusiastic solemnity communicates irrelevant tedium rather than sincere seriousness. Congregations ask no more and expect no less of a preacher than *truth expressed in a manner consistent with the personality of the preacher and reflective of the import of the message.* . . . The heightening (not changing) of your normal speech is the most natural and effective way to communicate important matters.[2]

I personally find great freedom in this concept of doing exposition within my own personality. It took me a long time to discover this freedom because I wanted to imitate those who were legendary preachers.

The issue of delivery and style falls under the category of *rhetoric*, which is the classical name for speaking publicly. Rhetoric basically means the art of speaking effectively in order to influence or persuade others.[3] In ancient times, rhetoric was a chief discipline along with respected studies such as mathematics and science. Not only did leaders need to know how to speak clearly and winsomely, but the common citizen did as well. For instance, people defended themselves in court many times, and thus the practice of rhetoric had practical benefits for the common individual. Arranging a logical and convincing argument was necessary for such an event. Further, the ancients praised rhetoric. They loved to hear their favorite orators, as we love to watch our favorite movies or cheer for our favorite teams.

One of the first preaching books was Augustine's *On Christian Rhetoric.* Augustine's work reflected books such as Quintilian's *Institutes of Oratory* and Aristotle's *On Rhetoric.* Augustine talked about interpretive principles for preaching along with various styles that are suitable for particular subjects. He taught that the speaker should seek to *teach, please,* and *persuade.*[4] According to Augustine,

[2] Bryan Chapell, *Christ-Centered Preaching*, 2nd ed. (Grand Rapids: Baker, 2005), 329–30.
[3] Vines and Shaddix, *Power in the Pulpit*, 229.
[4] Augustine, *On Christian Doctrine*, trans. D. W. Robertson Jr. (Upper Saddle River, NJ: Prentice Hall, 1997), 143.

the manner of delivery should be related to the content that is being delivered. He wisely taught that the speaker should speak in a *grand manner* when trying to move reluctant people to action; he should speak in a *subdued manner* when attempting to teach; and he should speak in a *moderate manner* when praising something.[5]

Today rhetoric is typically known as public speaking or "communicating." Often expositors cringe at the thought of "improving their preaching with secular communication ideas." But there are several reasons to improve your speaking skills. Paul apparently knew the importance of effective communication. He asked the Colossian church to pray for him that he would proclaim the mystery of Christ *clearly* (Col 4:2–4). We want to be clear, not to impress, but so that the gospel may be understood. Clarity is a moral issue, not a stylistic issue. It is an eternal issue. We should want to be clear because of what is at stake!

In my view, biblical exposition is the greatest form of communication because it has superior content and power. It is important to remember that while we may not add to the power of the message with impressive speaking skills, because the power is in the Word and Spirit, we can hinder the power of the Word coming through us by poor, distracting speaking habits. Therefore, the purpose of talking about style and persuasion is to think about some practices to avoid and some practices to consider so that the Word will go forth unhindered. It is good and right to desire both *faithfulness* (to the Word) and *effectiveness* (in delivery). Together, they lead to *fruitfulness* in our expositional ministry.

In today's post-everything world, people bristle at the idea of "persuasion" because to them it smacks of authority, arrogance, and manipulation. But we should not avoid persuasion because it is a necessary component in preaching. We are not manipulators, but we are contenders for the faith (Jude 1:3). It is okay to persuade someone about the truth. Granted, the Holy Spirit is the ultimate and decisive persuader; however, this should not prevent us from attempting to give sound reasons for belief in the gospel, as Paul himself did in the synagogues and marketplaces (Acts 17:1–4; 18:4). What Paul avoided was the showboat oratory of his day (1 Cor 2:1–5); but make no mistake, he desired to speak clearly and convincingly.

---

[5] Ibid.

PREACHING STYLE

The Spirit of God works through preachers and teachers who use various delivery styles. Just look at the prophets! They had unique backgrounds and unique ways of communicating the truth. When it comes to expressing your thoughts (style), choose a manner that fits who you are. Just remember to work at improving different elements of your style in order to avoid distractions and confusion.

What to Avoid

In Martin Luther's *Table Talk,* a collection of sayings and teachings from the Reformer, the editors noted Luther's ten points of a good preacher:

1. Be able to teach so that people can follow you.
2. Have a good sense of humor.
3. Be able to speak well.
4. Have a good voice.
5. Have a good memory.
6. Know when to stop.
7. Be sure of one's doctrine.
8. Be ready to venture body and blood, wealth and honor, for the word of God.
9. Suffer oneself to be mocked and jeered at by all.
10. Be ready to accept patiently the fact that nothing is seen more quickly in preachers than their faults.[6]

These ten points were probably spoken off the top of Luther's head while having a German beverage. So we should not think of these points comprising everything that Luther thought about preaching! However, these communication principles are still relevant. I love to reflect upon them. While the post-everything world that we live in is different than Luther's period, and calls for cultural contextualization (see next chapter), the principles for communication are not much different. These ten points are useful for thinking about speaking habits.

One timeless problem in preaching is *verbosity*. Preachers have a tendency to waste words and say more than what is necessary. Verbosity then leads to weariness and possibly snoring! In your sermon preparation time, work at cutting out unnecessary

---

[6] Quoted in Fred W. Meuser, *Luther the Preacher* (Minneapolis: Augsburg, 1983), 40.

material. Avoid talking way past your point. Make every word count. Remember Luther's point 6: "Know when to stop." In another list of preaching skills, Luther said that the preacher should "Stand up, speak up, and shut up."[7]

Dullness is another problem with communication. After preparing a sermon, I often think about how I can make it *dance*! Without going overboard into showmanship, think about how to express it in a livelier manner. Effective teachers maintain personality and variety. Luther said that we should have a "ready wit" or "a sense of humor." Learn how to read the audience and add some verbal spice when needed. Never bore anyone with the Bible.

A third danger is the *absence of rhythm and pace*. Young speakers have the tendency to speak in a rough and choppy manner. Work at developing a smooth pace and cadence that is easy for the hearers to follow. Luther called this "Be able to speak well." It is okay to practice your speaking skills. Just as writers have to work at developing their craft, speakers should do the same. Again, our goal is not to wow the audience; it is to communicate clearly.

A final problem is termed *circumlocution*. This mistake involves "saying many words but never really saying what you intend to say."[8] We must say what we mean. Think about what you are going to say and clearly state it. Politicians may be ambiguous in order to avoid stating their position, but as preachers, our job is to deliver God's message clearly and let the chips fall where they may.

What to Pursue

Simplicity and *clarity* are essential for expounding the Word effectively. If the children and the adults can understand the message (assuming that it is worth understanding), then you have achieved much as a communicator. Simplicity means that you use short words, few words, clear words, and plain words. It does not mean that you should avoid theological words, however. It means that when you use "propitiation," you should explain what it means so that everyone can understand it. You do not score any points for ambiguity. Be specific in your terminology.

Luther and the Puritans advocated a plain and simple style. Luther, who preached numerous times a week, said:

---

[7] Ibid.
[8] Vines and Shaddix, *Power in the Pulpit*, 232.

To preach plain and simple is a great art: Christ himself talks of tilling ground, of mustard seed, etc.; he uses altogether homely and simple similitudes. Cursed are all preachers that in the church aim at high and hard things, and neglecting the saving health of the poor unlearned people, seek their own honor and praise. . . . When I preach, I sink myself deep down. I regard neither Doctors or Magistrates, of whom, are here in this church above forty; but I have my eye to the multitude of young people, children, and servants, of whom are more than 2,000. I preach to those.[9]

Luther was also not one to quote Hebrew and Greek words from the pulpit but instead explained them in understandable language. He preached doctrine, of course, but he understood that you preach doctrine *to people*. Calvin also advocated a simple approach, saying, "I have not corrupted one single passage of Scripture, nor twisted it as far as I know. . . . I have always studied to be simple."[10]

Puritan William Perkins, whose preaching text influenced thousands of preachers such as Jonathan Edwards, stated that effective preaching involves reading the text clearly, explaining the meaning of the text, gathering some profitable points from the natural sense of the passage, and then applying the doctrines in "a straightforward, plain speech."[11] Again, plain speech does not mean boring or dull speech. It means to speak directly, clearly, and unmistakably.

Next, we should preach the Word with *Spirit-empowered boldness*. Consider the bold preaching of the early Christian preachers:

- "Now when they saw the boldness of Peter and John, and perceived that they were uneducated, common men, they were astonished. And they recognized that they had been with Jesus" (Acts 4:13 ESV).
- "And when they had prayed, the place in which they were gathered together was shaken, and they were all filled with the Holy Spirit and continued to speak the word of God with boldness" (Acts 4:31 ESV).

---

[9] Martin Luther, *The Table Talk of Martin Luther*, ed. Thomas S. Kepler (Grand Rapids: Baker, 1979), 253–54.

[10] John Calvin cited in John Stott, *Between Two Worlds* (Grand Rapids: Eerdmans, 1982), 128.

[11] William Perkins, *The Art of Prophesying*, rev. Sinclair Ferguson, repr. (Carlisle, PA: Banner of Truth Trust, 1996), 79.

- "So he went in and out among them at Jerusalem, preaching boldly in the name of the Lord" (Acts 9:28 ESV).
- "So they remained for a long time, speaking boldly for the Lord, who bore witness to the word of his grace, granting signs and wonders to be done by their hands" (Acts 14:3 ESV).
- "And he entered the synagogue and for three months spoke boldly, reasoning and persuading them about the kingdom of God" (Acts 19:8 ESV).
- "For the king knows about these things, and to him I speak boldly. For I am persuaded that none of these things has escaped his notice, for this has not been done in a corner" (Acts 26:26 ESV).
- "[Paul was] proclaiming the kingdom of God and teaching about the Lord Jesus Christ with all boldness and without hindrance" (Acts 28:31 ESV).
- "But though we had already suffered and been shamefully treated at Philippi, as you know, we had boldness in our God to declare to you the gospel of God in the midst of much conflict" (1 Thess 2:2 ESV).
- "And [pray] also for me, that words may be given to me in opening my mouth boldly to proclaim the mystery of the gospel, for which I am an ambassador in chains, that I may declare it boldly, as I ought to speak" (Eph 6:19–20 ESV).

Boldness is a mark of the Spirit. The early Christians prayed for boldness instead of the removal of persecution. Paul requested prayer not only for preaching clarity (Col 4:4) but also for holy boldness (Eph 6:18–20). We too should seek the fullness of the Spirit that we might proclaim the riches of Christ with boldness.

A third quality for powerful proclamation, which we will examine in the next chapter, is *contextualization*. By this, I mean making the gospel clear and engaging to particular people groups. We should not forget that preaching has a missional edge to it. We speak to different audiences in an attempt to make disciples of "all nations" (*panta ta ethne*, Matt 28:18–20). Of course, in today's global world, contextualization is needed across the street as much as it is needed across the seas. We should learn, like Paul, how to speak with cultural sensitivity to different groups of people in order that we may win some to Christ (1 Cor 9:23). When Paul spoke to the Jewish audience, he began with the Scriptures, and when he spoke

CHRIST-CENTERED EXPOSITOR

to the Greeks, he referenced their philosophers. With both audiences, he preached the resurrected Christ (Acts 17:3–5, 22–34).

Next, we should preach the Word with *variety*. We should assume various roles as preachers: warning like a prophet, teaching like a theologian, proclaiming like an evangelist, and applying wisdom like a sage (Col 1:28–29 ESV). Variety also means *holding the ear*. Some of the ways to keep listeners attentive include *rate* (maintain an appropriate speed), *pace* (have a consistent flow), *volume* (remember the whole audience), *stress* (emphasize the point), *pitch* (find your own), *inflection* (reflect what you want to say by how you say it), and *pauses* (speak with purposeful silence). Most of these qualities are obvious. I find, however, that few actually think about the purpose of the "pause." Pauses permit variety in our voices. They help us slow down. They keep us from going into the nervous realm, leaving us sounding as if we have not reached puberty. The pause naturally allows us to transition to the next point. They also allow listeners to think about heavy subject matter.[12] So before preaching the message, read through your notes and think about your pace and pauses.

Additionally, we should preach the Word *with body language and passion*. Lloyd-Jones, who described preaching as "theology on fire," once said that he heard a pastor preach on the prophet Jeremiah. He was talking about the fire that was in the prophet's bones. But Lloyd-Jones remarked, "The good man was talking about fire as if he were sitting on an iceberg."[13] We must never do explosion without passion. I agree with Lloyd-Jones that a "dull preacher" is a "contradiction of terms."[14]

While various surveys show different results about the importance of body language, everyone knows that we communicate a lot through our mannerisms. For this reason we should attempt to improve particular features about our body language. Eye contact is always quite important. If you use notes, work at using them by glancing occasionally at them. The challenge is to preach with notes *without* anyone noticing too much. Also think about your gestures. What are your hands saying to people? Avoid any distracting hand gestures, such as rattling your keys. Think about your facial

---

[12] See Vines and Shaddix, *Power in the Pulpit*, 321–22.
[13] D. Martyn Lloyd-Jones, *Preaching and Preachers* (Grand Rapids: Zondervan, 1971), 88.
[14] Ibid., 87.

expressions. Some researchers estimate that you have twenty thousand possible facial expressions.[15] Some guys that I watch preach seem as if they are always mad. I sometimes think, *Must you always preach on the love of God with a tight fist and an angry look?*

Posture is also something to check on for effective use of body language. The way you enter the pulpit, stand in it, and walk around it communicates. Stay relaxed yet confident, humble yet bold, casual yet serious. Stay away from swaying side to side, which results from nerves. Allow a friend or your spouse to help you maintain a posture that is not noticed because it is natural and non-distracting.

Next, *pursue a natural, conversational tone like you would normally speak to another person.* Even though public speaking requires the *heightening* of your normal conversational pattern, it should not be something that is totally out of character with your personality. Prepare the sermon in an oral form instead of in the form of a research paper. Keep in mind the previously mentioned ideas, but do not forget to be yourself and remember that you are preaching to human beings. A conversational tone does not mean that you speak without passion, of course. Even in a one-on-one conversation, you still speak with emphasis, passion, and variety. You can put someone to sleep in a conversation one on one or with a large group! Do not transform into a different species when you preach. Speak clearly and relationally, as a pastor who loves his people.

A final matter for us to consider in speaking effectively is *humor.* Presumably, evangelical preachers agree upon most of what I have said to this point. However, different views exist on the place of humor in the preaching event. I have heroes on both sides. On the one hand, Jonathan Edwards refrained from humor entirely. He said, "Resolved, never to speak anything that is sportive or a matter of laughter on the Lord's Day."[16] Spurgeon, on the other hand, reportedly told a lady who criticized him for using humor, "If you knew how much I held back you would not criticize me."

Surely there is a place for humor in preaching. Jesus used humor. Elton Trueblood pointed this out in *The Humor of Christ.* Jesus's form of humor was not knock-knock jokes or dugout humor, however. He used irony and sarcasm to make points. His description

---

[15] Loren Reid, *Speaking Well* (New York: McGraw-Hill, 1977), 243.
[16] Jonathan Edwards, *Resolutions,* ed. Stephen J. Nichols (Philipsburg, NJ: P&R, 2001), 21–22.

of those who "strain out a gnat but swallow a camel" (Matt 23:24) is funny and pointed. He talked about someone having a "log in their eye" to describe hypocrisy. Regarding Jesus's humor John Stott said, "It seems to be generally agreed that humor was one of the weapons in the armory of the Master Teacher."[17]

The misconception about humor is that it *only* consists of a *joke* or something that causes someone to *laugh*. Jokes, however, are only *one* of many forms of humor. In fact, not all humor makes you laugh. Some types of humor include anecdotes, witticisms, satire, hyperbole, irony, quips, examples, parables, sarcasm, sanctified imagination, understatement, metaphor, anticlimax, fables, mispronunciation, puns, or spoonerism (e.g., "tips of the slung!").

The type of humor that faithful preachers should avoid is humor that comes across in a way that communicates, "What I am saying is not very important." This approach communicates levity and flippancy. It is pointless humor. This includes opening jokes that serve no purpose to the sermon. Do not misuse humor with unrelated jokes. Throw them away. Spurgeon said, "Cheerfulness is one thing, and frivolity is another; he is a wise man who by a serious happiness of conversation steers between the dark rocks of moroseness, and the quicksands of levity."[18] In other words, let humor come naturally out of a cheerful heart. Avoid overusing humor and going outside your natural ability. If you are not funny, do not try to be. Maintain your personality.

The type of humor that communicates and instructs is "intelligent humor." By this, I mean irony, wit, sarcasm, an original metaphor, or exaggeration. I think this is what Luther had in mind when he said, "A good preacher needs a good sense of humor." I do not think the Reformer was reading joke books before he preached. He simply used his personality to relate the message.

Humor is a great tool for driving home a point. When you have the audience's attention, stick the truth to them. Humor also disarms people in tense situations. I find it useful for meetings that are stuffy. Humor may also break down barriers and serve as a commercial. I think guys who use humor effectively place it at appropriate points to maintain attention. Use different forms at different places

---

[17] John Stott, *Between Two Worlds* (Grand Rapids: Eerdmans, 1982), 287.
[18] Charles Spurgeon, *Lectures to My Students*, repr. (Grand Rapids: Zondervan, 1954), 151.

along the way, and it will assist in both holding attention and making points.

Communication Aids

In addition to our oral communication, other components may help us deliver the message to our people. You will have to develop your own philosophy on some of these nonverbal elements. I want to present the following communication ideas as questions for you to consider because I myself struggle with the need for some of them. I think the key is for you to consider your context, your personality, and the rationale for the following ideas.

Are your aesthetics at the church helping or hindering your message? Today we have a lot of debate over whether to have a pulpit. What is communicated if you do not have one? What is appropriate for your congregation and setting? Surely there are times when you will have to preach without a pulpit, such as on mission fields and other alternative locations. What about week by week in the local church?

While I use a table or pulpit normally, I do not think that guys who do not have a pulpit believe less in the authority of Scripture. Many preachers have pulpits but no exposition! Others have no pulpits and treat God's Word responsibly. I encourage men to do one primary thing: make the Word of God visible. I like to leave my Bible in my hand when I preach without a pulpit. Let people know where your message is coming from.

A related question has to do with your stage. What is your platform communicating? Could you communicate the message better with a thematic stage development? Do you have artistic people in your church to emphasize the truth that you are preaching? I think there is some benefit to incorporating these elements, as long as it is excellent. Some stage developments are cheesy. If you cannot do it well, then I suggest letting it go.

Another question to consider concerns the use of multimedia. Does your PowerPoint (or an equivalent) hinder or help the message? Some studies have shown that too many notes take away from the retention of the message. I think multimedia is great for pictures, charts, or other images. Too many notes on the screen may distract people and distort the message. Others argue that the use of such tools makes the sermon feel more like a classroom and prefer to use it for alternative purposes. You will have to wrestle with this issue. Of course, it is not a necessity.

One nonnegotiable communication aid is sound reinforcement. Do you have adequate sound quality? If I were to start a church, I probably would invest in a great system before making other large expenditures. Make sure your people can hear, and you are not losing your vocal chords. We do not have a job if we do not have a voice!

To really throw a firecracker in the crowd of church people, bring up the philosophy of clothing. It really is amusing to think about the ranges of clothing in today's church. What should you wear when you preach? A priestly collar? A robe? A Hawaiian shirt? A suit? A golf shirt? A collared shirt? A pair of jeans with flip-flops? Well, this is not an easy answer. Pastoral wisdom and discernment are quite important on this matter. Your attire does communicate, so it is not irrelevant. But much of it is personality, culture, and preference. I would not push the envelope on this matter when you go to a new church just because you are a young, hip, cool guy. I would think contextually and respectfully. What is appropriate for your setting? What does not distract from the message? Is it clean and modest? These are the questions that you should think about. Remember that your freedom in Christ should not be abused. Do not put a stumbling block in the way of the gospel.

PREACHING AND PERSUASION

A sermon is different from a lecture in that we are trying to persuade people to change. A lecture may sometimes only transfer information. Every sermon should have a goal. The text demands a response. These responses may differ, but there should always be a Christ-centered response. So how do you persuade the hearers?

We should always begin by knowing the truth that we are talking about. We are not trying to persuade someone to do something that is not rooted in Scripture. The Pharisees were known for adding extrabiblical rules to religion and putting unnecessary burdens on people. We are not Pharisees. We are truth tellers. Therefore, it is imperative that we call people to act on the truth, nothing but the truth, so help us God.

Furthermore, we must give the entire truth to people. A gospel without the problem of sin is no gospel at all. We must take truth to the problem, showing Christ as the great solution. Biblical integrity demands that we give the entire story. Manipulation occurs when we do not give the whole story. We must avoid this at all times.

Aristotle provided a useful way for analyzing persuasive messages. He listed three essentials: *logos, pathos,* and *ethos.* Logos refers to the logic and the content of the sermon, which is the gospel contained in the Scriptures. Pathos refers to the emotion or passion of the sermon that the speaker relates to the hearers. Effective preachers display intensity and communicate importance. Ethos means the character and credibility of the speaker. A preacher should persuade with his life and his message.

Great preachers employ each of these three classical elements. In fact, Paul referred to them (though he did not mention them precisely) saying, "For we know, brothers loved by God, that he has chosen you, because our *gospel* came to you not only in *word,* but also in *power* and in the Holy Spirit and with full *conviction.* You know *what kind of men we proved to be* among you for your sake" (1 Thess 1:4–5 ESV, my emphasis). Notice that the logos feature is the "gospel" and the "word." Pathos is implied in the phrase, "power in the Holy Spirit and with full conviction." Ethos is described in the last sentence as Paul described his proven character.

Logos

Logos is central to our task. We must proclaim the Word of God and Jesus as the Word, and we must do so clearly. After you understand your biblical faithful message, work at organizing it logically. Think about how the parts are related. Lead the people to see the relationship between the parts and call for a response. While God can and does work through poorly arranged material, we should accept our responsibility of showing the hearers how the sermon is brought to bear on their lives in a logical and reasonable way.

Rehearsing your sermon mentally or vocally will help you think through the movement of the sermon. It will also help you preach without notes or with little need for them. Effective transitional statements are important in this process, as well. Allow the hearers to follow you as you build to a climax. Think about a bottom-line question as you conclude.

A final word about logos is that we should always believe in our subject. Preach because you have something to say, not because you have to say something. Pore over your notes before you preach until you believe that your message is vitally important.

Pathos

I have mentioned pathos throughout this book. Pathos is critical because your hearers are not only listening to the subject; they are also listening to how you say it. Do you love what you are talking about? Do you believe in what you are talking about? Do you have a burden for the people for whom you are preaching?

Pathos is expressed in different ways such as volume, intensity, tears, sincerity, and concern. The prophets and the apostles preached with various forms of pathos. To preach without conviction and emotion communicates that your message is not that important. I pray for God to grant me deeper pathos every week. The simple gospel preached with passion changes lives. Ask God to do for you as he did for Paul in preaching the gospel with the Spirit's power and in full conviction. Do you burn on Sundays with fire? Envision your hearers coming with wet wood, asking you to take your torch and set their wood on fire. Only Spirit-wrought passion can do this.

Ethos

Paul mentioned that his hearers knew how he lived among them. In other words, his walk matched his talk. I cannot emphasize enough the need to maintain credibility as a preacher. I recently asked some students in a doctoral seminar which of these three Aristotelian categories are missing and most needed in preaching today. They all answered, "ethos." I concur. I am afraid that we have a lot of young people who look up at the preacher and do not disagree with his message, but they do dislike or distrust the messenger. If you preach solid messages but act like a jerk, you are hindering your persuasiveness and dishonoring God. Our lives must display holiness, honestly, humility, love, and deep affection for people.

The Bible is full of references that deal with ethos. For example, Paul constantly defended his lifestyle. To the Thessalonians he said, "But we were gentle among you, like a nursing mother taking care of her own children. So, being affectionately desirous of you, we were ready to share with you not only the gospel of God *but also our own selves*, because you had become very dear to us" (1 Thess 2:7–8 ESV, my emphasis). To Titus he said, "Show yourself in all respects to be *a model of good works*, and in your teaching show integrity, dignity" (Titus 2:7 ESV, my emphasis). To the Corinthians he said, "We put no obstacle in anyone's way, so that no fault may be found with our ministry, but as servants of God *we commend ourselves in every way*: by great endurance, in afflictions, hardships, calamities" (2 Cor 6:3–4 ESV, my emphasis). We too must preach the gospel with our lives.

So, cultivate holiness, a big heart for people, and a profound sense of humility. Haddon Robinson rightly said, "The audience does not hear a sermon, they hear a person—they hear you."[19] There is no place for us to hide. It is a painful reality. Pray for God's grace that people would hear a man with tremendous ethos.

In addition to your spiritual life, think about other factors such as your body. Yes, I mean your physical body. I heard about one professor who once scolded a seminary student because he was overweight. He told him that he would have to drop fifty pounds before anyone listened to him! While I know that many great preachers are overweight, and much of our bodies are due to poor inheritance, it does not go unnoticed by the hearers. I do not want to be harsh about this matter, or overemphasize its importance, but I do want to challenge you to think about the totality of your life. What are you saying without words?

The fact is more ministers are dismissed from congregations because of their lifestyle and relationship qualities than by the content of their sermons. Be likeable, transparent, believable, and authentic. When you play golf with members, check your temper. Do not argue with umpires at church league softball. Respond to critics with grace! In all things, reflect Jesus by the power of the Spirit. Embody the grace that you preach about.

SUMMATION

While all preachers will preach differently because of their personalities, there are some stylistic qualities to avoid and qualities to pursue. Avoid verbosity, dullness, absence of rhythm and pace, and circumlocution. Pursue the right volume, variety, contextualization, simplicity and clarity, boldness, passion and body language, and humor (if appropriate). Think also about helpful communication

[19] Haddon Robinson, *Biblical Preaching*, 2nd ed. (Grand Rapids: Baker, 2001), 25–26.

aids. Regarding persuasion, try to cultivate a striking balance of logos, pathos, and ethos so that the hearers may respond to the message positively.

QUESTIONS

1. What are Luther's ten points of a good preacher?
2. On the issue of style, what should preachers avoid?
3. On the issue of style, what should preachers pursue?
4. Explain your philosophy of humor in preaching and teaching.
5. What do *ethos, logos,* and *pathos* mean? What do they have to do with preaching?

14

CONTEXTUALIZE THE MESSAGE

I have become all things to all people, that by all means I might save
some. I do it all for the sake of the gospel, that I may share with them
in its blessings.

—1 Corinthians 9:22b–23 (ESV)

The prayer of many of us is that God would raise up a generation
of expository evangelists; preachers who understand biblical
exposition in missional terms; preachers whose hearts burst
with love for sinners; preachers who no longer dismiss biblical
exposition when they think of engaging culture; preachers
who no longer expound the Bible with disregard for the
unchurched people around them.[1]

—Zack Eswine

*C*ONTEXTUALIZATION HAS BECOME a bit of a buzzword that stirs up
much discussion and debate. I could simply call this chapter "How
to preach the Word both faithfully and effectively" because good
contextualization is simply about expounding the Word well within
a given context. Or, we could use John Stott's analogy of *bridge*
building to describe contextualization. Stott described how effective

---

[1] Zack Eswine, *Preaching to a Post-everything World* (Grand Rapids: Baker, 2008), 11–12.

bridge builders skillfully connect the biblical world to the contemporary world.

Many church planters whom I know already do a good job with the contemporary side of the bridge. They study culture. They have examples and stories to share about hip-hop culture, folk culture, pop culture, high culture, and youth culture. Most of my church planter friends are streetwise and savvy. They know how to speak in the language of the people and actually like to be around unbelievers.

But those who naturally "engage culture" need to constantly be reminded of the centrality of the gospel. The sad reality is, many who do this well often abandon the gospel.

Never abandon the gospel for the sake of being "engaging"! The gospel is of first importance, not our ability to "connect" with lost people. Besides this, we have abandoned contextualization if we abandon the gospel because what every group of people needs is Jesus. We have actually become irrelevant when we trade the gospel for something else.

Other pastors whom I know are really good with the gospel (the biblical world), but they have the personality of a brick wall. They have no real friendships outside the church, and they speak in Christianese, using the same tired clichés that the church has used for thirty years. They need to learn how to speak effectively to modern-day people, especially those with a non-Christian worldview.

The need to bridge build reminds me of the film *Gran Torino*, starring Clint Eastwood as Walt Kowalski.[2] Walt is a grumpy old widower—a blue-collar American living in Detroit (and owner of a sweet 1972 Gran Torino). His neighborhood is deteriorating, and social norms are not what they used to be. This bothers him. His family says Walt is stuck in the 1950s. Walt especially struggles to understand his next-door neighbors, who live totally within their ethnic Hmong community. Walt does not understand these Hmong people and has no interest in getting to know them. They feel the same way about Walt. Mutual incomprehension and animosity mark their relationship. What the two groups need is a communicator—a person who understands both parties, mediating between them. They need a *bridge builder*. In the movie, this is

---

[2] This illustration idea comes from Tim Keller, *Center Church* (Grand Rapids: Zondervan, 2012), 96.

what the teenage Hmong girl, Sue, becomes. As a bicultural girl, with streetwise skills, she is able to communicate effectively to both groups, and things change as a result of her efforts.

Preaching in the twenty-first century is challenging because a similar mutual incomprehension is taking place. The "old-fashioned Bible people" cannot understand why the newer generation has little regard for traditional beliefs. Meanwhile, the newer generation is perplexed by the rigidity of their old-fashioned predecessors. What is needed today perhaps more than ever are effective bridge builders.

The fact is, we all contextualize. We wear modern clothes, speak a particular language, use electricity, and benefit from many modern devices. The question is, are we contextualizing in a way that is both faithful to the gospel and effective in communication?

In order to think through these contextualization issues, let us work through three categories: *clarifications, foundations,* and *exhortations.*

CLARIFICATIONS

Let us begin with what I am not talking about when I refer to effective contextualization. I need to say these things because many have misconceptions about this issue. I am not talking about

- *Being hip.* Being cool is not the goal. Seeing people saved is the goal. This chapter is not an endorsement for skinny jeans or any other fashion trend.
- *Using foul language.* I am not advocating sin (Eph 5:4) nor encouraging adolescent behavior.
- *Using a table instead of a pulpit.* I want you to use a Bible above all.
- *Compromising the message.* This is not an option.
- *Fitting in with the sinful patterns of the world.* I am not encouraging you to change your view on marriage, gender, creation, or any other historic Christian belief.

When we talk about contextualization in the world of preaching, we are not talking about it exactly the same way that other disciplines talk about it either. While we share a lot in common with missiologists, and we must do the work of missiologists, they often talk about contextualization to describe the challenge of communicating the gospel across cultures within various ethnic groups. They have to address issues such as how do you translate "snow" for those who have never seen snow? How do you talk about different colors (Isa 1:18) when some cultures only have four basic colors or only speak of things being either shiny or dull? The Zulu people have 120 words for "walking," so how do you describe the walk to Emmaus or Jesus walking on water?[3] We share much of their struggle but not in these extreme linguistic ways. Our challenge involves crossing theological barriers rather than dialect barriers.

Church planters and pastors often talk about contextualization more in regard to ministries than in preaching. They try to understand the city were they reside and develop ministries to engage particular groups. For some churches, an outreach to prostitutes makes a lot of sense but maybe not for a church in the suburbs.

In the world of preaching, contextualization has to do with *audience sensitivity*. This sensitivity does not mean watering down the message. It means getting to know the idols of our people and learning to deconstruct them. It means showing people the relevance of the gospel. We do not make the gospel relevant; we show people why and how it is relevant. And we can only do this well if we understand their hopes, fears, dreams, and idols.

My friend Steve Timmis reminds us that to contextualize the message involves *establishing a point of contact with people and a point of conflict with them*. He says, "In every situation, there needs to be a point of contact with the people (understand their values, history, communication style) and a point of conflict that reveals how their own narrative conflicts with that of the Gospel. It is impossible to be 'context-neutral' so we need to be context savvy. While we can't be indifferent to culture, we also can't be enslaved by it because that will cause us to be blind to the point of conflict."[4] Effective expository evangelists establish this point of contact (by understanding the culture), but they also faithfully reveal the conflict (understanding the nature of the gospel). They show the hearer how their worldview is colliding with the gospel.

[3] David Sills, "Reclaiming Contextualization," accessed February 26, 2015, http://david-sills.blogspot.com/2009/05/reclaiming-contextualization.html.

[4] Steve Timmis, "How to Plant a Church," accessed February 26, 2015, http://www.acts29network.org/acts-29-blog/how-to-plant-a-church-five-principles-from-steve-timmis/.

FOUNDATIONS

To help us think in some biblical categories, let us consider some biblical *examples* of contextualization and a few biblical *applications.*

Biblical Examples

Where do we see both faithfulness and effectiveness displayed? The most cited text on this matter is probably in *1 Corinthians 9*, where we read the following:

> But I have made no use of any of these rights, nor am I writing these things to secure any such provision. For I would rather die than have anyone deprive me of my ground for boasting. For if I preach the gospel, that gives me no ground for boasting. For necessity is laid upon me. Woe to me if I do not preach the gospel! For if I do this of my own will, I have a reward, but if not of my own will, I am still entrusted with a stewardship. What then is my reward? That in my preaching I may present the gospel free of charge, so as not to make full use of my right in the gospel.
>
> For though I am free from all, I have made myself a servant to all, that I might win more of them. To the Jews I became as a Jew, in order to win Jews. To those under the law I became as one under the law (though not being myself under the law) that I might win those under the law. To those outside the law I became as one outside the law (not being outside the law of God but under the law of Christ) that I might win those outside the law. To the weak I became weak, that I might win the weak. I have become all things to all people, that by all means I might save some. I do it all for the sake of the gospel, that I may share with them in its blessings.
>
> Do you not know that in a race all the runners run, but only one receives the prize? So run that you may obtain it. Every athlete exercises self-control in all things. They do it to receive a perishable wreath, but we an imperishable. So I do not run aimlessly; I do not box as one beating the air. But I discipline my body and keep it under control, lest after preaching to others I myself should be disqualified. (1 Cor 9:15–27 ESV)

What has always struck me about this passage is not Paul's flexibility in "becoming all things to all people"; it is actually his *inflexibility* when it comes to preaching the gospel. Notice how many times Paul says something about "preaching" and "the gospel" in this famous contextualization passage. His emphasis on proclamation precedes and rises above his emphasis on adaptability.

Something else that is striking is that Paul follows his statement about cultural sensitivity with one of the strongest statements about *self-control* and *discipline* in the New Testament (9:24–27). Clearly, Paul did not see contextualization as a "license to sin." He ruthlessly sought to kill sin because he knew what was at stake.

With those two guardrails in place (not abandoning the gospel and not forsaking holiness), we can grasp and admire what Paul says about audience sensitivity and ministry flexibility. It is clear that Paul was not unaware of various cultures, theologies, social norms, and customs. He did not approach each group the same way. New Testament scholar Craig Blomberg applies this text saying,

> In light of verses 19–23, it is hard to justify the prevailing patterns of evangelism by formula: using identical tracts, sets of questions, or prepackaged approaches on everyone with whom we want to share Christ. Paul's model far more closely approximates "friendship evangelism"—coming alongside and getting to know unbelievers, valuing them as God's creation in his image in and of themselves, and not just as potential objects of conversions. Then as we become familiar with each person's unique hopes and fears, we may contextualize the gospel in such a way as to speak most directly to those concerns.[5]

Whether you care for the phrase "friendship evangelism" is of no consequence. The idea here, though, is quite important. Paul understood and valued people. We need to understand and value those whom we are addressing if we also desire effectiveness in exposition.

Paul's preaching in the *synagogues* and his preaching at *Mars Hill* also demonstrate audience sensitivity (see Acts 13:13–51 with 17:16–34). While Paul preached the same message (the resurrection!), his approach varied among Jews and non-Jews.

---

[5] Craig Blomberg, *1 Corinthians*, The NIV Application Commentary (Grand Rapids: Zondervan, 1994), 188.

Additionally, we see contextualization clearly in *the Epistles.* Every letter was practically written to address problems in particular churches. The writers of these epistles shared the same theology, but that theology was applied to different congregations.

The Gospels also highlight this same truth. Four Gospel writers describe the same basic narrative with differing emphasis determined by the audience. Matthew writes to a Jewish audience. So, when he traces the lineage of Jesus, he goes back to Abraham. Luke writes primarily to Gentiles. He traces the lineage of Jesus back to Adam. John writes to Greeks. He traces the lineage of Jesus back to Christ's preexistence. Mark writes to suffering Christians in Rome. He does not bother with a genealogy. He focuses on the Suffering Servant, immediately taking us to the cross. Matthew presents Jesus as the Jewish Messiah and King. Luke describes him as the Son of Man. John shows Jesus to be God in the flesh. Mark puts Jesus forward as the Suffering Servant. All four emphases are gloriously true and contextually fitting.

Within the Gospels, Jesus himself shows us the greatest picture of contextualization in *the incarnation.* He enters into a culture. He takes on customs. He takes up a language, and he communicated the words of life in ways that people understood. Praise God, Jesus contextualized the message! He helped us both see the good news and understand it.

Further, as Jesus prayed for his followers prior to the crucifixion, he prayed that we would follow his missional pattern of ministry: "I am not praying that You take them out of the world but that You protect them from the evil one. They are not of the world, as I am not of the world. Sanctify them by the truth; Your word is truth. *As You sent Me into the world, I also have sent them into the world*" (John 17:15–18, my emphasis). Jesus was a missionary. The Father sent him into the world, and he now sends us to follow his missionary way of life—to be separated from sin but not isolated from people. He has sent us with the sanctifying word to make disciples among the nations.

A final biblical example that I should mention is in *1 Corinthians 14.* As Paul takes up the issue of spiritual gifts in the corporate gathering, he insists that the worship experience be *intelligible* to everyone, including unbelievers (1 Cor 14:6–12; 16–17; 23–25). He wanted to make sure the message made sense, and that unbelievers would be drawn into the fellowship as they observed God's people worshipping and as they considered the gospel. We should desire this as well.

Biblical Applications

Three applications strike me as I look through these passages. *First, we should see contextualization as an act of love.* In 1 Corinthians 9, Paul says, "I have made myself *a servant* to all that I might win more of them" (v. 19, my emphasis). This sounds like Jesus, who humbled Himself, taking the form of a servant that people might be saved.

Every good parent contextualizes because every good parent loves each of their children. Good parents handle each child differently, without sacrificing inflexible values, out of love for the child. Every good coach knows that he has to treat players differently without giving up his core principles. And every good pastor-teacher will seek to make the message understandable to various types of people, if he truly loves them.

If you get lost in all of the philosophy of contextualization, come back to this point. If we love people the way Christ has loved us, then we will seek to establish this point of contact and point of conflict so that we might see all types of people saved.

Second, our identity must be firmly rooted in Christ, or else we will not address people from various cultures authentically or effectively. Why could Paul not make a big deal about Jewish and Gentile customs? It was because he was first and foremost a Christian! Those who take their political identity, national identity, racial identity, or economic identity as more important than their identity in Christ will never contextualize well. Jonah did not want to go to Nineveh because of his sinful prejudice. Perhaps you have something against the South or the North or against the Middle East. Will your ethnocentrism keep you from loving people and communicating the gospel effectively to them? Paul represented a different way. After citing his prized Jewish background in Philippians 3, he said it was "rubbish" compared to being found in Christ. It is good to value your city and your country, but do not let anything keep you from valuing your identity in the kingdom more! If you live with this kingdom-oriented, Christ-centered identity, you will be able to move in and out of cultures better and address your audience with sensitivity; and in so doing, you will actually be putting on display the unique beauty of the gospel as you demonstrate where your primary identity is found.

Finally, we should also seek the wisdom of God in order to be effective bridge builders. James tells us that God gives us wisdom when we ask for it (Jas 1:5). Trying to understand people in light of the gospel is often a challenge. It is a particular challenge when you preach in all sorts of settings. So pray that God will enable you to exegete your context so that you can faithfully exegete and apply the good news.

EXHORTATIONS

Therefore, let us strive to preach the gospel *faithfully* every week and preach the gospel *effectively* every week. We must be relentless in our commitment to make the gospel known, and we should also be mindful of our audience each time we stand up to deliver the Word.

Be Faithful

We must never overlook, assume, minimize, and/or replace the gospel with something else. Make the gospel *explicit.* Remember that it transcends cultures. Everyone needs it.

In 1 Corinthians 15, only a few chapters after his section on becoming all things to all men, Paul gives us a wonderful outline of the gospel, emphasizing this primary commitment in preaching.

> Now brothers, I want to clarify for you the gospel I proclaimed to you; you received it and have taken your stand on it. You are also saved by it, if you hold to the message I proclaimed to you—unless you believed for no purpose. For I passed on to you as most important what I also received: that Christ died for our sins according to the Scriptures, that He was buried, that He was raised on the third day according to the Scriptures, and that He appeared to Cephas, then to the Twelve. Then He appeared to over 500 brothers at one time; most of them are still alive, but some have fallen asleep. Then He appeared to James, then to all the apostles. Last of all, as to one abnormally born, He also appeared to me.
>
> For I am the least of the apostles, unworthy to be called an apostle, because I persecuted the church of God. But by God's grace I am what I am, and His grace toward me was not ineffective. However, I worked more than any of them, yet not I, but God's grace that was with me. Therefore,

whether it is I or they, so we proclaim and so you have
believed. (1 Cor 15:1–11)

Paul describes how the gospel is first *Christological.* Christ died,
was buried, and was raised (vv. 3–4). We are not preaching the gospel if we are not preaching Christ.

Second, he says the gospel is also *biblical.* Christ died for our sins
according to the Scriptures and was raised on the third day *according to
the Scriptures* (vv. 3–4). He preached this gospel from the Bible.

Third, we see that the gospel is *historical.* A real Jesus, a real
cross, a real tomb, and a real resurrection took place in human
history. Christ entered into this world through his incarnation, and
numerous people saw the resurrected Lord. We do not affirm "the
idea of Jesus" or the "idea of the resurrection" but the Jesus of history who lived among us and vacated a tomb bodily.

Fourth, the gospel is *doctrinal.* Christ did not merely die and
rise. He died *for our sins.* Christ dying and rising is historical; Christ
dying for our sins is doctrinal. We cannot abandon historical
Christian beliefs, such as the belief in substitutionary atonement.
For this is at the heart of Christianity, which gloriously teaches, in
contrast to other religions, that you get God's verdict *before* your performance, through faith in Christ. Do not abandon the best news
in the entire world; the very righteousness that God requires *from*
you is the very righteousness that God provides *for* you in Christ our
substitute (2 Cor 5:21). Some have not abandoned it theologically,
but they never say it publicly! They have substituted the substitute
with self-help and moralism. Reject this trend and make redeeming
love your central theme in your preaching. Fill your messages with
explanations of concepts such as sin, grace, repentance, propitiation, justification by faith alone, redemption, and personal and cosmic reconciliation.

Fifth, the gospel is *personal.* The gospel requires personal belief,
as Paul reminds us, "so we proclaim and so you have believed" (1
Cor 15:11). Individuals must respond to the good news with genuine, persevering faith (vv. 1–2). God has involved us in the process
of seeing people saved not because he needs us but because he
loves us. Faith comes by hearing and hearing through the Word of
God, and we get to be heralds who speak this good news to all kinds
of hearers (Rom 10:17). Marvel at this privilege and preach for the
glory of Christ and for the faith of your audience.

Sixth, the gospel is *practical.* Paul's words and testimony show us how the gospel does many wonderful things in our lives. The gospel makes us *humble.* Notice the humility in Paul's words: "I am unworthy to be called an apostle" (1 Cor 15:9). The gospel applied also leads to *hard work.* Paul can say, by God's grace, "I worked more than any of them" (v. 10b; see 15:58). Finally, the gospel maintains *unity* in the church. Gospel solidarity is woven throughout this text, and for the divided Corinthians, they desperately needed to be brought back to the center (see 1 Cor 1:10–17). As one scans this great chapter, and the rest of Corinthians, one observes how comprehensively practical the gospel really is. Paul addresses a variety of subjects but all of them in light of gospel ramifications. Keller says, "The gospel has supernatural versatility to address the particular hopes, fears, and idols of every culture and every person."[6] Do not abandoned this gospel in the name of contextualization because in that you are abandoning what every culture needs most—both for eternal salvation and for daily living.

Finally, the gospel is *doxological.* A true understanding of the gospel leads to praise. Paul gets to the end of this chapter, and he erupts into worship, saying:

Death is swallowed up in victory.
O death, where is your victory?
O death, where is your sting?
(1 Cor 15:54b–55 ESV)

He then cries out, "But thanks be to God who gives us the victory through our Lord Jesus Christ" (v. 57 ESV). How can we not praise the Savior? Our greatest problem has already been solved—and we did nothing to solve it! Christ accomplished it. And it is this vision that helps us see that our labor (in life and ministry) is not in vain (v. 58).

Faithfulness in the pulpit is all about *the main things, the plain things,* and the *same things.* Before plainly articulating the gospel (the main thing), Paul told the Philippians, "To write *the same things* to you is no trouble to me and is safe for you" (3:1). Repeating the gospel was no burden to Paul, and it was the best and safest thing for the Philippians to receive. Giving the gospel over and over was

---

[6] Keller, *Center Church,* 44.

an expression of Paul's love for the church; it was not the result of him lacking anything else to talk about. He made the main things the plain things because he loved them! Resolve to be a "same things" church and a "same things" preacher who plainly explains and reexplains the gospel to everyone.

Be Effective

Keller reminds us of the need to know our audience saying, "Sound contextualization shows people how the plotlines of the stories of their lives can only have a happy ending in Christ."[7] This implies that we need to be with others. We need to know the narratives of our culture and individuals. For we do not merely preach . . . we preach *to people.* As we listen and observe people, we will soon see some common challenges for contemporary preaching and teaching. Allow me to summarize some essentials for growing in effectiveness in the pulpit.

Expect different worldviews. Because we live in a melting pot of cultures, people will enter our gatherings with different theological and philosophical perspectives. Indeed, some think like postmoderns. They are skeptical of you when you open the Bible. They reject absolute truth claims. But I have met some classical modernists as well. They deny the reality of anything that they cannot see, taste, touch, or test. Premoderns are also present. They believe in unseen realities but do not understand the gospel. Therefore, we must not assume that everyone has a Christian worldview, that is, a belief in the one God who is Creator and Redeemer and one Mediator, Jesus Christ. Anticipate objections to your sermon in light of these views.

D. A. Carson challenges pastors to think like missionaries who aim to present the gospel to different cultures:

> The better seminaries have long included courses in the missions curriculum to help prospective missionaries "read" the culture they are about to enter. But such courses are rarely required of pastoral students in the pastoral track. The assumption is that these students are returning to their own culture, so they do not need such assistance. But the rising empirical pluralism and the pressures from globalization ensure that the assumption is usually misplaced . . . there is

---

[7] Ibid., 90.

a plethora of competing cultures in most Western nations, and many pastors will minister to several of them during their ministry.[8]

I concur. Most of us live in diverse settings, and in some places this cultural complexity is increasing rapidly. We cannot expect everyone to embrace our tertiary doctrines when they do not even embrace our primary doctrines. We have to explain some of our presuppositions and beliefs that were once assumed by the majority of the people entering Sunday gatherings because of the presence of differing worldviews. The more we know what they believe about these presuppositions, the better bridge builders we will become.

Assume biblical illiteracy. One of the advantages of studying *to be simple* (as Calvin put it) is that we will not assume that people know the Scriptures. The faithful expositor will assume that some of the listeners do not know who the prodigal son is or who the first Christian martyr was. Be mindful of these hearers. Tell them how to find a passage of Scripture. Explain the stories as if you were teaching to someone who lived on foreign soil and had no Bible. I get frustrated when I hear preachers say, "Now, you are familiar with the story of the Woman at the Well." Is everyone familiar with her? This practice communicates a lack of sensitivity toward the people who are biblically illiterate.

Further, the biblically knowledgeable people will benefit from this kind of sensitive exposition because it is refreshing to hear the message with childlike clarity. You also will demonstrate to the Christians how to explain the Bible to unbelievers. You do not have to be simplistic, only simple. You can go deep with unbelievers as long as you communicate the message carefully.

Preach the narrative of Scripture. One of the wonderful advantages of seeing the Bible as a coherent whole that points to Jesus as the hero, is that this understanding is practically useful when preaching to unbelievers. They need to understand the big picture. I regularly retell the story line of Scripture before I point the hearers to the particular text for the day because I want them to see where the selected text fits within the whole Bible. Helping people see how the Bible relates together also is important because the gospel is

---

[8] Quoted in Graham Johnston, *Preaching to a Postmodern World* (Grand Rapids: Baker, 2001), 10–11.

naturally woven into the message. Often at youth events I devote my first sermon at the event, or the introduction to my first sermon, entirely to an overview of the Bible. I find that many students respond to this positively. But I have also witnessed many mature believers also delighting in the breathtaking beauty of God's story of redemption.

Repeating the narrative of Scripture also responds to the postmodern idea that there is no "metanarrative" in life—that is, an overarching purpose to life and history. Perhaps some believe this because they have never been told the whole story. You can retell the biblical narrative in an introduction or within the body of the sermon as you explain the text.

Be redemptive. God gave us a gospel that transcends all of the competing worldviews and cultures. The gospel teaches people that they were made in the image of God, created for his glory, but because of sin have separated themselves from God and his purposes. But through the sinless, sin-bearing, and death-defeating Savior, we find salvation and hope. The Holy Spirit then indwells us and changes us. Preach the gospel every week! Make Jesus look glorious to the skeptic, the hedonist, or the atheist. The Spirit honors Christ and is able to break through the hardest of hearts and show them the way. And remember that believers also need to be reminded of who they are in Christ on a weekly basis.

This redemptive message should also be preached in a redemptive *manner.* Truth blended with grace is the pathway to the heart. Balance the art of playing the prophet and the priest, the sage and the evangelist.

Preach to your old self. Zack Eswine gives some great advice in *Preaching to a Post-everything World.* Eswine asks the great question, "Could I now reach who I once was?"[9] To those of us who were saved later in life, this is a great reminder that we were once the unmoved pagan and the skeptical cynic. How did you come to faith in Christ? What were your thoughts about church and preachers? What kind of worldview did you come with before you were converted?

To preach to your old self, you must remember that you are preaching to human beings, not other preachers or seminary students. Expand your target audience to include the person you used to be, not just the faithful saint who regularly serves in the church.

---

[9] Eswine, *Preaching to a Post-everything World,* 78.

Prepare your sermon and ask whether you would have understood this message before you were a Christian. Address the questions that you once had.

Furthermore, when you tell the congregation to find Leviticus, tell them that if they do not know where it is, that there was a time that you too did not know anything about the Bible, but in time they will learn.[10] Remind them that if they entered without a Bible that you are glad that they are there, and that they can have free copies. Be mindful of the presence of unbelievers. Treat outsiders as friends, not foes.

Utilize testimonies. Testimonies are one of the most powerful apologetics in the expositor's arsenal. I find it intriguing that Paul's testimony is reported so many times in Scripture. I am not suggesting that you replace the sermon with people's conversion stories (or your own) but, rather, that you integrate testimonies somehow in sermons. After presenting the testimony, "turn the mirror."[11] Let the hearers see themselves in light of the selected person's struggle and show them the same grace that he discovered. Capture imagination with stories of gospel transformation.

Keep listening, loving, and studying. The challenge of being faithful and effective is the journey of a lifetime. Let me encourage you to continue listening to our ever-changing world. Keep loving people enough to adapt where you can adapt. And keep studying this discipline. Keep meditating on biblical examples, like the apostle Paul. The apostle was a preacher, an evangelist, a missionary, an apologist, a contextualizer, a church planter, a mentor, a teacher, a prophet, and a Jesus-exalter. In his preaching he considered various worldviews as he presented the gospel. He also did not assume biblical knowledge when speaking to non-Jewish audiences. He preached redemptive sermons. He retold the narrative of Scripture. He referred to his old self and shared his conversion story constantly. He is a model for all of us.

SUMMATION

Preachers in every generation are bridge builders. While the gospel is unchanging and always relevant, we must connect with our

---

[10] Ibid., 85.
[11] Ibid., 93.

culture without conforming to the culture, and show them why and how the gospel is relevant. To be both faithful to the gospel and effective in communication, expositors need to establish a point of contact and a point of conflict with people. Building on the biblical foundations for contextualization, expository evangelists take up this challenge week by week. Some of the essentials for expositing the gospel in today's world include expecting different worldviews, assuming biblical cluelessness, being redemptive, preaching the story line of Scripture, and preaching to our old self and to keep learning, loving, and studying.

QUESTIONS

1. What does it mean to be an effective bridge builder?
2. Explain what *contextualization* in preaching involves.
3. List and briefly explain some passages to highlight the need to contextualize.
4. Why should we see contextualization as an act of love?
5. How can we be both faithful *and* effective?

CONCLUSION

Martin Luther preached his last sermon only three days before he died. He ended the sermon saying, "Much more could be said about this Gospel but I am too weak."[1]

What a gospel we have to preach! I want more than anything to go out like Luther, preaching the unsearchable riches of Christ. The work of exalting Christ from the Word will wear us out, but we can give our lives to nothing better than a lifetime of faithful exposition.

Luther's ministry truly was extraordinary. We praise God for those who are used in unusual ways to advance the gospel. But most faithful, Christ-centered expositors are unknown by most people. I pray for millions more of them. What we need is ten million "ordinary" pastors who love people and declare the Christ-centered Word faithfully, not ten more great conference speakers.

We need millions of faithful expositors who are willing to face persecution for rightly handling the Word of truth. Who knows how long we have in America before exposition is declared "hate speech"? May we handle God's Word faithfully as an act of worship to our great King, who vacated a tomb in the Middle East and occupies the throne in heaven. Apart from him we have no salvation, and by extension we have nothing to preach. But because of the Savior, let us rejoice if and when we face mockery, misrepresentation, threats, accusations, and even martyrdom. We are aligning

---

[1] Fred W. Meuser, *Luther the Preacher* (Minneapolis: Augsburg, 1983), 34.

ourselves with the faithful (Matt 5:10–12; Acts 5:41). We can rejoice when these trials come, not only now but even fifty billion years from now. We will look back on the hardships and consider it a small thing to suffer for his name.

There is much more gospel to preach. Let us keep exalting Christ until we see Christ.

A HISTORICAL SKETCH OF PREACHING

With its preaching Christianity stands or falls.[1]

—*P. T. Forsyth*

Preaching has always been the life-blood of the Christian church.[2]

—*David Larsen*

The fact that many preachers do not diligently study the history of preaching is a major reason for so many failures in the pulpit.[3]

—*G. Ray Jordan*

I HAD THE PRIVILEGE, AS a student and professor, to take part in the "Dead Preachers Society," an informal gathering of students who studied faithful preachers of the past. At our meetings, one of the students presented some gleanings from the life of a "dead preacher" whom God used in history. After about forty-five minutes of presentation and discussion, we spent the remainder of the time praying together. Our goal was both to learn from dead preachers and to be "dead preachers," dying to self and to this world.

The purpose of this little historical sketch is to introduce you to some representative "dead preachers" who continue to inspire and instruct us today. The follow list of preachers only scratches the surface of our rich heritage. Indeed, many preaching greats

---

[1] Quoted in Graeme Goldsworthy, *Preaching the Whole Bible as Christian Scripture* (Grand Rapids: Eerdmans, 2000), 31.

[2] David Larsen, *The Company of the Preachers* (Grand Rapids: Kregel, 1998), 14.

[3] G. Ray Jordan, *You Can Preach* (New York: Revell: 1951), 46.

are unknown to us (because of the lack of historical documentation, location, time, and our own biases and experiences). I simply want to highlight some key individuals and make some comments about those who have inspired me personally. As the next generation of preachers, it is important for us to remember the words of Hebrews 13:7: "Remember your leaders, those who spoke to you the word of God. Consider the outcome of their way of life, and imitate their faith" (ESV). While not all of the following preachers are exemplary to the same degree, they are all worthy of our attention. Perhaps you will find a few particularly interesting and seek to study them more on your own.

Charles Dargan, author of a classic work on the history of preaching, stated, "Christian preaching has its origin in ancient oratory, Hebrew prophecy, and the Christian gospel."[4] Hebrew prophecy, ancient rhetoric, and the gospel paved the way for the sermon as we know it today. Each of these foundations has been discussed in this book. The rest of church history demonstrates the incorporation of the three respectively.

Following the biblical period are four broad eras of preaching: (1) preaching among the Fathers and apologists (100–430), (2) preaching in the medieval period (430–1500), (3) preaching among the Reformers and Puritans (1500–1800), and (4) preaching in the evangelical age (1800–present). These (imperfect) classifications provide a reasonable way to reflect upon our heritage as evangelical preachers.

PREACHING AMONG THE FATHERS AND THE APOLOGISTS (100–430)

The early church fathers, who were often prominent bishops, generally preached simple homilies that retold the story of Christ. Preachers used Scripture throughout their sermons. Incidentally, these quotations show that the early church viewed the books of the New Testament as Holy Scripture. The peace of Rome provided a context for the freedom of preaching. Polycarp, Clement of Rome, Irenaeus, Papius, and Ignatius were among the early gospel preachers. Some of their letters remain today, but because of the lack of surviving sermons, little can be known about their preaching.

[4] E. C. Dargan, *A History of Preaching*, vol. 1 (Grand Rapids: Baker, 1954), 14.

More is known about the public ministry of the apologists. The leading Greek apologists included Justin (100–165), Clement of Alexandria (c. 160–c. 220), and Origen (185–254). These men were defenders of Christianity but not true expositors. Justin (Martyr) was more of a rhetorician and philosopher than a preacher. Nevertheless, he left us with an example of the importance of the preached Word in the public gatherings. He said:

> And on the day called Sunday, all who live in cities or in the country gathered together to one place, and the memoirs of the apostles or the writings of the prophets are read, as long as time permits; then, when the reader has ceased, the president verbally instructs, and exhorts to the imitation of these good things. Then we all rise together and pray, and, as we before said, when our prayer is ended, bread and wine and water are brought, and the president in like manner offers prayers and thanksgivings, according to his ability, and the people assent saying, Amen.[5]

Justin's description reminds us of the centrality of the Word in the corporate worship of the church.

Clement of Alexandria, a diligent student of the not-yet-canonized Scripture, was the first head of the Alexandrian school. One of the earliest sermons in existence is his homily on the wealthy in Mark 10:17–31. Origen could be labeled as an expositor, and he did create an interest in the biblical text, but he unfortunately employed the prevailing allegorical interpretation of the Scriptures of his day. We currently have many of his sermons.

The Latin apologists were also more controversialists, leaders, and writers than expositors. Many of the Latin apologists disdained the use of philosophy. A converted lawyer, Tertullian (150–220), gave us the term "sermon," and asked the famous question, "What does Athens [a center for philosophy] have to do with Jerusalem [a center for revelation]?" In *Apologeticus*, he defended Christianity in a time of Roman persecutions. Cyprian (200–258), who became bishop of Carthage in 248, followed after Tertullian as an orator and polemicist. He was also the first bishop to die as a martyr.

Preaching in the fourth and early part of the fifth centuries deserves great attention because of the rise of preaching in this

---

[5] Quoted in John Stott, *Between Two Worlds* (Grand Rapids: Eerdmans, 1982), 19.

period. Several factors contributed to this revival. Perhaps the greatest was Constantine's legalization of Christianity in the Western Empire in 313. The church gained a safe and respected standing in society. Further, the church recognized the canonical Scriptures. Doctrinal beliefs were clarified also with the labor of several theologians. In 325, Constantine held the First Council of Nicaea, held in Nicaea in Bithynia. Athanasius (296–372) won the day, arguing that Christ was the "same substance" as the Father, rather than "similar in substance" to the Father, as his opponent Arius was arguing. The majority of church leaders held to the deity of Christ. Athanasius reminds us of the importance of contending for the faith courageously in our day.

Gregory of Nazianzus (329–89) became a preacher of Constantinople when he was almost fifty years old. His fame as a theologian in the East gave him the nickname "Theologus." Basil the Great (d. 379), a friend of Gregory, helped found monastic institutions. Ambrose (340–97) was extolled in the West as a mighty orator. His works include commentaries and hymns. Most notably, he baptized Augustine on April 25, 387.

Two preachers in this period represent the apex of early preaching: Augustine in the West and John (Chrysostom) in the East. Augustine (354–430) began preaching at age thirty-six and later became bishop of Hippo. We presently have more than four hundred of his sermons, in addition to many of his classical theological works. His sermons could be called exegetical, but Augustine used allegorical interpretation too frequently to be labeled as a model of expository preaching.

Augustine wrote *De Doctrine Christianus* (*On Christian Doctrine*), which was the first influential homiletics book. He incorporated rhetorical and interpretive principles to discuss preaching. Augustine said, "There are two things necessary to the treatment of the Scriptures: a way of discovering those things which are to be understood, and a way of teaching what we have learned."[6] Preaching books today often follow this approach of combining the discipline of hermeneutics and homiletics. Young preachers should read all of Augustine's major works because of his theological reflection and personal devotion.

---

[6] Augustine, *On Christian Doctrine*, trans. D. W. Robertson Jr. (Upper Saddle River, NJ: Prentice Hall, 1958), 7.

John Chrysostom of Antioch (347–407), nicknamed "the golden mouth," stands as the premier patristic example for contemporary preachers. Chrysostom preached for twelve years in the Cathedral of Antioch before becoming bishop of Constantinople in 398. He wrote *On the Priesthood*, the first attempt at a book on preaching, but it dealt more with the pastor and his character. Chrysostom's sermons lasted for about an hour. We have more than seven hundred of his sermons today. He preached through books of the Bible normally, using faithful interpretative principles apart from allegory. Chrysostom also applied the text in a down-to-earth manner. In response to his popularity, Chrysostom exhorted his hearers to show their praise by obedience. Our prayer is the same today; namely, for our people to show their appreciation by obeying the commands of Jesus.

Preaching in the Medieval Period (430–1500)

After Rome fell in AD 476, drastic changes took place in the West, leading into the medieval period. The early part of the period is often referred to as the Dark Ages. War, arson, famines, plagues, unsafe travel, and the threat of vandals characterized this period. Politics, the arts, and education were in decline. Changes in culture, coupled with the changes in the church, such as the use of liturgies and the mass, deeply affected the state of preaching. James Stitzinger said, "The medieval period was perhaps the sparsest for expository preaching."[7] Consequently, the early part of the medieval period often is skipped in a cursory sketch of preaching history. However, before jumping to the pre-Reformers, it is important to take note of a few bright spots in this otherwise dark era.

Missionary preachers made a great impact in the early medieval period. Patrick (389–461) said that God called him to preach to the Irish in a dream. He planted many churches throughout Ireland. He stands as an inspirational example for contemporary church planters.

Missionaries came to England in 597. A Roman monk named Augustine (566–607) was an effective evangelist and missionary preacher who established the Roman church in England. He

---

[7] James Stitzinger, "The History of Expository Preaching," in John MacArthur Jr. and the Master's Seminary Faculty, *Rediscovering Expository Preaching* (Dallas: Word, 1992), 45.

founded the church in Canterbury and became the first arch-bishop there.[8]

Boniface (675–754) was an effective missionary preacher in Germany. He was slain later on a trip to the Netherlands by the very people he was trying to reach. Despite the efforts of some of these missionary preachers, the sermon basically was abandoned except for the "postils," a brief address offered at the end of mass.[9]

Preaching became a rallying point for the Crusaders in the latter part of the medieval period. Until the eleventh century, the Moslems controlled Jerusalem but still allowed pilgrimages. But when the Turks took over, they began to persecute Christians. In the effort to fight back and seize control of the city, preaching became a primary weapon. Peter the Hermit (1050–1115) and Bernard of Clairvaux (1091–1153) were among the leaders. Clairvaux, who had mastered techniques of sermon preparation, was probably the most influential during this period.

In the late medieval period, preaching among the Mendicant Orders, or "the preaching friars," impacted society. Francis of Assisi (1182–1226) wed poverty to preaching and insisted that the two must go together. His contemporary, Dominic (1170–1221), also placed a great emphasis on preaching. Following this time frame, a Dominican friar, Thomas Aquinas (1225–74), became the period's most influential theologian and one of the greatest philosophical minds in history.

The Age of Renaissance followed the medieval period and paved the way for the Reformation. Among the pre-Reformers in this era were Englishman John Wycliffe (1320–84), Bohemian John Huss (1369–1415), and an Italian Dominican, Girolamo Savonarola (1452–98). Wycliffe elevated preaching over the Eucharist. His passion to preach in the vernacular of the people and to put the Bible in the mother tongue changed history. He is known today as the "Morning Star" of the Reformation. Wycliffe said, "The high-est service that men may attain to on earth is to preach the Word of God."[10] Wycliffe is worthy of imitation in light of his desire to preach the Word in the language of the people, at great costs.

---

[8] Dewitte T. Holland, *The Preaching Tradition* (Nashville: Abingdon, 1980), 32.
[9] Ibid., 33.
[10] Stott, *Between Two Worlds*, 22.

Later, the humanist Erasmus (1469–1536) also championed the primacy of preaching over the sacrament. His most important work was on the editing and publishing of the Greek New Testament in 1516, one year prior to the Luther-initiated Reformation. It is often said that Erasmus "laid the egg that Luther hatched." While the two disagreed on important doctrines, they both understood the importance of the original languages. Their love for the languages reminds us of the great privilege that we have today with seminaries, computer software, and other available tools to learn and interact with the original languages of Scripture.

PREACHING AMONG THE REFORMERS AND THE PURITANS (1500–1800)

After the pre-Reformers emphasized the need to return to the Scriptures, a shift in authority occurred during the Reformation. Reformation doctrines such as *Soli Deo Gloria* ("glory to God alone"), *Sola Gratia* ("grace alone"), *Sola Fide* ("faith alone"), and *Sola Christus* ("Christ alone") were all based on the principle of *Sola Scriptura* ("Scripture alone"). Many significant theologians and preachers saw the Scriptures as authoritative, such as German Reformer Martin Luther (1483–1546), French Reformer John Calvin (1509–64), Swiss Reformer Huldreich Zwingli (1464–1531), Scottish Reformer John Knox (1513–72), and English Reformer William Tyndale (1494–1535). These men also practiced a more literal, grammatical, and redemptive-historical approach to biblical interpretation, in contrast to the allegory practiced in the medieval period. I find great encouragement when I read the biographies and books by these Reformers, and encourage you to read through them as well.

One cannot help but begin with Luther in understanding the scope of the Reformation. He was a converted Catholic monk who nailed a list of ninety-five arguments to the door of the church at Wittenberg on October 31, 1517, in response to the false teachings of the Catholic Church. He was upset particularly over the selling of indulgences. Through personal study (especially in the epistles of Romans and Galatians), Luther was convinced that the Scriptures taught "justification by faith alone." He wanted the common person to know this liberating truth. Of course, the church wanted Luther to recant on his teachings, but he responded, "My conscience is captive to the Word of God."[11] Luther's convictions changed the future of the church. We must never forget the price that was paid for preserving and passing on the gospel.

Luther was a theology professor—not a pastor—but he preached constantly. Between 1510 and 1546, he preached more than three thousand messages![12] He preached several times a week and often numerous times a day. Luther believed that the preaching of the Word should be central in corporate worship. In *Table Talk*, Luther insisted that the preacher should preach in "the plain mother tongue, which everyone is acquainted with."[13] He also believed that preaching should be expository in nature. The German word is *Shriftauslegend*—which is usually translated as "expository." *Auslegen* literally means to "lay out, exhibit or display, to make something evident or plain."[14] Luther's zeal for the Scriptures was recorded vividly on one particular occasion, as he commented on the Reformation; "I simply taught, preached, and wrote God's Word: otherwise I did nothing. . . . The Word did it all."[15] Luther's ministry teaches us to trust in the power of the Word. It can still bring another Reformation, which we desperately need.

Tyndale translated the New Testament into English because he too wanted the common man to understand God's Word. Tyndale was closely associated with Luther and actually printed many of his English Bibles in Wittenberg. His English translation was the first to draw directly from Hebrew and Greek texts. With the help of the printing press, like Luther and others, his text was distributed widely. In 1535, Tyndale was jailed outside of Brussels for more than a year. Then he was tried for heresy and eventually burned at the stake at age forty-two. His great desire was for every "plough boy" to know the Scriptures, not only the religious professionals. This passion inspires me to communicate the good news to every individual.

John Knox is considered as the founder of the Presbyterian denomination. He traveled to Geneva three times to learn from Calvin. In Geneva, Knox gained knowledge of Reformed theology and Presbyterian polity. He created a new order of service, which

[11] Quoted in R. C. Sproul, *The Holiness of God* (Wheaton, IL: Tyndale, 1985), 111–12.
[12] Fred W. Meuser, *Luther the Preacher* (Minneapolis: Augsburg, 1983), 19.
[13] Martin Luther, *The Table Talk of Martin Luther*, ed. Thomas S. Kepler (Grand Rapids: Baker Books, 1979), 244.
[14] Quoted in Meuser, *Luther the Preacher*, 46.
[15] Quoted in Ernest Gordon Rupp, *Luther's Progress to the Diet of Worms 1521* (London: SCM, 1951), 99.

was eventually adopted by the Reformed church in Scotland. Most of all, Knox was a fearless preacher who proclaimed the Word until his death, despite the criticisms of Queen Mary.

Ulrich Zwingli also taught the Scriptures plainly and responsibly. In 1519, he tried an unheard of thing: preach through a book of the Bible (Matthew). He later preached through many books of the Bible, but few of his sermons remain today because of his failure to write them out.

John Calvin provided the best example for expository preaching today. Christians generally know him more as a theologian than as a preacher. Calvin indeed wrote various types of theological books and tracts, but Dillenberger rightly stated, "[Calvin] assumed that his whole theological labor was the exposition of Scripture."[16] His love for biblical exposition is evidenced in his commentaries and in his writing on the subject.

For Calvin, the chief mark of identifying a true church was that the Word was preached. As a pastor in Geneva, Calvin preached twice on Sunday and every weekday on alternating weeks from 1549 until his death. His personal commitment to verse-by-verse exposition was illustrated in one vivid story. After preaching on Easter of 1538, he was banished by the City Council. He returned in September 1541 and picked up the series in the next verse (three years later)![17] He was a model expositor.

Calvin preached with a homily style, giving a running commentary of the text with simple and direct applications. He influenced many other preachers during his time. Other contemporary Reformers and expositors deserve attention, including Henry Bullinger (1504–75), Thomas Cartwright (1535–1603), John Jewel (1522–71), and Hugh Latimer (1485–1585). Latimer, an English Reformer, preached his best known sermon in 1548, in which he called out the unfaithful preachers of his day for not preaching the Scriptures.

The Puritan movement followed the Reformation throughout England, parts of Europe, and America. The Puritan age produced a great number of exemplary biblical preachers. These leaders sought to return the purity of Scripture to the life of the church. An early Puritan, William Perkins (1558–1602), was a mighty preacher and teacher of preachers. Ian Breward called him "the most widely

---

[16] John Dillenberger, *John Calvin: Selections from His Writings* (Scholars Press, 1975), 14.
[17] T. H. L. Parker, *Calvin's Preaching* (Edinburgh: T&T Clark, 1992), 60.

known theologian of the Elizabethan church."[18] Sinclair Ferguson said, "Christians throughout the world today owe a considerable but largely unrecognized debt to the great Puritan preacher and theologian William Perkins."[19]

The list of Puritans who held to a high view of biblical preaching included Joseph Hall (1574–1656), Thomas Goodwin (1600–1680), Richard Baxter (1615–91), John Owen (1616–83), Thomas Manton (1620–77), John Bunyan (1628–88), Stephen Charnock (1628–80), William Ames (1576–1633), Richard Sibbes (1577–1635), Jeremiah Burroughs (1600–1646), Samuel Rutherford (1600–1660), Thomas Manton (1620–77), Thomas Watson (1620–86), John Flavel (1628–91), and Matthew Henry (1662–1714). The lives of these ministers are worth reflecting upon.

Owen stands out as the leading theologian of the time. He entered Queen's College, Oxford, at the age of twelve and studied the classics, mathematics, philosophy, theology, Hebrew, and rabbinical writings. Among his recommended works are *Communion with God*, *The Mortification of Sin*, *Works of John Owen*, *The Death of Death in the Death of Christ*, and *Temptation and Sin*. Anytime I prepare to preach on personal holiness, I like to look at Owen's works. Perhaps no one understood the battle of indwelling sin and temptation as he did. He was a physician of the soul.

Richard Baxter and John Bunyan probably are the most popular Puritan pastors. Both remained in one local church their entire lives. They also faced imprisonment for their separatism. Baxter is now known more for his writings on pastoral ministry than on preaching. He ministered in Kidderminster for about sixteen years. Two of his books are read widely today: *The Saints' Everlasting Rest* and *The Reformed Pastor*. He preached with deep passion "as never sure to preach again, and as a dying man to dying men."

John Bunyan, a converted "tinker" and author of the classic *Pilgrim's Progress*, was a long-time preacher of sovereign grace in Bedford, England. When the theologian John Owen was asked why he went to hear this uneducated man, he said, "I would willingly exchange my learning for the tinker's power of touching men's lives."[20]

---

[18] Ian Breward, ed., *The Work of William Perkins* (Berkshire: Sutton Courtenay Press, 1970), xi.

[19] Sinclair Ferguson, "Foreword," in William Perkins, *The Art of Prophesying*, rev. Sinclair Ferguson, repr. (Carlisle, PA: Banner of Truth Trust, 1996), 7.

[20] Quoted in John Piper, *The Hidden Smile of God* (Wheaton, IL: Crossway, 2001), 54.

Matthew Henry was an exceptional expository preacher of a Presbyterian church in Chester, England, for twenty-five years. His devotional commentaries are still in circulation today. Other notable preaching works during the Puritan period included Andrew Hyperius's *On the Making of Sacred Discourse*, Richard Bernard's *The Faithful Shepherd*, Thomas Hooker's *The Soul's Preparation*, William Chappell's *The Preacher and the Art and Method of Preaching*, and Phillip Doddridge's *Lectures on Preaching*.

The Puritans' zeal for the Scriptures carried over into early America. David Larsen said, "In their courageous move from England to New England, the Puritans brought the centrality of the preached Word with them."[21] V. L. Stanfield classified colonial American preaching as: (1) intellectual yet emotional, (2) theologically conservative, (3) highly controversial, (4) ethically Puritan, (5) and biblically authoritative.[22] The early American preachers continue to inspire me today. Their work often influenced various fields of society, such as education and politics.

John Cotton (1585–1652) was touted as an orator and scholar who preached plain Puritan-style sermons. Thomas Hooker (1586–1647) came to America with Cotton. He was a pastor with deep concern for religious liberty and evangelical theology. David Larsen extolled Cotton Mather (1663–1728) as "the most brilliant and prolific thinker of his times."[23] Mather entered Harvard at eleven, did his MA thesis on the possibility of divine origin of the Hebrew vowel pointings, and later became one of the founders of Yale.[24]

Turnbull claimed that before 1750 a heavy Puritan and Calvinistic influence characterized preaching.[25] A revival of evangelistic preaching was present as well. The evangelistic emphasis of this day was evidenced in the preaching of the Great Awakening. The three most lionized preachers of the Awakening were Jonathan Edwards (1703–58), George Whitefield (1714–70), and John Wesley (1703–91).

Whitefield knew Wesley from the "Holy Club" at Oxford. The two disagreed on particular doctrines related to God's sovereignty

---

[21] Larsen, *The Company of the Preachers*, 293.
[22] V. L. Stanfield, *Notes on the History of Preaching*, 2nd ed. (New Orleans: NOBTS Printing Department, 1963), 172.
[23] Larsen, *The Company of the Preachers*, 298–99.
[24] Ibid.
[25] Ralph Turnbull, *A History of Preaching*, vol. 3 (Grand Rapids: Baker 1974), 51.

in salvation but remained long-time friends and encouragers. Whitefield was a greater orator and scholar with a booming voice. He studied with the Greek text. He loved to preach on the new birth. His sermons were more topical than verse by verse but were filled with biblical theology. When he died at age fifty-six, he had crossed the Atlantic sixteen times as a traveling evangelist. Every preacher should read a biography of Whitefield.

Wesley was an outstanding Oxford scholar whose preaching was quite organized and understandable. He too purposed to convert the hearers through preaching the gospel. He traveled for nearly sixty years and probably preached more times than anyone in history. Much of his preaching, like Whitefield, was in the open air. He also founded the Methodist movement.

Knoll stated that if Whitefield was the most important preacher in the Great Awakening, Jonathan Edwards had to be its most important apologist.[26] Edwards, a strong Calvinist, believed the preaching event was the primary means for conversion.[27] His best-known sermon was "Sinners in the Hands of an Angry God," preached at Enfield, Connecticut, in 1741, but this sermon does not represent his preaching adequately. Homiletically, Edwards developed the main points of doctrine from his text and then provided numerous applications at the end, following the instructions of William Perkins. Edwards is perhaps the greatest theological mind in American history. Among his recommended works include *Religious Affections, The Works of Jonathan Edwards,* and *Freedom of the Will.* Like John Owen, I recommend that young preachers read the works of Edwards thoroughly. His works have impacted contemporary pastors such as John Piper tremendously. It will take you a long time to work through much of Edwards, but it will be worth it.

PREACHING IN THE EVANGELICAL AGE (1800–PRESENT)

Dargan called the nineteenth century the greatest period in the history of preaching.[28] Preachers such as Charles Simeon (1759–

---

[26] Mark Knoll, *A History of Christianity in the United States and Canada* (Grand Rapids: Eerdmans, 1992), 95.

[27] Turnbull, *A History of Preaching,* 55.

[28] Dargan, *A History of Preaching,* 351. He ranks the fourth, thirteenth, and sixteenth centuries as the other three great periods of preaching.

1836), Henry Ward Beecher (1813–87), Phillips Brooks (1834–93), Joseph Parker (1830–1902), Frederick W. Robertson (1816–53), John Broadus (1827–95), Charles Spurgeon (1834–92), D. L. Moody (1837–99), John C. Ryle (1816–1900), Alexander Maclaren (1826–1910), G. Campbell Morgan (1863–1942), Gardner Taylor (1918–2015), and Martin Luther King Jr. (1929–68) are among the list of influential preachers in this age.

Beecher, pastor of Plymouth Congregational Church in Brooklyn, New York, was not known for exposition but rather illustrative and moving sermons on social issues, such as the evils of slavery. Stanfield called him the "greatest orator of the American pulpit."[29] Beecher also began the Lyman Beecher Lectures on Preaching at Yale in 1872, which made a lasting impact on homiletics. One of the lecturers was Phillips Brooks, an Episcopal minister in Boston, who gave us the great line that preaching is "truth through personality."

Regarding racial equality in America, no preacher was more important than Martin Luther King Jr. One can read about his theology and practice of preaching from homiletician Richard Lischer in *The Preacher King*. "In the quiet recesses of my heart, I am fundamentally a clergyman, a Baptist preacher,"[30] King declared. Lischer says of King's significance, "As no preacher in the twentieth century and no politician since Lincoln, he transposed the Judeo-Christian themes of love, suffering, deliverance, justice from the sacred shelter of the pulpit into the arena of public policy."[31]

In my opinion, the most important American preacher of this period was John Broadus. He was both a mighty preacher and devoted teacher of preachers. During his time at The Southern Baptist Theological Seminary, Broadus wrote the most influential book on preaching up to his time, *On the Preparation and Delivery of Sermons* (1871). The book has undergone four revisions and is still read and relied upon today. Broadus laid a homiletical foundation for effective biblical preaching for years to come. Other renowned scholar-preachers who followed Broadus were B. H. Carroll (1843–1914) and E. Y. Mullins (1860–1928).

---

[29] Ibid.
[30] Richard Lischer, *The Preacher King* (New York: Oxford Press, 1995), Kindle edition.
[31] Ibid.

Charles Spurgeon is the most popular preacher from England during this period. Spurgeon's sermons from the Metropolitan Tabernacle in London are penetrating and biblical. He was more Puritan in form, taking a theological truth from the text and dividing it into parts. His combination of intellect, Reformed theology, wit, and oratory is well documented. Spurgeon produced more literature than any Christian in history. My own call to pastoral ministry came as I was reading a biography on Spurgeon. I have a Spurgeon bust in my office reminding me of his faithfulness to God through the midst of enormous sufferings, such as gout, a sickly wife, Baptist associational problems, and depression. I spent an entire summer reading nothing but the Bible and Spurgeon, and it had a dramatic effect on my life.

Prior to Spurgeon, Charles Simeon set the example for endurance in ministry. Simeon, a lifelong friend of contemporary William Wilberforce, became the vicar at Holy Trinity Church in Cambridge in 1782. He was initially met with opposition. Despite the opposition, Simeon (single his whole life) remained for fifty-four years. He eventually won the hearts of his people and left a legacy of faithful expository preaching and a passion for global missions. His *Expository Outlines* are available today. Simeon also translated Jean Claude's *Essay* on preaching, which is found at the end of his *Expository Outlines*. Simeon was known as "the Luther of Cambridge." His aim in ministry was to "humble the sinner, exalt the Savior, and to promote holiness."[32] John Stott often refers to the example of Simeon as an example for modern preachers. His whole life was devoted to the Word of God and the mission of God.

Alexander Maclaren was a legendary expository preacher who spent forty-five years at Union Chapel in Manchester, England. He developed a rigorous study schedule, and his sermons demonstrated the fruit of his discipline. His thirty-two-volume sermons in *The Expositor's Bible* can still be read today. MacLaren had a gift for rightly dividing the text into natural divisions and explaining its meaning.

---

[32] Russell Levenson, "'To Humble the Sinner, to Exalt the Saviour, to Promote Holiness': Reflections on the Life, Ministry, and Legacy of Charles Simeon," *Sewanee Theological Review* (1998): 47.

G. Campbell Morgan, a powerful expositor of the Word, preached in the nineteenth and twentieth centuries at Westminster Chapel in London (serving as pastor twice). I have heard both Maclaren and Morgan exalted as "the Prince of Expositors." His study habits consisted of reading the Bible book from which he was preaching numerous times. Like Maclaren, Morgan had a gift for developing simple and biblically faithful outlines.

Following Morgan was D. Martyn Lloyd-Jones (1899–1981). I have quoted this hero of mine throughout this book. His commentaries on Romans and Ephesians display his theological passion and careful attention to the biblical text. He believed that there was no substitute for biblical preaching and that a revival of preaching is the greatest need for another awakening. I could not agree more.

Toward the end of the century, more books on biblical preaching emerged than in any other period. Examples include Merrill Unger's *Principles of Expository Preaching* (1955), Donald Miller's *The Way to Biblical Preaching* (1957), Lloyd Perry's *Biblical Preaching for Today's World* (1973), Haddon Robinson's *Biblical Preaching* (1980), William Thompson's *Preaching Biblically* (1981), and John Stott's *Between Two Worlds* (1982). More recent and excellent insights on preparing expositional sermons are John MacArthur and The Master's Seminary Faculty's *Rediscovering Expository Preaching* (1992), Bryan Chapell's *Christ-Centered Preaching* (2005), Sidney Greidanus's *The Modern Preacher and the Ancient Text* (1988), Wayne McDill's *The Twelve Essential Skills* (1994), and Jerry Vines and Jim Shaddix's *Power in the Pulpit* (1999).

John R. W. Stott, John MacArthur, Tony Evans, Bryan Chapell, Jim Shaddix, Sinclair Ferguson, Mark Dever, Thabiti Anyabwile, H. B. Charles, Alistair Begg, D. A. Carson, and John Piper are among my personal list of exemplary expositors in the recent era. My Baptist brothers also place W. A. Criswell, Adrian Rogers, and Jerry Vines (among many others) as historical preaching heroes. Many other pastors, such as Rick Warren, have influenced thousands worldwide through preaching and writing. I could also rattle off the names of a host of men around the current age of forty who are having a tremendous impact in evangelicalism. May the Lord continue to use them and raise up the younger generation to carry faithfully the baton of this gospel-preaching relay race.

THE NEXT GENERATION

Time will only tell what will be said of preaching in the twenty-first century. We face many new challenges today, such as globalization, postmodern thinking, biblical illiteracy, secularization, and the need for many more churches in urban cities. We also have wonderful opportunities and resources via technological advances (no one could podcast Luther five hundred years ago!). My prayer is for our generation to follow the example of these greater periods of preaching. I am reminded of Stott, who commented on Simeon saying, "On many occasions I have had the privilege of preaching from his pulpit in Holy Trinity Church, Cambridge, and standing where he stood, have prayed for a measure of his outstanding faithfulness."[33] I have never preached in the pulpits of Calvin, Edwards, or Stott, but I too pray for a measure of their outstanding faithfulness to God, his Word, his calling, and his mission for the glory of King Jesus.

---

[33] Stott, *Between Two Worlds*, xxvii.

APPENDIX 2

ADVICE ON DOING EXPOSITION IN NON-PULPIT CONTEXTS

WHILE MUCH OF THIS book has focused on the weekly expository sermon prepared by a pastor of a local congregation, we should also look to expound the Bible in various other contexts. Below are some common questions that I receive for these "non-pulpit" settings.

1. What advice would you give for delivering a wedding message?

Before talking about the actual message, be sure to take the couple through good biblical counseling. There are a number of ways to do this. After an initial meeting, we usually have the couple read *The Meaning of Marriage* by Tim Keller and also suggest a few more books. We then give them five to six sermons to listen to on the subject. We give some homework following these sermons. We also have conversations with the couple regarding basic marriage challenges such as finances, communication, parenting, sex, and roles.

Prior to the wedding ceremony, I prefer to have someone else handle all the logistics if possible. I tell them that I am not a wedding coordinator! Of course, I share some opinions about the order of service, mainly to ensure that it is Christ-honoring and that it flows well.

Concerning the wedding sermon, I encourage you to keep a few things in mind.

First, be biblical. While you could expound on a number of passages, I typically do Ephesians 5 because so much is there.

Second, be brief. I shoot for absolutely no longer than fifteen minutes. Remember that people are standing and are uncomfortable. I had a bride almost pass out once because she was all snugged in her dress and the lights were burning her up. An average service should not be longer than forty-five minutes. The sermon structure that I normally use is a homily—a running commentary (normally on Ephesians 5). I hit the high points and offer running application until I get to the end of the passage.

Third, be personal. Begin with something personal and pastor them in the moment. Additionally, make sure you remember their names! Write the names of the bride and groom at the top of your notes if necessary. Also, tell the congregation that you are mainly speaking to the bride and groom, but that you want to invite the audience into the discussion because everyone needs to hear of Jesus's love, everyone needs to have an elevated view of the church, and everyone needs to know the biblical view of marriage. Then speak to the couple throughout the sermon.

Fourth, be Christ-centered. Remind them that the Bible begins and ends with a wedding, that Jesus's first miracle was at a wedding, and one day, we will take part in the ultimate marriage union. Make the sermon ultimately about Jesus, our Great Groom. With that said, emphasize Jesus's covenantal love for His bride.

Finally, be practical. The wedding sermon is not a time to lecture or drone on forever, but it is OK to address practical matters quickly. Remind the couple of the sufficiency of God's grace to enable them to forgive, communicate, express love, repent, and rejoice in suffering and to have a marathon marriage. As you mention these things, consider including them in the vows—vows that should reflect the truths and grace of your message.

2. What advice would you give for delivering a funeral message?

I typically get more involved with the planning of the funeral than I do with the planning of the wedding. Often people are well intended, but their suggested readings/testimonies/songs are simply inappropriate for a funeral service, and I try to gently steer them into more Christ-honoring options.

Once the service begins, I open with a word of welcome and state the purpose of the occasion. Then I usually read a psalm or a text that mingles grief and hope, followed by an opening prayer. After the prayer, I will then introduce any song or personal biography that has been prepared. I prefer to stay close to the podium and help move the service along, and also guard against any inappropriate actions. Once the songs and words are offered, I will then give a funeral homily.

Remember *these important guidelines* for your message.

Comfort with gospel hope. You are there not only to honor the deceased person but also to comfort the living. Your attitude, posture, disposition, and subject should be one of peace and comfort, rooted in the reality of a crucified Lamb, an empty tomb, an occupied throne, and the presence of the Holy Spirit.

Be brief. While you have a little longer for a funeral sermon than a wedding sermon, I would shoot for less than twenty minutes (unless the family says otherwise, and you deem it necessary to go longer).

Praise God more than the person. If you want to commend the person, that is certainly fine and good, but remember to hold the cross higher than the person's good works.

Avoid theological lectures. This is a time to hold the cross high and point people to Jesus, not to get into speculative end-times matters, the problem of evil, and so forth. Make the main things the plain things, and the plain things the main things.

Remember that ultimately only God knows the hearts of people. We are not there to render a verdict but ultimately tell everyone the good news and to comfort the suffering. It is true that believers will show fruit, but the thief on the cross reminds us that some find mercy in dying moments; and though we may have serious doubts about a particular deceased person, we ultimately do not know if he joined that thief in paradise. So be quite careful about offering people either false assurance or no hope. Point them to the gospel.

Speak gospel truths simply. Avoid "church speak" because a lot of unchurched people will usually be present. Make the message theologically clear and understandable.

Regarding *the content of the message*, below are some things to keep in mind.

First, begin with something personal. Let the family know that you care for them. Address them directly and gently. If possible, I like to preach from the Bible of the deceased person. This adds a nice personal touch, and the family normally appreciates it. Just try to avoid exaggeration.

Second, tie the personal reference to a text/theme. This may be easy to do if you knew the deceased personal well (or if the person's Bible is all marked up). I like to use a text that somehow reflects the life of the person. While the sermon itself should not be focused on the deceased person, an opening connection between your text and the beloved prepares the audience to hear the rest of the message in light of the occasion.

Third, develop the hope Christians have in light of this theme and comfort believers with this hope. Those themes could include the joys of heaven, the end of suffering, resurrection, God's promises, ultimate reunion, or Christ's triumph.

Finally, end with the focus being on Christ. End the message by telling everyone that they are looking at their destiny (death), but Christ has offered us a way to triumph over our great enemy through his cross work and glorious resurrection.

For examples on preaching funeral messages, see *The Hardest Sermons You'll Ever Have to Preach,* edited by Bryan Chapell.[1]

Following the message, I will end in prayer and offer myself to the family and friends for further conversations. At the graveside, I usually select a passage dealing with God's promises in the gospel (e.g., 1 Corinthians 15) or a particular psalm to comfort the grieving. The message is usually no more than ten minutes, and a prayer follows it. If I am serving with another minister, I will ask him to do the graveside portion.

3. What advice do you give to "worship leaders" (worship pastors) regarding the role of the Word?

Generally speaking, lead/senior/preaching pastors need to think more about worshipping, and worship leaders need to think more about pastoring. Pastors often view the church as a "preaching arena." They often give little attention to acts of worship such as corporate reading of Scripture (woefully neglected today!), prayers, the Lord's Supper, song selection, audience participation, and so on. Plus, the entire sermon (as pointed out previously) should be an offering of worship (it does not come *after* worship). We should preach in such a way that people want to sing!

---

[1] Bryan Chapell, ed., *The Hardest Sermons You'll Ever Have to Preach* (Grand Rapids: Zondervan, 2011).

As for worship leaders, I prefer the title "Pastor for Corporate Worship." The worship leader is doing the work of a pastor. He is shaping minds, putting truth in people's mouths, leading in prayer at times, reading Scripture, and offering short exhortations. That is the work of a pastor—to care for, train, equip, and encourage the saints through the Word. Good worship leaders are more than song leaders. They are more than artists, more than performers, more than program directors—and not *mood creators*. It is true that they need to choose good music (artists), do music with excellence (performers), and oversee a band/choir (program coordinators). But they are more than this. And the idea that the worship leader can somehow usher in God's presence is more than anyone can offer. God's presence is a gift; we cannot manufacture or manipulate the presence of God.

Music is portable theology. People receive tunes filled with gospel truth. Therefore, I want qualified pastors selecting these songs, and I want qualified pastors shepherding the people through the corporate worship service. Not every church will have an individual like this—who is qualified as a pastor—but I still maintain that this is the goal. And if a church does not have a pastor for worship, then the lead/senior/preaching pastor should be more active in leading the congregation in the acts of worship (stepping aside at various moments to let others sing, read, pray, etc.). Further, we should be raising up pastors for corporate worship, not only bands that can play music and ignite a crowd.

When the pastor for corporate worship has an opportunity to read a passage out loud, recite a creed with the congregation, or do a brief exposition before a song, he should prepare for this act. He should also work with the lead pastor in order to be on the same page and stay tied to a particular theme. I usually work with my pastor for corporate worship all week. As I develop notes and ideas for my sermon, I pass them along to him. He then selects songs, readings, and other elements based on these notes. We also talk during the week about particular applications that our people need to hear. It is a tremendous blessing to work with a guy who loves the Bible and is even more of a pastor than he is a musician/artist (and he is exceptional musically). Our pastor for corporate worship performs related duties common to our other pastors, such as oversight, counseling, attending meetings, weighing in on decisions, and so forth.

Therefore, my advice to those leading in corporate worship is simple: elevate your vision. Realize that you are more than a song leader. Shepherd the people with other shepherds. Read the Bible corporately. Select great gospel-saturated songs. Savor what you are singing. Exhort the people with prepared comments. Encourage the downcast with soul-nourishing truth. See the flock from Christ's perspective. Set people's gaze upon Christ. And when the worship gathering is finished, realize there is more shepherding to be done.

4. What advice would you give to small group leaders?

It depends on the type of small group. One may choose to do an open group, a closed group, a missional community, a group focused on a particular curriculum, or a sermon-based small group (to name only a few categories). In each of these groups, however, it is important to have a good leader. The last thing a church needs is a maverick small group. Small groups can become places where the seeds of false doctrine or division are sown. Therefore, it is imperative that small group leaders be on the same page with the church's leadership, that they hold the same theology, and that they know how to maintain the unity of the Spirit. This assumes that the leaders are above reproach and able to teach at some level.

Our particular church follows a sermon-based model, as outlined by Larry Osborne in *Sticky Church*.[2] Pastor Osborne says, "The ultimate goal of a sermon-based small group is simply to velcro people to the two things they will need most when faced with a need-to-know or need-to-grow situation: the Bible and other Christians."[3] We do about seven different activities in our sermon-based groups, which meet in homes scattered across our area: (1) have a meal together, (2) hang out together, (3) pray and do accountability together, (4) do ministry projects together, (5) plan for ways to connect with each other outside the meeting, (6) discuss the sermon together, and (7) reinforce important church announcements and initiatives.

The goal of the sermon discussion is simple: apply the sermon text. The *application grid* in chapter 11 may be helpful for group leaders to consider. We also give some overarching questions that

---

[2] Larry Osborne, *Sticky Church* (Grand Rapids: Zondervan, 2008).
[3] Ibid., Kindle edition.

groups can always consider: (1) What in the sermon was easy to believe? (2) What in the sermon was difficult to believe—and why? (3) What are specific ways we can apply this sermon to our lives? Another set of questions (or perhaps additional questions) includes (1) What does this text teach us about God? (2) What does this text say about sinful man? (3) What does this text say about the gospel? And (4) in light of what it says about the gospel, what should we do about it? The small group leader also has freedom to chase down cross-references and to even digress when it benefits the group so long as the general theme of the sermon is being considered.

We also meet with small group leaders once a month and try to keep everyone up to speed on the sermon series and on the church's initiatives and updates. In many ways, the small group leader is a mini-pastor of a home church. Each small group leader has an assistant, and once the group gets too big (more than 12–15), we commission the assistant to start a new group, made up of the newest people in the group (the long-time group members ideally will stay together, though we are flexible on this).

The sermon-based discussion has several advantages. Osborne says that more people take notes; more people pay attention (because they know they will discuss the sermon); more people get involved in the discussion (unlike in a curriculum-based discussion); it creates a churchwide focus; more people try to get the recording of the sermon when absent on a Sunday; and it allows people to dig deeper into particular truths that they may not have fully grasped after initially hearing the sermon.[4] We have observed all of these to be true.

However, I do not want to insist that this is the one true way to do a small group! There are downsides. Some people want to study something different. And we do. Once a year (for about six weeks), we select a small book to study together as a church within our groups (such as Bonhoeffer's *Life Together*). We also have occasional studies going on in the church (though they are not required nor emphasized like our small groups). Others want better community life, and others want more ministry projects together. These are all challenges we try to address. Some of our groups are better at different aspects of the group life, reflective of the leader and the members.

---

[4] Ibid., Kindle.

One of the reasons we chose this model is that we want to have a ministry model that is *replicable*. We are a church plant, and like most church plants, we started with quite a small budget. We are also sending out literally hundreds of people all over the world, and we want to give them a pattern they can actually follow. This particular approach only requires a Bible and people! You do not need a budget for curriculum, and you do not need a classroom in a church building. Furthermore, it can be used as a church planting strategy. A small group (perhaps one that meets a good distance away from other groups) could become a core team for a church plant. Two or three small groups such as this could also combine to form a congregation.

APPENDIX 3

SERMON OUTLINE SHEET

I. Introduction
   a. *Opener* [note the type of introduction you will give]
   b. *MPT:* [state the main point of the text]
   c. *MPS:* [state the main point of the sermon]
   d. *Title:*
II. Body
   [sketch an outline that supports the MPS; include a two-sentence description of each functional element for each point]
III. Conclusion
   a. *Summation* [give a way to recap]
   b. *Response* [list the type of response that you will give]

SERMON EVALUATION FORM

Speaker

    Text _____

    Title _____

    Date _____

                                          Poor   Excellent

I. Scripture Reading

    a. Read with expression   1 2 3 4 5 6 7

    b. Read with clarity   1 2 3 4 5 6 7

    Comments:

II. Introduction

    a. It incited interest.   1 2 3 4 5 6 7

    b. It established relevancy   1 2 3 4 5 6 7
        (for the believer and unbeliever).

    c. It introduced the MPT.   1 2 3 4 5 6 7

    d. It introduced the MPS.   1 2 3 4 5 6 7

    e. It contained a redemptive quality. 1 2 3 4 5 6 7

    f. It included the preacher's
        expectations.   1 2 3 4 5 6 7

    g. It was not too long.   1 2 3 4 5 6 7

What was the opener?

Did the introduction give momentum to the rest of the sermon?

                                          Poor   Excellent

III. Body

    a. Main headings/points/divisions
        supported the MPS.   1 2 3 4 5 6 7

b. Main headings/points/divisions were
    derived from the text.   1 2 3 4 5 6 7
c. Each point contained some if not all
    of the functional elements.   1 2 3 4 5 6 7
d. Functional elements were used with
    equality.   1 2 3 4 5 6 7
e. Text was explained well,
    demonstrating research.   1 2 3 4 5 6 7
f. Illustrations were inspirational and
    instructional.   1 2 3 4 5 6 7
g. Application was tied to the text.   1 2 3 4 5 6 7
h. Specific and transformative
    application was given.   1 2 3 4 5 6 7
i. Application was used throughout
    the sermon.   1 2 3 4 5 6 7
j. The gospel was integrated in the
    sermon naturally and responsibly.   1 2 3 4 5 6 7

What was the most effective element(s) of the expositional items in this sermon?

What was the weakest element(s) of the expositional items in this sermon?

How was Christ exalted in this sermon?

IV. Conclusion

	Poor	Excellent

Summation
a. Content was summarized clearly.   1 2 3 4 5 6 7
b. Summation did not contain new
    information.   1 2 3 4 5 6 7
c. Summation led to the response
    smoothly.   1 2 3 4 5 6 7

How was the content summarized?

	Poor	Excellent

Response
d. Speaker was clear on how the hearers
    should respond.   1 2 3 4 5 6 7
e. Response was tied to the MPS.   1 2 3 4 5 6 7
f. Hearers were pointed to Christ.   1 2 3 4 5 6 7

What type of response was offered?

		Poor					Excellent

V. Delivery and Style

		Poor ←					→ Excellent
a.	Sermon was clear.	1	2	3	4	5	6 7
b.	Sermon was not dull.	1	2	3	4	5	6 7
c.	Passion was demonstrated.	1	2	3	4	5	6 7
d.	Authenticity was demonstrated.	1	2	3	4	5	6 7
e.	Eye contact was maintained well throughout the message.	1	2	3	4	5	6 7
f.	Sermon maintained good pace and momentum.	1	2	3	4	5	6 7
g.	Humor was appropriate and purposeful.	1	2	3	4	5	6 7
h.	Communication aids helped not hindered.	1	2	3	4	5	6 7
i.	Preacher spoke with humble confidence.	1	2	3	4	5	6 7
j.	Preacher spoke with credibility.	1	2	3	4	5	6 7
k.	Preacher spoke with pastoral care.	1	2	3	4	5	6 7
l.	Preacher related well to the audience.	1	2	3	4	5	6 7

What was the most effective element(s) of the delivery and style items in this sermon?

What was the weakest element(s) of the delivery and style items in this sermon?

VI. Overall Comments

SELECTED BIBLIOGRAPHY

BOOKS

Akin, Daniel, David Allen and Ned Mathews, eds. *Text-Driven Preaching*. Nashville: B&H, 2010.

Akin, Daniel, Bill Curtis and Stephen Rummage. *Engaging Exposition*. Nashville: B&H, 2011.

Ash, Christopher. *The Priority of Preaching*. Reprint. London: Proclamation Trust Media, 2010.

Augustine. *On Christian Doctrine*. Translated by D. W. Robertson Jr. Upper Saddle River, NJ: Prentice Hall, 1997.

Azurdia, Arturo, III. "Reforming the Church Through Prayer." In *Reforming Pastoral Ministry*. Edited by John H. Armstrong. Wheaton, IL: Crossway, 2001.

———. *Spirit Empowered Preaching*. Ross-Shire, Scotland: Christian Focus, 1998.

Barth, Karl. *Homiletics*. Translated by Geoffrey W. Bromiley and Donald E. Daniels. Louisville: WJK, 1991.

Baxter, Richard. *The Reformed Pastor*. Edited by William Brown. First published in 1656. Reprint. Carlisle, PA: Banner of Truth Trust, 1996.

Beeke, Joel. "The Utter Necessity of a Godly Life." In *Reforming Pastoral Ministry*. Edited by John H. Armstrong. Wheaton, IL: Crossway, 2001.

Begg, Alistair. *Preaching for God's Glory*. Wheaton, IL: Crossway, 1999.

Blackwood, Andrew W. *Expository Preaching Today*. Grand Rapids: Baker, 1975.

———. *The Preparation of Sermons*. New York: Abingdon, 1948.

Blomberg, Craig. *1 Corinthians*. The NIV Application Commentary. Grand Rapids: Zondervan, 1994.

Bohannon, John. *Preaching and the Emerging Church*. 2010.

Boice, James Montgomery. *Psalms*. Volume 3. Grand Rapids: Baker, 1998.

Bonar, Andrew A., ed. *Memoirs of McCheyne.* Reprint. Chicago: Moody, 1978.

———. *Robert Murray M'Cheyne.* Reprint. London: Banner of Truth Trust, 1972.

Bounds, E. M. *E. M. Bounds on Prayer.* Compilation. New Kensington: Whitaker House, 1997.

———. *Power Through Prayer.* Uhrichsville, OH: Barbour, 1984.

———. *Prayerful and Powerful Pulpits.* Grand Rapids: Baker, 1994.

Breward, Ian, ed. *The Work of William Perkins.* Berkshire: Sutton Courtenay Press, 1970.

Broadus, John A. *On the Preparation and Delivery of Sermons.* Fourth edition. Revised by Vernon L. Stanfield. San Francisco: Harper and Row, 1979.

———. *On the Preparation and Delivery of Sermons.* New and Revised by Jesse Burton Weatherspoon. New York: Harper and Brothers, 1944.

———. *A Treatise on the Preparation and Delivery of Sermons.* Philadelphia: Smith, English & Co., 1870. Reprint, Philadelphia: H. B. Garner, 1884.

Brooke, Stopford A. *Life and Letters of Frederick W. Robertson.* New York: Harper and Brothers, 1865.

Brooks, Phillips. *Lectures on Preaching.* New York: E. P. Dutton & Co., 1877. Reprint. Grand Rapids: Baker, 1969.

Bruce, F. F. *Commentary on the Book of Acts.* Grand Rapids: Eerdmans, 1970.

Bryson, Harold T. *Expository Preaching.* Nashville: B&H, 1995.

Bryson, Harold T., and James C. Taylor, *Building Sermons to Meet People's Needs.* Nashville: Broadman, 1980.

Bullock, C. Hassell. *An Introduction to the Old Testament Prophetic Books.* Updated. Chicago: Moody, 2007.

Burton, Joe W. *Prince of the Pulpit.* Grand Rapids: Zondervan, 1946.

Calvin, John. *Institutes of Christian Religion,* 2:323. Translated by Henry Beveridge. Grand Rapids: Eerdmans, 1957.

Carson, D. A. *A Call to Spiritual Reformation.* Grand Rapids: Baker, 1992.

———. "Contemporary Challenges and Aims." In *Preach the Word.* Edited by Leland Ryken and Todd A. Wilson. Wheaton, IL: Crossway, 2007.

———. *The Cross and Christian Ministry.* Grand Rapids: Baker, 2003.

———. *New Testament Commentary Survey.* Sixth edition. Grand Rapids: Baker, 2007.

———. *Scandalous.* Wheaton, IL: Crossway, 2010.

———. "Systematic Theology and Biblical Theology." In *New Dictionary of Biblical Theology.* Edited by T. Desmond Alexander, Brian S. Rosner, D. A. Carson, and Graeme Goldsworthy. Downers Grove, IL: InterVarsity, 2000.

Chapell, Bryan. *Christ-Centered Preaching.* Second edition. Grand Rapids: Baker, 2005.

———. "The Future of Expository Preaching." *Preaching Magazine* 20, no. 2 (September-October, 2004): 42–43.

———, ed. *The Hardest Sermons You'll Ever Have to Preach.* Grand Rapids: Zondervan, 2011.

———. *Using Illustrations to Preach with Power.* Wheaton, IL: Crossway, 1992.

Clowney, Edmund. *Preaching and Biblical Theology.* Grand Rapids: Eerdmans, 1961.

———. "Preaching Christ from all the Scriptures." In *The Preacher and Preaching.* Edited by Samuel T. Logan. Phillipsburg, NJ: P&R, 1986.

Cummings, Asa. *A Memoir of the Rev. Edward Payson.* New York: America Tract Society, 1830.

Dallimore, Arnold. *George Whitefield.* Volume 1. Edinburgh: Banner of Truth Trust, 2001.

———. *Spurgeon.* Chicago: Moody Press, 1984.

Dargan, Edwin Charles. *A History of Preaching.* Volume 1. Grand Rapids: Baker, 1954.

Dever, Mark, and Greg Gilbert. *Preach.* Nashville: B&H, 2012.

Dever, Mark, and Paul Alexander. *The Deliberate Church.* Wheaton, IL: Crossway, 2005.

Dillenberger, John. *John Calvin, Selections from His Writings.* Missoula, MT: Scholars Press, 1975.

Dowden, Landon. "An Examination of Pneumatological Content in Southern Baptist Homiletic Theory Since 1870." PhD dissertation. New Orleans Baptist Theological Seminary, 2007.

Driscoll, Mark. *The Radical Reformission.* Grand Rapids: Zondervan, 2004.

Driscoll, Mark, and Gerry Breshears. *Vintage Jesus.* Wheaton, IL: Crossway, 2007.

Duduit, Michael, ed. *Handbook of Contemporary Preaching*. Nashville: Broadman, 1992.

Edwards, Brian. *God's Outlaw*. Sixth edition. Darlington, England: Evangelical Press, 1988.

Edwards, Jonathan. *A History of the Work of Redemption*. In *The Works of Jonathan Edwards*. Volume I. Sixth printing. Peabody: Hendrickson, 2007.

———. *Resolutions*. Edited by Stephen J. Nichols. Phillipsburg, NJ: P&R, 2001.

Ehrman, Bart. *Misquoting Jesus*. San Francisco: HarperCollins, 2005.

Erickson, Millard J. *Christian Theology*. Second edition. Grand Rapids: Baker, 2000.

———. *Postmodernizing the Faith*. Grand Rapids: Baker, 1998.

Eswine, Zack. *Preaching to a Post-everything World*. Grand Rapids: Baker, 2008.

Fee, Gordon D., and Douglas Stuart. *How to Read the Bible for All Its Worth*. Third edition. Grand Rapids: Zondervan, 2003.

Ferguson, Sinclair. *Inside the Sermon*. Edited by R. A. Bodey. Grand Rapids: Baker, 1990.

Geisler, Norman L. *Christ: The Theme of the Bible*. Chicago: Moody, 1968.

Goldsworthy, Graeme. "Biblical Theology as the Heartbeat of Effective Ministry." In *Biblical Theology*. Edited by Scott J. Hafemann. Downers Grove, IL: InterVarsity, 2002.

———. *Preaching the Whole Bible as Christian Scripture*. Grand Rapids: Eerdmans, 2000.

Gordon, T. David. *Why Johnny Can't Preach*. Phillipsburg, NJ: P&R, 2009.

Green, Joel B., and Mark D. Baker. *Recovering the Scandal of the Cross*. Downers Grove, IL: InterVarsity, 2000.

Greidanus, Sidney. *The Modern Preacher and the Ancient Text*. Grand Rapids: Eerdmans, 1988.

———. *Preaching Christ from the Old Testament*. Grand Rapids: Eerdmans, 1999.

Grudem, Wayne. *Christian Beliefs*. Edited by Elliot Grudem. Grand Rapids: Zondervan, 2005.

———. *Systematic Theology*. Grand Rapids: Zondervan, 2000.

Heisler, Greg. *Spirit-Led Preaching*. Nashville: B&H, 2007.

Holland, Dewitte T. *The Preaching Tradition*. Nashville: Abingdon, 1980.

Horton, Michael. *Christless Christianity.* Grand Rapids: Baker, 2008.

Hughes, Kent. *Disciplines of a Godly Man.* Revised. Wheaton, IL: Crossway, 2001.

Hughes, Kent and Barbara. *Liberating Ministry from the Success Syndrome.* Wheaton, IL: Tyndale House, 1988.

Johnson, Dennis. *Him We Proclaim.* Phillipsburg, NJ: P&R, 2007.

Johnston, Graham. *Preaching to a Postmodern World.* Grand Rapids: Baker, 2001.

Juel, Donald. *Messianic Exegesis.* Philadelphia: Fortress, 1988.

Kaiser, Walter C., Jr. *Toward an Exegetical Theology: Biblical Exegesis for Preaching and Teaching.* Grand Rapids: Baker, 1981.

Keller, Timothy. *Center Church.* Grand Rapids: Zondervan, 2012.

———. *Counterfeit Gods.* New York: Dutton, 2009.

———. *Prayer.* New York: Dutton, 2014.

———. *Preaching.* New York: Viking, 2015.

———. *The Reason for God.* New York: Dutton, 2008.

Knoll, Mark. *A History of Christianity in the United States and Canada.* Grand Rapids: Eerdmans, 1992.

Larsen, David L. *The Anatomy of Preaching.* Grand Rapids: Baker, 1989.

———. *The Company of the Preachers.* Grand Rapids: Kregel, 1998.

Lawrence, Michael. *Biblical Theology.* Wheaton, IL: Crossway, 2010.

Levenson, Russell. "'To Humble the Sinner, to Exalt the Saviour, to Promote Holiness': Reflections on the Life, Ministry, and Legacy of Charles Simeon." *Sewanee Theological Review* (1998): 47.

Lischer, Richard. *The Company of Preachers.* Grand Rapids: Eerdmans, 2002.

———. *The Preacher King* (New York: Oxford Press, 1995), Kindle edition.

Lloyd-Jones, D. Martyn. *Preaching and Preachers.* Grand Rapids: Zondervan, 1972.

Longman, Tremper, III. *Old Testament Commentary Survey.* Fourth edition. Grand Rapids: Baker, 2007.

Lowry, Eugene. *The Homiletical Plot.* Louisville: John Knox, 1980.

Luther, Martin. "A Mighty Fortress Is Our God." Translated by Frederick H. Hedge. In *The Baptist Hymnal.* Nashville: Convention Press, 1991.

———. *The Table Talk of Martin Luther.* Edited by Thomas S. Kepler. Grand Rapids: Baker, 1979.

MacArthur, John, Jr., and the Master's Seminary Faculty. *Rediscovering Expository Preaching.* Dallas: Word, 1992.

———. "Rightly Dividing the Word of Truth." In *Preach the Word.* Edited by Leland Ryken and Todd A. Wilson. Wheaton, IL: Crossway, 2007.

Mahaney, C. J. *Humility.* Sisters, OR: Multnomah, 2005.

———. "The Pastor's Priorities: Watch Your Life and Doctrine." In *Preaching the Cross.* Edited by Mark Dever, J. Ligon Duncan III, R. Albert Mohler Jr., and C. J. Mahaney. Wheaton, IL: Crossway, 2007.

Mayhue, Richard L. "Introductions, Illustrations, and Conclusions." In *Rediscovering Expository Preaching.* John MacArthur Jr. and the Master's Seminary Faculty. Dallas: Word, 1992.

McDill, Wayne V. *The Twelve Essential Skills for Great Preaching.* Nashville: B&H, 1994.

Merida, Tony. *Proclaiming Jesus.* E-book. Gospel-Centered Discipleship, 2012.

Metaxas, Eric. *Bonhoeffer: Pastor, Martyr, Prophet, Spy.* Nashville: Thomas Nelson, 2011.

Metzger, Bruce M. *The Text of the New Testament: Its Transmission, Corruption, and Restoration.* Third edition. New York: Oxford University, 1992.

Meuser, Fred W. *Luther the Preacher.* Minneapolis: Augsburg, 1983.

Meyer, F. B. *Expository Preaching: Plans and Methods.* London: Hodder & Stoughton, Ltd., 1912. Reprint. Eugene, OR: Wipf and Stock, 1974.

Miller, Donald G. *The Way of Biblical Preaching.* New York: Abingdon, 1957.

Montoya, Alex. *Preaching with Passion.* Grand Rapids: Kregel, 2000.

Moo, Douglas J. *The Letters to the Colossians and Philemon.* In *The Pillar New Testament Commentary.* Grand Rapids: Eerdmans, 2008.

Moule, H. C. G. *Charles Simeon.* London: InterVarsity, 1948.

Murray, Ian. *D. Martyn Lloyd-Jones: The First Forty Years.* Third edition. Carlisle, PA: Banner of Truth Trust, 1982.

Murrow, David. *Why Men Hate Going to Church.* Nashville: Nelson, 2005.

Oden, Thomas C. *Pastoral Theology: Essentials of Ministry.* San Francisco: HarperOne, 1983.

Olford, Stephen F., and David L. Olford. *Anointed Expository Preaching.* Nashville: B&H, 1998.

Osborne, Larry. *Sticky Church.* Grand Rapids: Zondervan, 2008.

Owen, John. *Overcoming Sin and Temptation*. Edited by Kelly M. Kapic and Justin Taylor. Wheaton, IL: Crossway, 2006.

Packer, J. I. "Foreword." *The Unfolding Mystery*. By Edmund Clowney. Colorado Springs: NavPress, 1988.

———. *God Has Spoken*. London: Hodder and Stoughton, 1965.

———. *My Path of Prayer*. Edited by David Hanes. Worthing, West Sussex: Henry E. Walter, 1981.

Parker, T. H. L. *Calvin's Preaching*. Edinburgh: T&T Clark, 1992.

Perkins, William. *The Art of Prophesying*. Revised by Sinclair Ferguson. First published in Latin in 1592 and English in 1606. Reprint, Carlisle, PA: Banner of Truth Trust, 1996.

Perry, Lloyd M. *Biblical Preaching for Today's World*. Chicago: Moody, 1973.

Piper, John. *Brothers, We Are Not Professionals*. Updated and Expanded. Nashville: B&H, 2013.

———. *The Hidden Smile of God*. Wheaton, IL: Crossway, 2001.

———. *Let the Nations Be Glad!* Grand Rapids: Baker, 1993.

———. *The Supremacy of God in Preaching*. Revised edition. Grand Rapids: Baker, 2004.

Reid, Loren. *Speaking Well*. New York: McGraw-Hill, 1977.

Robinson, Haddon. *Biblical Preaching*. Second edition. Grand Rapids: Baker, 2001.

———. "The Heresy of Application." *Leadership* (Fall 1997): 21.

Rosner, B. S. "Biblical Theology." In *New Dictionary of Biblical Theology*. Edited by T. Desmond Alexander, Brian S. Rosner, D. A. Carson, and Graeme Goldsworthy. Downers Grove, IL: InterVarsity, 2000.

Rosscup, James E. "The Priority of Prayer and Expository Preaching." In John MacArthur Jr. and the Master's Seminary Faculty, *Rediscovering Expository Preaching*. Dallas: Word, 1992.

Rupp, Ernest Gordon. *Luther's Progress to the Diet of Worms 1521*. London: SCM, 1951.

Saucy, Robert. *Scripture*. Nashville: Word, 2001.

Schreiner, Thomas R. *Galatians*. Zondervan Exegetical Commentary on the New Testament. Grand Rapids: Zondervan, 2010.

———. *Interpreting the Pauline Epistles*. Second edition. Grand Rapids: Baker, 2011.

Shaddix, Jim. *The Passion-Driven Sermon*. Nashville: B&H, 2003.

Smith, Robert, Jr. *Doctrine That Dances*. Nashville: B&H, 2008.

Smith, Steven W. *Dying to Preach*. Grand Rapids: Kregel, 2009.

———. *Recapturing the Voice of God: Shaping Sermons Like Scripture.* Nashville: B&H, 2015.

Smith, Thomas N. "Keeping the Main Thing the Main Thing." In *Reforming Pastoral Ministry.* Edited by John Armstrong. Wheaton, IL: Crossway, 2001.

Sproul, R. C. *The Holiness of God.* Wheaton, IL: Tyndale, 1985.

Spurgeon, Charles. *An All-Round Ministry.* Reprint. Carlisle, PA: Banner of Truth Trust, 2002.

———. *Autobiography.* Edinburgh: Banner of Truth Trust, 1973.

———. *Lectures to My Students.* Reprint. Grand Rapids: Zondervan, 1954.

———. *The Metropolitan Tabernacle Pulpit.* Volume 25. Reprint. Pasadena: Pilgrim Publications, 1980.

———. *The Power in Prayer.* New Kensington, PA: Whitaker House, 1996.

———. *The Soulwinner.* New Kensington, PA: Whitaker House, 1995.

———. *Spurgeon at His Best.* Compilation by Tom Carter. Grand Rapids: Baker, 1988.

Stanfield, V. L. *Notes on the History of Preaching.* Second edition. New Orleans: NOBTS Printing Department, 1963.

Stanley, Andy, and Lane Jones. *Communicating for a Change.* Colorado Springs: Multnomah, 2006.

Stetzer, Ed. *Planting Missional Churches.* Nashville: B&H, 2006.

Stitzinger, James. "The History of Expository Preaching." In John MacArthur Jr. and the Master's Seminary Faculty, *Rediscovering Expository Preaching.* Dallas: Word, 1992.

Stott, John R. W. *Between Two Worlds.* Grand Rapids: Eerdmans, 1982.

———. *Guard the Truth.* Downers Grove, IL: InterVarsity, 1996.

———. *The Preacher's Portrait.* London: Tyndale, 1961.

Swindoll, Chuck. *Growing Strong in the Seasons of Life.* Grand Rapids: Zondervan, 1994.

Thomas, I. D. E. *A Puritan Golden Treasury.* Edinburgh: Banner of Truth Trust, 1977.

Thompson, James. *Preaching Like Paul.* Louisville: WJK, 2001.

Thompson, William. *Preaching Biblically.* Nashville: Abingdon, 1980.

Tozer, A. W. *The Knowledge of the Holy.* San Francisco: Harper, 1961.

Tripp, Paul. *Dangerous Calling.* Wheaton, IL: Crossway, 2012.

Turnbull, Ralph. *A History of Preaching*. Volume 3. Grand Rapids: Baker 1974.

Unger, Merrill F. *Principles for Expository Preaching*. Grand Rapids: Zondervan, 1955.

Vines, Jerry, and Jim Shaddix. *Power in the Pulpit*. Chicago: Moody, 1999.

Vos, Geerhardus. *Biblical Theology*. Grand Rapids: Eerdmans, 1948. Reprint, Carlisle, PA: Banner of Truth Trust, 1975.

Ware, Bruce. *Father, Son, and Spirit: Relationships, Roles, and Relevance*. Wheaton, IL: Crossway, 2005.

Warfield, B. B. *The Religious Life of Theological Students*. Reprint. Phillipsburg, NJ: P&R, 1992.

Williams, Jessica. *Fifty Facts That Should Change the World 2.0*. New York: Disinformation, 2007.

Wright, Christopher J. H. *Knowing Jesus Through the Old Testament*. Downers Grove, IL: InterVarsity, 1995.

———. *The Mission of God*. Downers Grove, IL: InterVarsity, 2006.

———. *Sweeter Than Honey*. Carlisle, PA: Langham, 2015.

Cassettes

Carson, D. A. "The Primacy of Expository Preaching." Bethlehem Conference for Pastors, 1995.

Online Resources

"The Baptist Faith and Message, 2000." Accessed February 13, 2015. http://www.sbc.net/bfm2000/bfm2000.asp.

Carson, D. A. "People Don't Learn What I Teach Them; They Learn What I'm Excited About." Article accessed February 15, 2015. http://www.thegospelcoalition.org/blogs/justintaylor/2010/11/19/carson-people-dont-learn-what-i-teach-them-they-learn-what-im-excited-about/.

———. "The Temptation of Joseph." Sermon preached from Genesis 39 at Champion Forest Baptist Church on April 28, 2013. Accessed February 5, 2015. https://www.youtube.com/watch?v=oS0iVA5UtN4.

Chalmers, Thomas. "The Expulsive Power of a New Affection" Accessed February 25, 2015. http://manna.mycpanel.princeton.edu/rubberdoc/c8618ef3f4a7b5424f710c5fb61ef281.pdf.

Chapell, Bryan. "Why Expository Preaching?" The Gospel Coalition. Accessed February 5, 2015. http://resources.thegospelcoalition.org/library/why-expository-preaching.

Davis, Andrew. "An Approach to Extended Memorization of Scripture." Article accessed August 26, 2008. http://www.fbc durham.org/pages.php?page_id=5.

Ferguson, Sinclair. *Preaching Christ from the Old Testament.* PT Media. PDF available at http://www.proctrust.org.uk/dls/christ_paper .pdf.

Hayden, Eric. "Did You Know?" The Spurgeon Archive. Accessed March 12, 2015. http://www.spurgeon.org/spurgn2.htm.

Keller, Tim. "Applying Christ to the Heart in Preaching." Article accessed February 24, 2015. http://static1.squarespace.com /static/5315f2e5e4b04a00bc148f24/t/5410791ae4b0c1ca62ec 04a0/1410365722378/Applying+Christ+to+the+Heart+in+Pre aching.pdf.

————. "Ministry and Character." Article accessed February 14, 2015. http://static1.squarespace.com/static/5315f2e5e4b04a00bc 148f24/t/537a7280e4b0d45559686de9/1400533632260/ Ministry+and+Character.pdf.

————. "Preaching in a Secular Culture," Article accessed February 25, 2015. https://static1.squarespace.com/static/5315f2e5e4b04a00 bc148f24/t/537a728fe4b0d45559686e07/1400533647273/ Preaching_in_a_Secular_Culture.pdf.

————. "Scraps of Thoughts on Daily Prayer." Accessed February 11, 2015. http://www.thegospelcoalition.org/article/scraps-of -thoughts-on-daily-prayer.

LaRue, John, Jr. "The Internet: Blessing or Curse for Pastors?" Article accessed July 28, 2008. http://www.christianitytoday .com/yc/2001/002/18.88.html.

Miller, Kevin. "Can Pastors Really Be Happy?" Article accessed July 28, 2008. http://www.christianitytoday.com/leaders/newsletter /2001/cln11205.html.

Mohler, Albert. "Has God Called You?" Article accessed June 30, 2016. www.albertmohler.com/2013/07/19/has-god-called-you-discerning -the-call-to-preach-2.

Piper, John. "Books Don't Change People; Paragraphs Do." Article accessed February 25, 2015. http://www.desiringgod.org/articles /books-don-t-change-people-paragraphs-do.

————. "Charles Spurgeon: Preaching Through Adversity." Accessed February 16, 2015. http://www.desiringgod.org /biographies/charles-spurgeon-preaching-through-adversity.

————. "The Essential and Prominent Place of Preaching in Worship." Sermon preached at Southeastern Baptist Theological Seminary. Accessed February 5, 2015. https://www.youtube .com/watch?v=P8CMrjT62Vo.

————. "Where and How Did You Learn to Preach?" Desiring God Ministries. Accessed February 5, 2015. http://www.desiringgod .org/interviews/where-and-how-did-you-learn-to-preach.

Rinne, Jeramie. "Biblical Theology and Gospel Proclamation." Accessed February 12, 2015. http://9marks.org/article /biblical-theology-and-gospel-proclamation/.

Robinson, Haddon. "The Heresy of Application: An Interview with Haddon Robinson." Article accessed February 24, 2015. http:// www.christianitytoday.com/le/1997/fall/7l4020.html?start=4.

Sills, David. "Reclaiming Contextualization." Article accessed February 26, 2015. http://davidsills.blogspot.com/2009/05 /reclaiming-contextualization.html.

Spurgeon, Charles. "Election: Its Defenses and Evidences." Sermon accessed July 10, 2008. http://www.biblebb.com/files/spurgeon /2920.htm.

————. "To You." Sermon accessed February 15, 2015. http://www .spurgeongems.org/vols49-51/chs2899.pdf.

Timmis, Steve. "How to Plant a Church." Article accessed February 26, 2015. http://www.acts29network.org/acts-29-blog/how-to -plant-a-church-five-principles-from-steve-timmis/.

NAME INDEX

Alexander, Paul, 105
Alexander, T. Desmond, 53, 146
Armstrong, John H., 34, 99, 102
Ash, Christopher, 8
Augustine, 212, 248
Azurdia, Arturo, III, 52, 88, 90, 91, 94, 95, 99, 102, 156
Baker, Mark D., 61
Barth, Karl, 11
Beale, G. K., 146
Beeke, Joel, 34
Begg, Alistair, 8
Beveridge, Henry, 85
Blackwood, Andrew W., 15, 102
Blomberg, Craig, 232
Bodey, R. A., 101
Boice, J. M., 32
Bonar, Andrew A., 38
Bounds, E. M., 40, 99
Breward, Ian, 254
Broadus, John A., 11, 14, 52
Bromiley, Geoffrey W., 11
Brooke, S. A., 101
Brooks, Phillips, 11
Brown, Seth, 190
Bruce, F. F., 90
Bryson, Harold T., 15, 155
Bullock, C. H., 6
Burton, J. W., 101
Calvin, John, 85, 216, 253
Carson, D. A., 8, 15, 20, 48, 53, 59, 93, 107, 110, 144, 146, 149
Chalmers, Thomas, 183
Chapell, Bryan, 14, 145, 147, 157, 158, 163, 193, 194, 195, 212, 264
Cummings, A., 101
Dallimore, Arnold, 79, 106
Daniels, Donald E., 11

Dargan, E. C., 246, 256
Davis, Andrew, 33
Dever, Mark, 5, 14, 105, 186, 190
Dillenberger, John, 253
Dowden, Landon, 81
Edwards, Brian, 47
Edwards, Jonathan, 68, 187, 219
Ehrman, Bart, 42, 43
Erickson, Millard, 44, 46
Eswine, Zack, 74, 227, 240
Fee, Gordon D., 135
Ferguson, Sinclair, 51, 101, 216, 254
Geisler, Norman, 52
Gentry, Peter J., 149
Gilbert, Greg, 5, 14, 190
Goldsworthy, Graeme, 53, 54, 146, 245
Gordon, T. David, 1, 157
Green, Joel B., 61
Greidanus, Sidney, 9, 14, 54
Grudem, Elliot, 44, 45
Grudem, Wayne, 44, 45
Hafemann, Scott J., 54
Hanes, David, 99
Hayden, Eric W., 79
Heisler, Greg, 83, 95
Holland, Dewitte T., 250
Horton, Michael, 62
Hughes, Barbara, 124
Hughes, R. Kent, 104, 124
Johnston, Graham, 239
Jones, Lane, 151, 156, 164, 202
Jordan, G. Ray, 245
Juel, Donald, 52
Kapic, Kelly, 26
Keller, Tim, 2, 17, 36, 39, 61, 66, 70, 98, 121, 183, 185, 186, 187, 188, 228, 237

Kepler, Thomas S., 216, 252
Knoll, Mark, 256
Larsen, David, 96, 100, 245, 255
Larson, Kevin, 131
Lawrence, Michael, 190
Levenson, Russell, 258
Lischer, Richard, 257
Lloyd-Jones, D. Martyn, 11, 82, 84, 86, 92, 100, 128, 188, 218
Longman, Tremper, III, 144
Lowry, Eugene, 172
Luther, Martin, 216, 252
MacArthur, John, Jr., 14, 101, 102, 149, 192, 249
Mahaney, C. J., 94
Martin Luther, 32
Mayhue, R. L., 192
McDill, Wayne, 140
M'Cheyne, Robert Murray, 25, 38
Metaxas, Eric, 76
Metzger, B. M., 45
Meuser, Fred W., 84, 214, 243, 252
Meyer, F. B., 15
Mohler, Albert, 85
Montoya, Alex, 90
Moo, Douglas J., 74
Moule, H. C. G., 101
Murray, Ian, 65
Nichols, Stephen J., 219
Oden, Thomas C., 85
Olford, David, 143
Olford, Stephen F., 143
Osborne, Larry, 266
Owen, John, 26
Packer, J. I., 25, 47, 53, 99, 120
Parker, T. H. L., 253
Payson, Edward, 101
Perkins, William, 51, 170, 216, 254
Piper, John, 10, 11, 46, 79, 112, 118, 121, 171, 192, 254
Reid, Loren, 219
Rinne, Jeramie, 53
Robertson, D. W., Jr., 212, 248
Robertson, Frederick W., 101

Robinson, Haddon, 14, 151, 181, 182, 225
Rosner, Brian S., 53, 146
Rosscup, James E., 101, 102
Rupp, Ernest Gordon, 252
Ryken, Leland, 48, 149
Saucy, R., 46
Schreiner, Thomas R., 140, 141
Shaddix, Jim, 12, 14, 16, 50, 100, 115, 118, 138, 142, 154, 169, 173, 175, 177, 193, 202, 205, 211, 212, 215, 218
Sills, David, 230
Simeon, Charles, 258
Smith, Robert, Jr., 116
Smith, Steven W., 93, 136
Sproul, R. C., 252
Spurgeon, Charles H., 26, 65, 79, 81, 84, 86, 88, 92, 94, 97, 99, 102, 105, 106, 108, 220
Stalker, James, 34
Stanfield, Vernon L., 11, 255
Stanley, Andy, 151, 156, 164, 202
Stitzinger, James, 249
Stott, John, 7, 12, 14, 30, 37, 60, 104, 123, 126, 127, 133, 152, 167, 176, 199, 209, 216, 220, 247, 250, 260
Stuart, Douglas, 135
Swindoll, Chuck, 32
Taylor, James C., 155
Thompson, James, 49
Timmis, Steve, 230
Tozer, A. W., 119
Tripp, Paul, 36
Turnbull, Ralph, 255, 256
Vines, Jerry, 12, 14, 16, 100, 138, 142, 154, 169, 173, 175, 177, 193, 202, 205, 211, 212, 215, 218
Ware, Bruce, 41, 57, 117
Warfield, B. B., 39
Wellum, Stephen J., 149
Whitefield, George, 106
Wilson, Todd A., 48, 149
Witherspoon, Jesse, 14, 52
Wright, Christopher J. H., 52, 75

SUBJECT INDEX

A

Anointed preaching (see Spirit-
empowered preaching, anointing
of Holy Spirit)

B

Biblical authority, 45
    Early church leaders and
        Reformers, 46
    Implications, 46
Biblical inspiration
    Author's definition, 43
    Clarity of Scripture, 45
Biblical revelation
    Difference between biblical
        preachers and today's
        preachers, 47, 48
    New and old, 48
    Similarities between biblical
        preaching and today's
        preaching, 48
Biblical sufficiency, 49
    Avoiding emotional sensational-
        ism, 50
    Avoiding pragmatic moralism, 51
    Benefits of Scripture, 50
Biblical Theology, 52

C

Communication aids, 221
    Church clothing, 222
    Multimedia, 221
    Pulpit, 221
    Sound system, 222
    Stage, 221
Congregation
    Cultivating hunger for exposi-
        tion, 136

Developing gospel-centered
    worldview, 73, 164
Different worldviews, 238
Prayers of, 95
Unity, 95
Contextualizing the message, 227
    Clarifications, 229
    Exhortations, 235
    Foundations, 231
        Gospels, 233
        Jesus, 233

E

Evangelism, 10
Exegetical process (see Preparation,
    exegetical process)
Exhortation, 10
Expositor's role, 51, 71, 116
Expository preaching
    Alternative approaches, 20
        Dialogical, 21
        Topical felt-need, 21
    Benefits, 17
    Content, 13
    Dangers
        Christ-less sermons, 20
        Detail overload, 19
        Dullness, 19
        Intellectual pride, 19
        Irrelevancy, 19
        Monotony, 19
    Definitions, 12, 15
        Author's, 16
    Process, 13
    Style, 13
Exultation, 10

F
Faithful prayer, 98
Faithful preaching
　Author's definition, 9
　Church growth, 124

G
Glory of God
　People's need to behold, 120
　Preacher's quest for, 119
　Relevance and, 121
God as preacher, 5
Great Awakening, 256

H
Holy Spirit
　As teacher, 95, 135
　Necessities for obtaining in
　　preaching, 93
　Need for in preparation, 87, 95
　Role in preaching, 57
Homiletics, 11, 99

L
Luther's points of a good preacher,
　214

M
Message
　Apply wisdom, 72
　Christ, 61
　Christless Christianity, 62
　Clarifications, 67
　For sanctification, 75
　Proclaim, 70
　Teach, 72
　Warn, 71
Multimedia use, 203, 221

P
Postmodernism, 238
Pragmatic moralism and the Bible,
　51
Prayer
　As conversation with Father, Son,
　　Spirit, 98

Essential part of homiletics, 99
Fasting, 94, 112
Hindrances
　Common excuses, 107
　Sinful actions, 109
Practical tips, 110
Preacher and
　Appropriate language, 180
　Body language and passion,
　　218
　Boldness, 216
　Communication (see Preacher
　　and, rhetoric)
　Competition and jealousy, 123
　Contextualization, 217
　Experience, 3
　Fasting, 94, 112
　Gifts, 3
　Holiness, 4
　Humor, 219
　Illumination, 102
　Indwelling sin, 122
　Instruction, 5
　Intercession, 102
　Love for people, 3
　Love for the Word, 2
　Memorization and meditation of
　　Scripture, 31
　Mentor, 3
　Obsession with church growth,
　　124
　Persuasion, 213
　Posture, 219
　Praise of men and fear of men,
　　123
　Prayer, 4, 94
　Ranting, 9
　Rhetoric, 212
　Simplicity and clarity in speech,
　　215
　Spirit of God, 5
　Training for godliness, 29, 34
Preacher's
　Aspiration, 85
　Calling, 5, 84
　Character, 86, 127

Confirmation of calling
    External, 85
    Inward, 85
Courage, 128
Humility, 128
Illumination, 95
Leadership gifts, 86
Lifestyle, 86
Limitations, 89
Message, 125
Motives, 122
Passion, 127
Personal godliness/holiness, 26,
    94
Personality, 19
Prayer for multitudes, 94
Responsibility, 2, 223
Sincerity, 127
Preaching
    Christ from all the Scriptures,
        54
    Content, 11
    God as primary audience, 123
    Growth in effectiveness, 148
    Passion, 211
    Public, 48
    Rhetorical elements, 49
    Style
        Circumlocution, 215
        Combating dullness, 215
        Speaking well, 215
        Verbosity, 214
    Trinitarian, 12
    Variety, 218
    Word in worship, 252
    Work of Spirit, 12, 89
    Worship, 125
Preaching among
    The Fathers and apologists, 246
    The Reformers and Puritans, 251
Preaching and Persuasion
    Ethos, 223, 224
    Lifestyle, 224
    Logos, 223
    Pathos, 223, 224
    Truth, 222

Preaching in
    Evangelical Age, 256
    Medieval period, 249
        Age of Renaissance, 250
        Missionary preachers, 249
        Original languages, 251
    Truthless culture
        Assumed biblical illiteracy,
            239
        Differing worldviews, 238
        Diverse settings, 239
        Like Paul, 241
        Narrative of Scripture, 239
        Preaching to old self, 240
        Redemptive messages, 240
        Testimonies, 241
Preparation
    Application, 180
        Placing, 188
        Specific, 181
        Stating, 190
        Transformative, 182
    Conclusions, 199
        Invitation options, 205
        Response, 205
        Summation, 204
    Exegetical process, 138
    Explanation, 177
        Contemporary concepts, 179
        Cross-references, 179
        Present the facts, 179
        Read text with emphasis, 180
        Retell story, 179
        Visual aids, 180
    Illustrations, 192
        Cautions, 195
        Finding, 193
    Introductions, 199
        Purposes and qualities, 201
        Types, 202
    Manuscript use, 207
    Outlines, 163
        Benefits
            Biblical teaching, 165
            Congregational guidance,
                166

Doctrinal instruction, 165
Multiplication, 166
Sermon unity, 167
Expository, constructing
Approaches, 169
Extended, 208
Sermon, principles for developing
Ideas to consider, 168
Problems to avoid, 167
Reading, 193
Selecting a sermon title, 161
Selecting the text, 136
Sermon briefs, 208
Studying the text, 134
Background information of text, 139
Commentary use, 144
Cross-references, 143
Dissecting the passage, 140
False interpretations, 139
Implications
Personal application, 149
Theological significance, 149
Interpretation, 139
Redemptive integration, 145
Structural diagram, 140
Unifying theme of text, 151
Develop main point of sermon (MPS), 152, 155
Benefits, 160
Fallen condition focus, 157
Develop redemptive MPS, 157
Identify main point of text (MPT), 152
Recurring ideas, 155
Surrounding context, 155
Why an MPT, 153

R
Relationships within the Trinity, 117

S
Scripture
Centrality of Christ, 136
Bible as unified book, 52
Jesus as hero, 51
Centrality of worship, 126
Context, 135
High view of, 41
Literary genre, 135
Sensationalism, 50
Sermons (see Preparation)
Sin
Believers, 89
Presence and effects, 88
Unbelievers, 88
Spirit-empowered preaching
Also Christ-exalting, 92
Anointing of Holy Spirit, 89
Apostolic, Christ-centered preaching, 55
Biblical foundation, 90
Descriptions of, 92
Evidence of, 93
Misunderstandings, 91
Use of "Spirit" over "anointed" terminology, 90
Spiritual disciplines
Growing in ministry, 38
Humility, 36
Living in community, 36
Prayer and repenting, 35
Scripture reading, 34
Self-examination, 38
Setting an example, 37

T
Topical preaching, 13
Topositional sermon, 15

W
Westminster Confession, 118

SCRIPTURE INDEX

Genesis
3:15 *147*
12–13 *205*
49:10 *147*

Exodus
20:14 *181, 182*
20:22 *6*

Numbers
11:16–30 *90*
11:29 *xvii*

Deuteronomy
6 *63*
18:21–22 *6*
25:4 *44*

Joshua
1:1–9 *153, 155, 156, 160, 161*
1:6–7 *9, 155*
2:1 *56*
4 *205*
9 *108*
9:14 *108*

Ruth
3:12 *177*

1 Samuel
3:19 *6*
12:23 *104*

2 Samuel
23:2 *44, 90*

1 Kings
18:1–40 *179*

2 Chronicles
24:20 *90*

Ezra
9–10 *205*

Nehemiah
8 *48, 126, 136*
8:1 *6*
8:1–8 *10*
8:8 *151*
8–9 *48, 205*
9:30 *90*

Psalms
2:7 *55*
9 *31*
16 *55*
16:10 *55*
19 *50, 119*
19:7 *45*
34 *109*
96:3 *118*
99–100 *31*
110 *55*
115:4–5 *5*
119 *31, 32, 33*
119:9–11 *50*
119:11 *31, 181*
119:18 *95, 102, 135*
119:24 *42*
119:72 *33*
119:97 *42*
119:105 *50*
119:140 *42*

Proverbs
21:13 *110*

25:11 *32*

Isaiah
1:18 *230*
6:5 *xii*
6:8–13 *125*
6:9–13 *6*
7:14 *142*
8:11 *44*
49:6 *55*
53 *55, 76, 146*
55:3 *55*
59:2 *109*
61:1–2 *90*
64:6 *xii*
66:2 *128*

Jeremiah
1:7–9 *6*
15:16 *50*
21 *6*
23 *6*
23:29 *50*
30:4 *44*

Ezekiel
2:4 *6*
11:5 *90*

Daniel
4 *62*

Joel
2:28–32 *xvii*

Amos
8:11 *44*

Micah
1:1 *170*

Habakkuk
1:5 *55*

Matthew
3:1 *6*
4 *44*

4:1–11 *44*
4:12–17 *5*
4:17 *90*
5 *182*
5:8 *27*
5:10–12 *244*
5:17 *47*
5:18 *179*
6:1 *123*
6:6 *98*
6:9 *98*
6:12 *110*
6:14–15 *110*
6:16 *112*
7:11 *98*
8:27 *119*
10:19–20 *140*
10:28 *123*
13:52 *171*
16:18 *142*
18:15–20 *140*
18:20 *140*
18:21–35 *110*
23:24 *220*
23:27–28 *27*
23:34 *75*
24:35 *44*
28:16–20 *193*
28:18–20 *xvii, 217*

Mark
1:32–34 *100*
1:35 *98, 100*
1:37–38 *8*
3:14 *8*
4:18 *90*
4:35–41 *172*
4:40 *172*
4:41 *172*
10 *xii*
10:17–31 *247*
11:25 *110*

Luke
1:13–15 *91*
1:39–41 *91*
1:42–45 *91*

1:67–79 *91*
4:1 *91*
4:14–22 *6*
4:16–21 *48*
4:16–22 *126*
4:18 *90*
4:18–19 *8*
4:20–21 *54*
5:16 *100, 111*
6:12 *100*
7:46 *90*
9:18a *100*
10:7 *44*
10:42 *107*
11:9–10 *108*
15:1–2 *11–32, 186*
15:11–32 *70*
17:10 *xii*
18:1–8 *108*
22:40 *109*
24:25–27 *20*
24:25–49 *6*
24:27 *xi, 48, 54, 145*
24:32 *50, 72, 135*
24:44 *44, 54*
24:49 *90*
32 *48*
43–44 *6*
44–47 *20*

John

1:1 *143, 178, 179*
1:14 *47, 117*
2:2 *90*
3:8 *93*
5:39 *54*
5:46 *54*
6:66 *125*
8:58 *143*
9:11 *90*
14:6 *180*
14:12–14 *94*
15:5 *xiii, 87, 94, 112*
15:7 *111*
15:26 *57, 92*
16:13 *135*
16:14 *57, 92, 93, 117*

17:2–3 *57*
17:2 *4, 117*
17:15–18 *233*
17:17 *31, 50*
20:28 *47*

Acts

1:4–5 *8, 90*
1:14 *106*
1:16 *43*
1:24 *106*
2 *xvii*
2:2–4 *91*
2:12 *xvii*
2:14–34 *55*
2:14–36 *57*
2:14–47 *5*
2:16 *xvii*
2:17 *xvii*
2:21 *139*
2:22–36 *xvii*
2:37–41 *93*
2:38 *139, 205*
2:41 *94*
2:42 *xviii, 106*
3:18–25 *55*
3:19 *139*
4 *93*
4:4 *94*
4:8 *91*
4:12 *70, 119*
4:13 *216*
4:20 *119*
4:26 *90*
4:29–31 *106*
4:31 *91, 216*
4:32–37 *156*
5:1–11 *156*
5:3–4 *178*
5:14 *94*
5:41 *244*
5:42 *xviii, 48, 60*
6:1 *94*
6:3 *91*
6:4 *35, 97, 98, 113*
6:5 *91*
6:7 *xviii, 94*

7:55 *91*
8 *55*
8:4 *xviii, 9*
8:8 *94*
9:17 *91*
9:28 *217*
9:31 *94*
9:35 *94*
9:42 *94*
10:1–11:19 *153*
10:36–38 *90*
11:21 *94*
11:24 *xviii, 91, 94*
12:5 *106*
12:24 *xviii, 94*
13 *55, 65, 70*
13:1–3 *106*
13:5 *70*
13:8–11 *91*
13:13–51 *232*
13:17–41 *7*
13:38–39 *139*
13:43 *49*
13:48 *94*
13:49, *xviii*
13:52 *91*
14:1 *94*
15:9 *139*
16:1–3 *85*
16:5 *xviii, 94*
16:14 *57, 88, 95*
16:31 *139*
17:1–3 *49*
17:1–4 *126, 213*
17:2–3 *49, 55*
17:3–5 *218*
17:4 *94*
17:11–12 *94*
17:16–34 *89, 232*
17:17 *49*
17:22b–23 *199*
18:4 *49, 213*
18:5 *55*
19:8 *49, 217*
19:12 *135*
19:20 *xviii, 94*
20:17 *28, 179*

20:17–35 *xix*
20:20–21 *139*
20:27 *51*
20:28 *28*
20:31 *71*
26 *49*
26:18 *78*
26:22–23 *55*
26:26 *217*
26:28 *49*
28:23 *55*
28:23–24 *49*
28:30–31 *xviii*
28:31 *217*

Romans

1:1b–3 *55*
1:10 *110*
1:15 *8*
1:16 *70*
1:19–20 *47*
3:9–19 *88*
8 *74, 181*
8:13 *122*
8:18 *74*
8:26 *98*
8:29 *28, 51, 142*
8:32 *73*
10:14 *8*
10:17 *50, 236*
11:36 *117*
12:1–2 *142*
12:2 *18*
12:3–8 *87*
12:7 *xviii*
12:12 *108*
15:14b *xviii*
15:20 *75*
16:25–27 *55*
16:25a *76*

1 Corinthians

1:10–17 *237*
1:18–2:5 *8*
1:22 *70*
2:1–2 *93*
2:1–5 *61, 90, 93, 213*

2:2 *61, 89*
2:3 *89, 94*
2:3–5 *81*
2:4 *89, 94*
2:5 *94*
2:9–11 *92*
2:9–12 *87*
4:14 *71*
6:19b–20 *117*
9 *231, 234*
9:15–27 *231*
9:16 *8, 86*
9:19 *234*
9:19–23 *232*
9:22b–23 *227*
9:23 *217*
9:24–27 *232*
10:31 *118*
12 *87*
12:10 *xviii*
13:1–3 *127*
14 *233*
14:6–12 *233*
14:16–17 *233*
14:23–25 *233*
14:37 *44*
15 *235, 264*
15:1–8 *8*
15:1–11 *236*
15:3 *61*
15:3–4 *61, 236*
15:9 *237*
15:10 *77*
15:10b *78, 237*
15:11 *236*
15:54b–55 *237*
15:57 *237*
15:58 *237*

2 Corinthians

1:21–22 *90*
3:18 *32, 76, 188*
3:18–4:6 *116*
4:4 *88*
4:4–6 *78, 90*
4:5–6 *66, 122*
4:5a *78*

4:6 *78*
4:7 *89*
5:15 *37*
5:16–21 *178*
5:21 *xiii, 236*
6:3–4 *225*
8:9 *73, 183*
11:23–27 *77*

Galatians

1:6–17 *6*
1:10 *123*
3:1b *71*
3:24 *xiii*
4:19 *51, 75*
5:16 *123*
5:19–23 *127*
5:22–23 *93*
6:14 *37*

Ephesians

1:1–14 *178*
1:15–16 *103*
1:16 *110*
2:1–4 *88*
2:4 *140*
2:18 *98*
3:8 *67*
3:14 *168, 176*
3:14–21 *168*
3:15–19 *168, 176*
3:20–21 *168, 176*
4:1 *83*
4:7 *86*
4:11 *xviii, 83*
4:12 *83*
4:17–18 *88*
4:17–24 *153, 156, 159, 160, 161*
4:24 *180*
4:25–32 *95*
4:30 *95*
4:32 *110*
5 *261, 262*
5:4 *229*
5:25 *73*
6:12–17 *103*
6:17a *32*

6:18 *98, 103*
6:18–20 *90, 93, 95, 103, 108, 217*
6:19 *103*
6:19–20 *217*

Philippians
1:3–5 *104*
1:18 *124*
1:18a *66*
2:5–11 *67*
2:7 *173*
2:11 *117*
2:12–13 *34*
3 *234*
3:1 *137, 237*
3:7–8 *120*
3:10 *121*
3:10–11 *119*

Colossians
1 *69*
1:6 *74*
1:9 *72*
1:9–10 *104*
1:9–14 *111*
1:10 *72*
1:15–17 *69*
1:15–23 *69*
1:16 *47*
1:18–19 *69*
1:19–23 *69*
1:24 *74*
1:24–2:5 *69*
1:24–29 *60, 69*
1:28 *60, 69, 74, 77*
1:28–29 *59, 69, 80, 218*
1:28a *74*
1:28b *74, 75, 77*
1:28c *74*
1:28d *74*
1:29 *60, 77*
1:29b *78*
2:1 *77*
2:3 *72*
2:6–7 *76*
3 *73*
3:4 *72*

3:10–11 *75*
3:11 *73*
3:12 *73*
3:13 *73*
3:15 *73*
3:16 *31*
3:16a *xviii*
3:24 *73*
4:2–4 *213*
4:3–4 *211*
4:4 *217*
4:5 *xviii*
28 *69*

1 Thessalonians
1:2 *110*
1:2–3 *104*
1:4–5 *223*
2:2 *217*
2:7–8 *224*
4:3 *27*
4:17 *142*
5:12 *71*
5:14 *71*
5:17 *98*
5:19 *95*
5:25 *95*

2 Thessalonians
3:15 *71*

1 Timothy
1–7 *xviii*
1:12 *84*
2:1–7 *150*
2:1–8 *98*
2:5 *34, 98*
3 *xviii*
3:1 *86*
3:1–7 *28, 179*
3:2 *86*
3:11 *142*
3:16–17 *158*
4:6 *33*
4:6–10 *29*
4:6–16 *29*
4:6a *29*

4:6b *30*
4:7 *30*
4:10 *34*
4:11 *13, 29*
4:11–16 *174, 196*
4:12 *29, 37, 127, 196*
4:13 *7, 10, 36, 48, 126, 196*
4:13 *15, 1*
4:14 *38, 85*
4:14–15 *29, 197*
4:15 *38*
4:16 *25, 28, 29, 38, 197*
4:16a *94*
5:3–6:2 *155*
5:3 *17, 155*
5:17 *175*
5:17–18 *176*
5:18 *44*
6:1 *155*
6:3–11 *38*
6:11 *127*
7 *34*
12b *38*

2 Timothy

1:3 *104, 110*
1:3–2:13 *155*
1:3–14 *155*
1:6 *85, 86*
1:6–7 *93*
1:13–14 *48*
2:1–2 *161*
2:1–7 *153, 159, 160*
2:1–10 *210*
2:2 *48, 155, 156, 159, 163, 166*
2:8 *66*
2:14 *137*
2:14–26 *162*
2:15 *95, 133*
2:21 *94*
3:2 *36*
3:14–17 *8, 41, 50*
3:15 *55*
3:16 *43*
3:16–17 *179*
3:17 *49*
4:1–2 *41*

4:1–4 *10*
4:2 *8, 126*
4:13 *30*

Titus

1:5 *7, 179*
1:5–9 *xviii*
1:7–9 *28*
2:1 *7*
2:1 *15, 48*
2:7 *225*

Hebrews

1:9 *90*
4:12 *50*
4:14–16 *108*
10:19 *98*
10:19–25 *36*
13:7 *xviii, xix, 246*
13:17 *77*
13:22 *7*
17 *xix*

James

1:5 *235*
1:18–27 *173*
1:21 *50*
1:27 *179, 181, 190*
2:1 *154*
2:1–13 *153, 154, 156, 160, 161, 169, 203*
2:2–4 *154*
2:5–7 *154*
2:8–13 *154*
2:13 *160*
2:14–16 *171*
2:14–26 *169*
3:1 *xix*
3:1–12 *169*
4:3 *109*
5:13–18 *98*

1 Peter

1:3ff *76*
1:13 *26*
1:13–2:3 *26*
1:13–14 *26*

1:15 *28*
1:15–16 *26*
1:17 *26*
1:18–21 *26*
1:22–25 *26, 50*
1:23–25 *93*
2:1 *26, 28*
2:1–2 *50*
2:2 *26, 45*
2–4 *28*
2:9 *119*
2:9–12 *28*
2:11 *26*
2:13–17 *28*
2:22 *27*
3:1–7 *28*
3:7 *109*
3:8 *109*
3:12 *109*

3:13–17 *28*
3:15 *xviii*
4:7 *109*
4:8–12 *28*
4:10–11 *xviii, 115*
4:11 *7, 118*
4:12–19 *28*
5:1–5 *28*
5:2–3 *86*
5:5 *128*
5:6 *128*

2 Peter
1:20–21 *43, 47*
3:1 *137*
3:16 *44*

Jude
1:3 *213*